Additional Praise for
Reclaiming Participation

"Cynthia Peters Anderson has written a remarkable, timely book because she is so unconcerned to be timely. By mediating and evaluating Barth and Balthasar's soteriology through Cyril of Alexandria, she demonstrates the importance of deification and participation in God for navigating modern and post-modern theological abandonments of the christological analogy of being. The final chapter, "Reclaiming God's Vision for Human Life," proves the point. Her work will benefit not only Barth and Balthasar studies but also anyone committed to theological substance and its place in the church and the world."

D. Stephen Long | Marquette University

"In this ambitious and carefully honed study, Cynthia Peters Anderson places Cyril of Alexandria's single-subject Christology into critical and constructive dialogue with Karl Barth and Hans Urs von Balthasar, noting their similarities and differences while appreciating Barth but agreeing more with Balthasar. Readers certainly will learn a great deal about how these three important theologians think about nature, grace, deification, the *imago dei*, analogy, justification, and sanctification, as well as the relationship between the immanent and economic Trinity. This thoughtful book surely will challenge readers to think through their understanding of Christology and soteriology once again."

Paul D. Molnar | St. John's University, Queens, New York

Reclaiming Participation

Reclaiming Participation

Christ as God's Life for All

Cynthia Peters Anderson

Fortress Press
Minneapolis

RECLAIMING PARTICIPATION

Christ as God's Life for All

Cover image: Descent into Hell. Russian icon, 16th c. / Art Resource

Cover design: Laurie Ingram

Library of Congress Cataloging-in-Publication Data

Print ISBN: 978-1-4514-7817-4

eBook ISBN: 978-1-4514-8956-9

The paper used in this publication meets the minimum requirements of American National Standard for Information Sciences — Permanence of Paper for Printed Library Materials, ANSI Z329.48-1984.

Manufactured in the U.S.A.

This book was produced using PressBooks.com, and PDF rendering was done by PrinceXML.

Contents

Introduction 1

1. Deification in the Early Church and Cyril of Alexandria 15

2. Barth 75
Elected for Covenant-Partnership with God

3. Balthasar 147
The Christological Analogy of Being

4. Realizing the Promise 211
Barth's and Balthasar's Conceptions of Participation in the Life of God

5. Reclaiming God's Vision for Human Life 253

Bibliography 267

Index of Authors 281

Index of Subjects 285

Introduction

"For having become partakers of him through the Holy Spirit, we were sealed with his likeness, and we mount up to the archetypal form of the image, according to which the divine Scripture says that we were made . . . . Therefore we mount up to a dignity above our nature on account of Christ, but we also will be sons of God, not according to him identically, but through grace in imitation of him."

—Cyril of Alexandria, *Commentary on John*[1]

Peter lowered his voice to a whisper. "The Buddha said, 'You are God yourself.' Jesus taught that 'the kingdom of God is within you' and even promised us, 'The works I do, you can do . . . and greater.' Even the first antipope—Hippolytus of Rome—quoted the same message, first uttered by the Gnostic teacher Monoimus: 'Abandon the search for God . . . instead, take yourself as the starting place.' ". . . . "A wise man once told me," Peter said, his voice faint now, "the only difference between you and God is that you have forgotten you are divine."

—Dan Brown, *The Lost Symbol*[2]

---

1. Cyril, *Commentary on John*, 1:12, trans. Daniel A. Keating from texts in Pusey, ii, 133, in Keating, *The Appropriation of Divine Life in Cyril of Alexandria* (Oxford: Oxford University Press), 183.
2. Dan Brown, *The Lost Symbol* (New York: Doubleday, 2009), 492.

The transformation of human life, the concept of humans becoming more than they currently are, has occupied pagan and religious thought for thousands of years. The captivating idea that humans are destined for something different, something more, is certainly not confined to the past. From modern and post-modern philosophy and science to an array of popular novels and films, this theme of a metamorphosis of human life pulsates deeply through western culture's veins despite the increasing secularization of western society.

It is a particularly poignant yearning in a postmodern landscape littered with the violent ravages of the twentieth century and the ongoing clashes of the twenty-first. The postmodern philosophical responses of deconstructionism and nihilism are set in an oscillating counterpoint with an ongoing post-Enlightenment humanism that refuses to give up the ghost. In this landscape, the Christian affirmation of human participation in the life of God's truth, beauty, and goodness offers hope and meaning for humanity that is secured by God's participation in human life through Jesus Christ. However, particularly in light of the vast array of neo-gnostic interpretations of deification that riddle popular culture with the idea that we are gods of our own making, it is crucial that Christianity recover an authentic conception of what it means for humanity to participate in God's life—one that accounts for a full transformation of human life through the grace of Jesus Christ, while retaining the real distinction between God and human.

This distinctively Christian affirmation is critical in a Western world that searches to find any secure source of hope and seems to have come loose from any moorings. Some, looking for a more hopeful end, have turned to a neo-Enlightenment humanism that places its faith in the inherent capacities of humans to become gods—whether through science, education, nature, the arts, or the endless stream of self-improvement programs and debates about ethics that pervade popular culture. Others, faced with the ongoing evidences of humanity's atrocities, both large and small, move in the direction of a Nietzsche-influenced philosophical nihilism that is caught in an endless cycle of deconstruction, with meaning endlessly deferred and the telos of human life envisioned as one of continual assertion of the will-to-power in an inherently violent and conflicted world.

A word here about the understanding of postmodernity in this project is necessary.[3] In referring to postmodern philosophy, I am making reference to that line of thought that traces itself to Frederich Nietzsche's critique and deconstruction of the Enlightenment and the ensuing modern era, including many of the epistemological, metaphysical and hermeneutical foundations on which it was built. Gianni Vattimo argues that Nietzsche deconstructed a modernity that was founded on the Enlightenment assumptions of universal reason built upon human knowledge and will. Nietzsche exposed modernity as an era of "overcoming" characterized by a preoccupation with progress, a pursuit of the "new" that incessantly grows old and must be replaced by the still newer. Ultimately, given what Nietzsche terms an excess of historical consciousness, there is nothing truly "new" enough to satisfy the constant demand for

---

3. Frederick Bauerschmidt argues that there are two distinct versions of postmodernity—one as the end of metanarratives and the other as the end of suspicion, both of which can be too easily identified with nihilistic accounts of truth. Bauerschmidt argues that the idea that postmodernity is the end of metanarratives, with the death of meaning and endlessly deferred interpretation, is really nothing but a continuation of the modern's narrative of emancipation, the turn to the subject collapses in on itself in the pursuit of an endless freedom from any certain meaning or interpretation. Bauerschmidt argues that postmodernity's assertion that metanarratives are at an end should be met with suspicion because it too is simply another truth claim designed to serve interests. If Christianity accepts such a claim, then the Christian story can no longer compellingly be told in ways that proclaim hope that the world might be redeemed. Rather, we are left with a truncated mission of service to the world, which remains secular and independent despite all the service. See Frederick Bauerschmidt, "Aesthetics: The theological sublime" in *Radical Orthodoxy*, eds. John Milbank, Catherine Pickstock and Graham Ward (London: Routledge, 1999), 202–204.

novelty—what appears is merely a repetition of the same disguised as the new.[4] Any pretense to reason is simply a disguise of the will-to-power. Within this concept of modernity, truth becomes unmoored from any metaphysical grounding in Being after Nietzsche's unveiling of the death of God. With no metaphysical foundation to secure it, being is reduced to the new; truth is reduced to value; and both being and truth are seen as events, subject to constant reinterpretation.[5] This reduction to mere value, which is really just opinion or perspective, ultimately results in truth dissolving itself.[6] Now humans can never truly know things in and of themselves. There are no foundational certainties and the mere idea of *any* foundation is emptied of content.[7]

The failure of modern philosophy to address Nietzsche's critique has given rise to postmodernity. In the 1970s, Jean-Francois Lyotard began defining the postmodern as the end of master narratives. Modernity's master narrative of human reason is shown to be a failure. All signs and all language are deconstructed, negating any stable meanings. Joining Lyotard, Vattimo draws extensively on the thought of Heidegger as well as Nietzsche and argues that modernity—characterized by degradation of the metaphysical concept of being into the new and the reduction of truth to value—cannot be overcome.[8] Postmodernity is not the end of

---

4. Gianni Vattimo, *The End of Modernity* (Baltimore: John Hopkins, 1988), 166.
5. Vattimo, *The End of Modernity*, 20–22, 167–168.
6. Vattimo, *The End of Modernity*, 167-171.
7. Nietzsche's most serious point of conflict with Christianity is rooted in the metaphysical realism of Judaism and the Christian tradition. The world as divinely created order exists independent of human thinking and doing. For humans to judge and desire rightly, they must be in alignment with the divine purpose for the created order. Nietzsche's rejection of the distinction between what is real and what is only apparent—there is no real for Nietzsche and everything is only apparent—is in direct conflict with this metaphysical realism. In the Christian tradition, the concept of rationality is embedded in theology rather than abstracted from it. See Alasdair MacIntyre, *Three Rival Versions of Moral Enquiry: Encyclopaedia, Genealogy and Tradition* (Notre Dame: University of Notre Dame Press, 1990), 66–67.
8. Vattimo, *The End of Modernity*, 2–3, 20–23, 99–101.

modernity in the sense of a new, emerging sense of history, but rather is an experience of "the end of history" itself.[9] Since the entire concept of overcoming is rooted in a metaphysics that has died, though not completely faded, postmodern philosophy cannot seek to overcome modernity without falling prey to the very constructs it seeks to expose and deconstruct.[10] Rather, postmodernity is left with the ironic option of twisting and deconstructing modernity by endlessly playing with language and aesthetics to expose modernity's errors and drain it of strength.

Postmodernity sees the modern era in its impoverishment and the cruel irony of its inescapability. With the collapse of the modern master narrative of human reason secured by the human subject alone, there are no more metanarratives and there are no unifying, universal categories of meaning. Rather, there is only deconstruction and endless deferral of meaning in which language and sign are never stable because they can always be placed in another context and made to mean something else. There is only play and, for some, an aesthetics that attempts to make the horror of modernity more beautiful or bearable by its very exhibition.

While postmodernity assures us there is no metaphysically secure foundation, it seems to found itself on a violence that takes on ontological shape and weight. Difference and absence are conceived as inherently conflicted and violent. This originating violence constitutes the possibility of being and knowing.[11] Given this context

---

9. Vattimo, *The End of Modernity*, 4–5.

10. Vattimo, *The End of Modernity*, 1–13, 166–167.

11. See John Milbank, *Theology and Social Theory: Beyond Secular Reason* (Oxford: Blackwell, 1990) for a thorough tracing of this position. See also Graham Ward, "Introduction, or, A Guide to Theological Thinking in Cyberspace" in *The Postmodern God: A Theological Reader*, ed. Graham Ward (Oxford: Blackwell, 1997), xli. In seeking to break the hold of immanence and rationalistic metaphysics, however, these postmodern thinkers posit a difference that cannot be overcome. Difference offers us a trace of the heterogeneous origin of all things, but this in itself cannot overcome a metaphysics based on human reason because philosophy cannot

for understanding the world, postmodern philosophy seems fascinated with a sublime it is sure cannot be represented or made to secure reality. In attempts to show modernity's enslavement to the metaphysics of Enlightenment reason secured by the human subject, postmodernity is left with a modern sublime that is fragile, unrepresentable, and a trace that is seen only in the trauma and violence of its otherness and absence. Yet in this proposal by Vattimo and others, one hears only the echo of the modern—the constant pursuit of the new, now called hermeneutic interpretation and disguised as persuasive rhetoric and the will-to-power. Ultimately, despite assertions against master narratives and protestations that everything can be deconstructed, postmodernity itself seems still caught in the modern master narrative of freedom and will-to-power grounded in a nihilistic violence that is given an ontological reality. The only thing that seems sure and stable in postmodernity is that there is no meaning and that the world is endlessly caught in violence and trauma.[12] The most we can hope for is to find moments of terrible beauty—Nietzsche's "artistic taming of the horrible"—in the process of exposing the ugliness around and within. There is nothing more than this.

Yet, despite the best efforts of Nietzsche and his followers, the Enlightenment confidence in the inherent capacity and power of humans to improve themselves and the world, to continually rise to greater heights of achievement on all fronts, still stubbornly hovers over western culture. It can be seen in the arts, sciences, technology, and perhaps most tellingly, in popular culture, embedded in successful books and movies for all ages. Whether it's a blockbuster like *Avatar* or the latest bestselling Dan Brown novel, the message

overcome itself. The language of western philosophy is built upon the very metaphysics it seeks to overcome.

12. See Bauerschmidt, "Aesthetics: The theological sublime" for his discussion of this issue.

that humanity will eventually figure things out and live up to its inherent potential, unlocking the secret knowledge within and ushering in peace and harmony for all is deeply pervasive.

It is particularly in light of these movements within western culture—and the permutations of the concept of deification and the telos of human life that come with it—that Christians must struggle to properly understand and reappropriate the Christian understanding of human life as a participation in the life of God. For the Christian story requires a long, hard look at humanity's sinfulness and the consequences that flow from it. The Christian narrative carries out its own form of deconstruction on a residual Enlightenment confidence that humanity can self-sufficiently overcome all obstacles by reliance on inherent strength and capacity. But that reminder always comes within an even more powerful proclamation that God has created humanity for life with God and that God has insured that telos by the very gift of God's self, which overcomes all that can separate us from God. Humanity is created, called, and securely claimed for a life with God—not out of any inherent capacity, but solely as a gracious gift of a God who loves. Our source of secure hope lies outside ourselves, but it lies securely in the gracious love and purposes of God, who can be known in the revelation and self-giving of God's self in Jesus Christ. It is a narrative that must be reclaimed and confidently reappropriated in the current age.

To begin that reappropriation, we turn to the fifth century, particularly to Cyril of Alexandria. While Cyril is best known for his role in the christological controversies with Nestorius, Cyril's thought offers rich resources for recovering a Christian vision of redeemed and restored human life, a vision that offers hope and a teleological sense of purpose to a world that questions both. There has been much recent discussion of Cyril's work as a response to theological conceptions of a passible God.[13] But the fruitfulness of his understanding of participation in the life of God is just beginning to be reexamined and reappropriated in response to postmodern deconstructions of modernity and religion. These deconstructions are troublesome not only because they leave suffering and violence unredeemed, but because they result in a loss of hope and any teleological vision of the human life as an ongoing participation in the life of God that begins in the here and now through the power of the Holy Spirit.

We will examine the rich resources of Cyril's adamant insistence on the single subject of the incarnation as the divine Son who, through his mode of existence as a fully human being, overcomes sin and death itself in his one person and refashions humanity so that humans might be restored to life with God. Until recently, one of the reasons for Cyril's passionate insistence on the one person has often been overlooked: it is only through the unity of humanity and divinity in Christ that a transformed life is made possible for all creation. In addition, Cyril insisted on a dynamic view of this participation, involving both an ontological transformation that made humanity truly and fully human, and an empowerment for an ongoing dynamic growth in Christian living within the pattern of Christ.

In Cyril we see the affirmation that there is real hope for humans to be fully and authentically human, and that human life has profound purpose and meaning. But this hope is grounded not in humanity's own ability to find purpose or achieve potential from within itself. Instead Cyril reminds us that humanity finds its completion, fullness and purpose only in relationship to God through Christ and that we truly do participate in God's life through the life, death and resurrection of Jesus made present and real in human life through

13. See for instance the work of Thomas Weinandy, Paul Gavrilyuk, Herbert McCabe, and John O'Keefe.

look at his use of dialectic and analogy as he continually strives to emphasize the covenant relationship of God and humanity while also keeping the divine and human in confrontation. In addition, we will examine Barth's understanding of the relationship between nature and grace and the role this understanding plays in his conception of human life in God—including his explicit rejection of deification in favor of the theme of exaltation. Finally, we will explore his conceptions of the relationship between divinity and humanity before and after Christ's life, death, and resurrection and the ways in which his insistence on maintaining a firm divide between divine and human even after Christ illuminates these key themes.

Chapter 3 will turn to an examination of Balthasar and the key conceptions that form the framework for his understanding of deification and human participation in God's life. Balthasar's theological conceptions are analogical through and through. He honed his discussion of the analogy of being against Barth's adamant rejection of the concept and in conversation with Barth's proposal of the analogy of faith, in which knowledge of God is grounded in the prior revelation of God. Balthasar takes the concept of the analogy of being and gives it a christological structure. This christological analogy of being pervades his theological conceptions and allows him to radicalize and stretch Cyril's conception of the one person of Christ and the wondrous exchange in Christ as he places before us the dramatic event of God's irruption into human history in Jesus Christ. We will examine Balthasar's argument that in the one person of Christ, God assumes the absolute depths of human alienation from God—even to the depths of suffering in hell—in order to bring humanity into the heights of a life with God, to the point of seeing creation as a non-necessary enrichment in the life of God itself. We will explore Balthasar's conceptions of sin and the fall, his confidence that grace perfects nature, and his conviction that God in Christ assumes everything that can separate humanity from God, overcoming sin and death in order to free humanity to become truly human and to play a real role in Christ's ongoing work in the world.

In chapter 4, we will bring together an analysis of Barth and Balthasar in light of Cyril. Both Barth and Balthasar take seriously the impact of Christ's life, death, and resurrection on creation and both seek to give an account of the human response to this event. While their christological positions have much in common, their treatments of the way in which humans participate in the divine life differ substantially. Barth provides a detailed exposition of human ethics with a rich discussion of humanity as God's covenant partners. However, he adamantly refuses even to consider the concept of deification in any serious way. He conceives of deification as a concept that would blur the sharp distinction between humanity and divinity, which he is determined to preserve. On the other hand, Balthasar rarely discusses specific ethical issues in detail. However, he does sing of the saints, and his Christology itself is based on analogical participation in mission. While Barth refuses deification, Balthasar is open to ideas of deification and participation that can speak of creation as an enrichment in the life of God. This chapter brings together the work of the previous three by analyzing the conceptions of Barth and Balthasar and their visions of human life as a participation in God's life through the lens of Cyril's understanding of deification. The similarities between Barth and Balthasar have been noted by a number of scholars.[14] However, they have different conceptions of the role and acting spaces for human beings, different perspectives on how and to what extent humans participate in the divine life, and different understandings of the effects of that

14. See for example the work of Stephen Wigley, *Karl Barth and Hans Urs von Balthasar: A Critical Engagement*, as well as Mark McIntosh's and Edward T. Oakes's works on Balthasar, which note similarities and differences between the two theologians.

participation. Comparisons to Cyril's Christology help illuminate the differences between Barth and Balthasar in these key areas. In this chapter, we examine to what extent each of them captures Cyril's insights into the redemptive and transformative union of humanity and divinity in Jesus Christ that draws humanity into the life of God.

Finally, a brief concluding chapter will summarize findings and point toward opportunities for further study and conversation. Christianity provides the possibility of envisioning the redemption of a postmodern world caught in a seemingly endless cycle of falsely placed hope and the despair that follows. In ways subtle and overt, postmodern culture promotes an ontology of suffering and violence, which is troublesome not only because it leaves suffering and violence unredeemed, but because it results in a loss of hope and any teleological vision of human life. In contrast, Cyril, Barth, and Balthasar place before us theology that sees creation as a gift of God, in which humans are held and transformed by the gracious, redeeming, and sustaining love of the Trinity. This vision of human life as a participation in the life of God made possible by Jesus Christ through the power of the Holy Spirit offers postmodernity a counter-ontology of transformed humanity made possible by the sheer gift of God's grace, and urges us to purposeful and holy living as God's people.

These three theologians remind us that in Jesus Christ, God has overcome sin, death, and violence and restored creation to its intended harmonious relationship of participation in the life of God. They call us to place on the horizon once again the classical Christian conception of real and true participation in the life of God, made possible by Christ through the power of the Holy Spirit, who draws humanity toward an inexhaustible light. Cyril, Barth, and Balthasar remind us, each in their own way, that if Christ's salvific work is truly effective, then all of life has changed and humans now have the possibility of a radically new life—both here and now, and eternally. This ancient affirmation of Scripture and the Christian tradition provides a teleological hope and direction that gives meaning to life now and moves us toward the future with faith and confidence in God's redemptive purpose and power.

1

––––––

Deification in the Early Church and Cyril of Alexandria

It is therefore manifest, in my view, and plain to all that it is especially for these reasons that, being God and by nature from God, the Only-begotten became man in order to condemn sin in the flesh, kill death by his own death and make us sons of God, regenerating those on earth in the Spirit and bringing them to a dignity that transcends their nature.[1]

—Cyril of Alexandria, *Commentary on John*

Cyril of Alexandria was passionately convinced that if we want a true and faithful understanding of Christology, if we are to worship and live rightly as followers of Christ, then we must start with the economy of salvation and God's intended telos for humanity. The "why" of the incarnation remains Cyril's focal point throughout

1. Cyril, *Commentary on John*, trans. Norman Russell, from the text of P. E. Pusey, *The Commentary of St. John*, Vol. 1, Library of the Fathers of the Church 43 (Oxford: James Parker, 1874) in Russell's *Cyril of Alexandria* (New York: Routledge, 2000), 18–19.

his writing—before, during, and after his contentious debate with Nestorius. For Cyril, the telos of human life *is* deification. The Word becomes flesh to "reconstitute our condition within himself."[2] It is the unique union of divine and human in the one person of Jesus Christ that makes this possible.

This intimate connection between Christology and soteriology is key to understanding Cyril's theological work and his adamant confrontation with Nestorius. For Cyril, that argument was not a hypothetical debate about the finer points of systematic theology as an academic exercise—for him nothing less than the salvation of humanity was at stake in affirming that there is only one subject: the second person of the Trinity, the Word, is the sole subject of all of Jesus' words and actions. Cyril's single subject Christology is inextricably linked to his soteriology. The Word became human to share what we are so that we might be given a share of the divine life through his life, death, resurrection, and ascension. For Cyril, salvation is participation in the divine life, made possible by the fact that the Word became flesh. Through his life, death, and resurrection Christ opened a way for humanity to be raised to life with God. As Cyril notes, ". . . he came down into our condition solely in order to lead us to his own divine state."[3] God became human so that sin and death would be defeated and humanity would be transformed—both ontologically and morally.

It is this soteriological conviction that fuels his strict rejection of any conception that threatens the unity of divine and human in the one subject of the incarnation. Failing to see or affirm the unique union of divine and human in the incarnation undoes the entire economy of salvation. This is the central issue at stake in Cyril's

2. Cyril, *On the Unity of Christ*, trans. John Anthony McGuckin, *St. Cyril of Alexandria: On the Unity of Christ* (Crestwood, N.Y.: St. Vladimir's Seminary Press, 1995), 62.

3. Cyril, *On the Unity of Christ*, trans. McGuckin, 63.

debate with Nestorius and indeed with any theological conception that fails to see how the incarnation is linked to nothing less that the transformation of humanity into those who participate in God's life.

However, having said that, there are immediately a number of questions and issues that arise regarding deification itself, and certainly there is no small number of theological concepts intrinsic to Cyril's theology that have been and continue to be the subject of debate. If we are to use Cyril's conceptions as a lens through which to examine Karl Barth and Hans Urs von Balthasar, a number of issues need to be addressed in this chapter, including a brief exploration of whether deification is a viable and faithfully Christian concept, as well as a thorough understanding of Cyril's Christology and his conception of participation.

We will begin with an examination of the concept of deification, which itself has become an incredibly complex issue and has developed differently in the Western and Eastern traditions of the church since the Middle Ages—indeed it has become one of the factors that continually causes friction between the two traditions.[4] A good number of Western theologians (including Barth) reject the concept of deification itself. They often argue, like Adolf von Harnack, that it is a Greek Hellenistic import into Christianity that should be jettisoned, or worry that embracing deification necessarily entails impingement on the real distinction between God and humanity, either by violating divine transcendence or by evacuating

---

4. It is beyond the scope of this study to explore the complex and highly nuanced differences regarding the understandings of deification, or participation, that have developed in the Eastern and Western traditions since the Middle Ages, particularly through the traditions linked with Aquinas in the West and Palamas in the East. For a thorough exploration of Aquinas and Palamas on *theosis*, including an argument that the two traditions share more in common than is often thought, see A. N. Williams, *The Ground of Union: Deification in Aquinas and Palamas* (Oxford: Oxford University Press, 1999). For an account of participation and deification in modern Catholic thought, see Adam G. Cooper, *Naturally Human, Supernaturally God: Deification in Pre-Conciliar Catholicism* (Fortress, 2014).

humanity of its properly human nature. Our study will examine the origins of the concept of deification and its development in the early church. We will see that this concept is a central and strong affirmation of the early church's soteriology and vision for human life in Christ, which Cyril receives and develops.

After exploring deification, we will turn to Cyril of Alexandria himself. Cyril's theology during the modern era has been studied or cited for his emphasis on single subjectivity, but often without sufficient attention to the scope of his thought and the intricate linking of his Christology to his soteriology and pattern of redemption. Fortunately, a number of studies in recent years have rectified this deficit.[5] As we begin our study, then, it will be important to spend time understanding the background and scope of Cyril's Christology within the context of his debate with Nestorius—which is fundamentally a debate about the relationship of Christology to soteriology—before we turn to an examination of Cyril's conception of deification itself.

As we develop our understanding of Cyril, the approach will be first to examine the context of Cyril's debate with Nestorius—and the nuances of Theodore of Mopsuestia's thought on which Nestorius drew—in order to understand Cyril's position as it was hammered out in that controversy. We will examine the differences in language and conceptual framework between the two theologians to see what light those divergences cast on what was at stake in the debate, particularly related to their soteriological patterns and their vision for human life in Christ. Taking the time to explore this background will also aid us in subsequent chapters, because, as we shall see, the

---

5. I am particularly indebted to Daniel Keating whose work on Cyril's emphasis on the appropriation of the divine life has greatly informed my understanding of the intimate connection between Cyril's Christology and soteriology.

issues between Cyril and Nestorius have not disappeared in modern theological discourse.

Finally, we will be in a position to examine Cyril's understanding of deification, focusing on the way in which this concept is linked inseparably to his Christology, as well as looking at the role of the Holy Spirit in human participation in divine life. Throughout we will note the careful distinctions and boundaries he places around deification—boundaries that protect the real distinction between divine and human and the real fullness of each, while also allowing for a real participation and a transformed human life.

Is Deification Even Christian?

Those of us in the western tradition of the church have inherited a distrust of the very word deification in the large and sustained wake of Harnack's attack on it as a purely pagan and Hellenistic concept imported into Christianity with deleterious results.[6] Harnack argued that the exchange formula so critical to Alexandrian Christology—that God became human so that we might become "what he is himself," as Irenaeus put it—was a miraculous transformation of human nature that altered its natural state in ways that were contrary to the gospel narratives.[7] The question arises as to whether Barth's rejection of deification may at least in some measure be due to this inheritance from Harnack. Before we move to Cyril's conceptions, it seems wise to begin by taking a closer look at deification itself, with a brief review of several recent studies that

6. See Adolf von Harnack, *History of Dogma*, vol. 1, trans. Neil Buchanan from third German edition (Boston: Little, Brown, and Company, 1902), 45–57. Harnack's thesis was that when the gospel was rejected by the Jewish people it became altered by the Hellenistic culture of the Gentiles who accepted the message but imposed Hellenistic philosophical concept upon it in ways that perverted or obscured the original message.

7. See Norman Russell, *The Doctrine of Deification in the Greek Patristic Tradition* (Oxford: Oxford University Press, 2004), 3 for an extensive discussion of this issue.

have cast serious doubt on Harnack's thesis and instead assert that deification is a thoroughly Christian concept.

Scholars such as Norman Russell, John Meyendorff, and Robert Wilkin have recently argued that this supposed Hellenization of Christianity is more myth that reality. Yes, the early Church used the language and some conceptual frameworks of the Greek world, but they also radically transformed them in the process.[8] While the early church fathers were influenced by Platonism—incorporating ideas related to participation—the idea of deification itself and the vocabulary that grew up around it were developed primarily within Christianity.[9]

In addition, the charge of Hellenistic distortion of the New Testament overlooks the deeply Jewish roots of Christian ideas. Russell notes, for instance, that the concept of transcendent life beyond death developed over time in Judaism itself.[10] Carl Mosser also has argued that the Christian patristic writers drew on Jewish interpretive tradition, particularly related to Psalm 82, as they developed the concept of deification. Mosser notes that the patristic writers considered themselves faithful to their Jewish roots, not to pagan Hellenistic conceptions in developing the concept of deification.[11] Further, faithfulness to these Jewish roots meant the early church theologians remained firm in asserting that participation in God does not mean that humans become God. The human's

---

8. Russell, *The Doctrine of Deification*, 8. See also John Meyendorff, *Byzantine Theology: Historical Trends and Doctrinal Themes* (New York: Fordham University Press, 1974) 23–25, and Robert L. Wilkin, *The Spirit of Early Christian Thought: Seeking the Face of God* (New Haven: Yale University Press, 2003).

9. Russell, *The Doctrine of Deification*, 52.

10. See Russell's argument in *The Doctrine of Deification*, 57–61.

11. See Carl Mosser, "The Earliest Patristic Interpretations of Psalm 82, Jewish Antecedents, and the Origin of Christian Deification," *Journal of Theological Studies*, NS, 56, Pt. 1 (April 2005): 30–74.

individual identity as human is retained and is not changed at the level of essence.[12]

Moving from this framework, the Christian scriptures themselves speak of participation through Christ in God's new creation as bringing with it a real change. The idea of a new creation is seen in a number of facets in the New Testament, particularly in Paul's concept of participatory transformation and union and in John's emphasis that all who believe in Christ possess such life in the present. Because Jesus actually is life himself, all who participate in him through belief and Baptism also receive eternal life as a supernatural gift through the Holy Spirit.[13] By the time Cyril began writing to Nestorius, these scriptural themes had developed into a kind of shorthand—the exchange formula—through which these early theologians gave expression to the link between who Christ is and what he does, between Christology and soteriology, particularly around Christ's restoration of humanity to the image and likeness of God culminating in a participation in Christ as a new creation.[14]

Emerging against a Jewish backdrop and given expression in the Christian Scriptures, the concept of deification as a participation in Christ leading to a new creation surfaced as a central theme early in the church's life as a way of giving expression to the salvific work and purpose of the Trinity on behalf of the creation.[15]

12. See Russell's discussion, *The Doctrine of Deification*, 59–65. See also Khaled Anatolios, *Athanasius: The Coherence of His Thought* (London: Routledge, 1998) for an extensive discussion of the way Athanasius developed and used the concept of participation to express the relationship between God and creation.

13. Russell, *The Doctrine of Deification*, 79–89. This theme resonates through the early church in theologians such as Irenaeus, Athanasius, and, later, Cyril.

14. Donald Fairbairn argues that this soteriological pattern that emphasizes God's "personal presence" was the predominant one across the early church. See Fairbairn, *Grace and Christology in the Early Church* (Oxford: Oxford University Press, 2006).

15. Bruce McCormack echoes Harnack's characterization of this concept as a "Platonic ontology of participation" imported into Christianity with damaging results. See McCormack, "What's at Stake in the Current Debates over Justification" in *Justification: What's at Stake in the Current Debates*, ed. Mark Husbands and Daniel J. Treier (Downer's Grove, Ill.: Intervarsity, 2004)

Key Concepts in Understanding Deification:
Sin, Death, Nature and Grace

To understand the concept of deification that developed in the early church, particularly in the Eastern tradition out of which Cyril emerged, it is important to understand the theological importance of the fall and its consequences of sin and death. If deification is the restoration of humanity as the image and likeness of God, how did the fall affect that image and how does deification restore it?

There are a number of scholars who have noted a pattern of redemption common to the early church, in which the story of salvation moves from creation, in which humans are created in the image of God as the recipients of grace who are designed to grow ever more into likeness and fellowship with God through obedience, which is the gift of the Spirit. Human disobedience breaks this spirit-filled and empowered relationship, distorts human's likeness to God and results in sin and death. In Christ God personally enters into the creation and, through the union of divine and human in the incarnation, overcomes sin and death in himself through his death and resurrection, imbuing humanity with the indwelling of the Spirit through Christ and restoring it to participation in the life of God.[16]

104–106. Russell and Wilken have disagreed, arguing that such themes have their roots deeply in Judaism and the earliest Christian tradition. See also David Bentley Hart's work for his insistence that themes of analogical participation have their roots in the biblical accounts and that these early Christian theologians worked with Greek ontological concepts but actually subverted their metaphysical understandings. See David Bentley Hart, *The Beauty of the Infinite: The Aesthetics of Christian Truth* (Grand Rapids: Eerdmans, 2003). See especially, 250–260, 349–360.

16. See Athanasius, *On the Incarnation of the Word* (www.ccel.org/athanasius/incarnation/html.) chapters 1and 2 and Cyril, *Commentary on the Gospel of John*, in Library of the Fathers (London: W. Smith, 1885), two volumes, translated by P. E. Pusey, Vol. 1 and T. Randall, Vol. 2; also available at archive.org. (Author's note: In the Pusey translations, I have substituted modern versions of the older English words for readability – i.e. partakes instead of partaketh.) See also Fairbairn, *Grace and Christology in the Early Church,* Daniel Keating, *The Appropriation of the Divine Life in Cyril of Alexandria* (Oxford: Oxford University Press, 2004), Veli-Matti Kärkkäinen, *One with God: Salvation as Deification and Justification* (Collegeville, Minn.:

John Meyendorff argues that, for the Greek patristic tradition of Athanasius and Cyril, participation in the life of God undergirds all of human anthropology. Humans are created to live in a graced relationship with God and outside of this relationship they are not authentically human.[17] As Meyendorff and Veli-Matti Kärkkäinen note, mortality, not guilt, was seen as the main problem facing humanity. For those in the Greek tradition, all of humanity is affected by the death and corruption that resulted from Adam's disobedience, but sin is viewed as the ongoing consequence of this distortion brought about by death and corruption, which have broken humans' ability to be who they truly are—participants in God's life. As a result of death and corruption, humans have an increasing propensity to exercise their free will in sinful ways and they bear responsibility for this personal sin, but death and the corruption it brings are the primary problems.[18] Death, not sin, is *the* critical enemy.[19] Through his death and resurrection, Christ conquered death and opened the door for humanity to be renewed, to be empowered for progress in the moral life, and to attain likeness to God and once again participate in a life of intimate relationship with God.

In addition, it is important to understand the relationship between God's gracious initiative and human free will and response. God's grace is always primary and initiative, yet humans have a genuinely free will to respond to that grace, though even this responsiveness is a graced gift. Grace is what provides the ground for the cooperation between God's will and humans' freedom of choice and continued growth toward God's intention for human life. Grace does not remove human freedom or responsibility.[20] Kärkkäinen notes,

---

Liturgical, 2004), and Meyendorff, *Byzantine Theology* for extensive studies of these themes in the early church.

17. Meyendorff, *Byzantine Theology*, 137–138.
18. Meyendorff, *Byzantine Theology*, 143–146.
19. Kärkkäinen, *One with God*, 21.

"Theosis is the mystery of human nature's perfection in Christ, not its alternation or destruction, because theosis is the mystery of eternal life in communion with God in the divine Logos."[21] ✳

Deification in the Early Church

Within the matrix of these scriptural, theological and anthropological frameworks, the concept of deification continued to develop in the early centuries of the church. A. N. Williams notes that from the third century forward, deification became the "dominant model of the concept of salvation."[22]

A brief survey using the work of Russell, Meyendorff, and Khaled Anatolios is helpful in order to place Cyril's conception of deification within the larger framework of the developing tradition, particularly in the work of Irenaeus and Athanasius. The theme of human life as a life intended for participation in God's life was deeply embedded in Greek patristic thought.[23] In Irenaeus we see the most extended early treatment of deification with the emergence of the exchange formula: the Son became human in order to make us "what he is himself."[24]

---

20. Meyendorff, *Byzantine Theology*, 139. See also the discussion on 38–40.
21. Kärkkäinen, *One with God*, 25, citing Kenneth Paul Wesche's work in "Eastern Orthodox Spirituality: Union with God in Theosis," *Theology Today*, 56, no. 1, (1999), 31.
22. Williams, *The Ground of Union*, 27. Donald Fairbairn also argues that the Alexandrian conception of God's personal presence in the incarnation was a predominant way of understanding the incarnation and salvation across the church even during the conflict between Cyril and Nestorius. Through an extensive study of both Alexandrian and Antiochene writers, including John of Antioch and John Chrysostom, Fairbairn argues that the vast majority of these early theologians held to a concept in which, through the incarnation, and the life, death, and resurrection of Jesus Christ, who is the true presence of God, humanity is transformed and restored to a life of participation with God. For a thorough discussion of this issue, see Donald Fairbairn, *Grace and Christology*, 221–226.
23. See Meyendorff, *Byzantine Theology*, 32.
24. Irenaeus: *Against Heresies*, ed. and trans. Alexander Roberts and James Donaldson. *Ante-Nicene Fathers* I (Edinburgh: T&T Clark and Grand Rapids, Eerdmans, 1996): cited in Russell, *The Doctrine of Deification*, 106. Russell argues that Irenaeus's exchange formula has its roots in Pauline thinking (as in Phil. 2:6-8; 2 Cor. 8:9).

This formula would become a central concept of Christology and soteriology for the early church. Fighting against Gnosticism, Irenaeus argued that there was an ontological and true union of God and humanity in the incarnation. This had to be the case if the incarnation's saving purpose was to effectively recover the image of God lost at the fall, an image that becomes regenerated in humans through participation in the incarnate Logos through the Spirit, through the practices of the church and the sacraments.[25]

However, Russell argues that it is important to note that as early as Irenaeus, "the 'exchange' signifies precisely that: an exchange of *properties,* not the establishment of an identity of *essence.*"[26] There is no miraculous overruling or evacuation of human nature—it does not become divine at the level of essence.[27]

With Athanasius, whose thought would be so influential for Cyril, Daniel Keating argues that there are additional developments that govern how participation is understood and used in the early church.[28] As Athanasius debated against the Arians, he refutes the subordinationist concept that the divine Son receives his divinity from the Father through participation. Instead, Athanasius asserts that the Son is fully of the same essence as the Father. What possesses the same essence has no need to participate. It would be a participation

25. For a discussion of this theme see Williams, *The Ground of Union,* 28 and Russell, *The Doctrine of Deification,* 108. Irenaeus was responding to the gnostic conception that God was removed from creation and would not interact with physical and earthly matter, which was conceived as evil. Emphasizing the real, ontological character of the union of God the Son with actual human flesh was an important Christian counter to this gnostic conception.

26. Russell, *The Doctrine of Deification,* 108. See also Williams's discussion of the emergence, as early as Irenaeus of an emphasis on balancing of the "unbreachable divide" between divine and human essence and the participation by the human in the divine by grace. *The Ground of Union,* 28. See also Anatolios, *Athanasius,* 80–83, for Anatolios's exposition of Athanasius use of predication to speak of the exchange of properties in the incarnation.

27. Russell, *The Doctrine of Deification,* 113. Athanasius and Cyril repeatedly stress this point throughout their writings.

28. Keating, *The Appropriation of Divine Life,* 153.

in oneself. Humanity shares in the Sonship of Christ by participation and grace, but not in any way essentially or by nature.[29]

In Athanasius, the Word deifies the body he assumes and humanity now shares in that deified flesh. Human nature is exalted in Christ and this exaltation is its deification.[30] The Word makes human nature his own and humanity is taken into the incarnate Word to share in the exchange of attributes between God and humanity.[31] This exchange of attributes—divinity to Christ's humanity and humanity to Christ's divinity—is crucial to Athanasius's understanding. Neither divine nor human are erased or improperly mixed through this participation. Further, the Son in his divine nature needs no deification because he is completely divine himself. Only the flesh he assumes is deified.[32]

It is also important to note that central to Athanasius's view of humanity is its receptivity.[33] Khaled Anatolios argues that, for Athanasius, humanity in its intended orientation to God is primarily receptive. It is oriented to the reception of grace and relationship with God.[34] Russell also notes that the role of Jesus' passive receptivity for Athanasius: "The sin of ordinary human beings lies precisely in their

29. See Athanasius's arguments throughout *Contra Gentes and De Incarnatione*, and Anatolios, *Athanasius*, 50–61, 104–109, 124 for a fuller exposition of Athanasius's understanding and use of the concept of participation as the way in which humanity is transformed into likeness to God by the incarnation without erasing the distinction between God and creature. Cyril also repeatedly returns to this argument in the Commentary on John. See Keating, *The Appropriation of Divine Life*, 153–154.

30. See Athanasius, Orations Against the Arians, in *The Trinitarian Controversy*, translated and edited by William G. Rusch (Philadelphia: Fortress Press, 1980) 107–113. See also Russell, *The Doctrine of Deification*, 171.

31. See Athanasius, *Orations Against the Arians*. See also Thomas G. Weinandy, *Athanasius: A Theological Introduction* (Farnham: Ashgate, 2007) 37–38 for a discussion of this exchange, and Anatolios, *Athanasius*, 80–83, 142–155, for a discussion of Athanasius's use of a model of predication to speak of this exchange. See also Russell, *The Doctrine of Deification*, 171–172.

32. See Weinandy, *Athanasius*, 32–37 and Russell, *The Doctrine of Deification*, 173–178. See also Anatolios, *Athanasius*, 70–73, 140–163 for an extensive discussion of the soteriological importance of Jesus' full humanity

33. See Athanasius, *Orations Against the Arians*, 105–109.

34. Anatolios, *Athanasius*, 2, 155–161.

failure to be receptive. Christ by contrast, was *totally* receptive to the Word, so that we can say that the Word was the single subject of all Christ's saving acts."[35] Anatolios also notes that it is Christ's perfect reception of divine grace as a human that makes it possible for us to be receptive to the Spirit and deification. The incarnation becomes the axial ground for the indwelling of the Spirit in humanity and the transformation of human being. Our receptivity is dependent upon Christ's receptivity.[36]

These developments through Athanasius became the foundation of the Alexandrian conception of deification that Cyril would take up in his debate with Nestorius and we will see Cyril take these themes and develop them during the controversy with Nestorius. We conclude this brief tracing of the development of the concept of deification with Russell's summarization of its four-characteristic features: 1) A strong emphasis on transcendence and immanence coming together in the one person of Christ. Christ, as the first fruits of humanity and the pattern we are to follow, makes possible our participation in the divine life. 2) A heavy use of participation as an ontological sharing of being in Being. In this understanding, humanity retains its finite, limited status but dynamically shares in the divine through the power of the Spirit, who moves humans toward a moral life in the image and likeness of God. 3) Further, this concept is an emphatic rejection of any attempt to erase the distinction between God and creation. God does not become less God, but rather humans participate in the exaltation of Christ's humanity. 4) The ecclesial context for deification is given a central place and moves the conception away from a merely contemplative exercise toward the practices of the sacraments and the virtues in communal life.[37]

---

35. Russell, *The Doctrine of Deification*, 186.
36. Anatolios, *Athanasius*, 157–161.
37. Russell, *The Doctrine of Deification*, 203–204.

Deification is never an innate human quality. It is a gift of participation in the divine life as a gift of grace in Christ through the Spirit.

Cyril of Alexandria:
Dynamic Participation in the Life of God

We are now in a place to turn to Cyril as he develops this tradition he received and defends this christological and soteriological understanding in his dispute with Nestorius. As we will see, Cyril picks up Athanasius's ideas and further develops them by emphasizing the two-fold aspects—corporeal and spiritual, ontological and moral—of dynamic participation in the divine life. However, to properly understand Cyril's conceptions, it is critical to see them within the context of his single subject Christology and against the backdrop of his pneumatological reading of the creation and fall story.[38] For Cyril, Christology and soteriology are mutually interrelated and determinative within the Trinity's plan of salvation for creation. His insistence on a single subject Christology is driven not by abstract metaphysical speculation but rather by the economy of salvation through which God becomes truly human so that humans can be given new birth and participation in the divine life. "In short, he took what was ours to be his very own so that we might have all that was his."[39] In his debates with Nestorius, nothing less was at stake. And it is against this background of his controversy with Nestorius that his views can be clearly seen.

---

38. I am greatly indebted to Daniel Keating's in-depth study of these aspects of Cyril's thought. Here see, Keating, *The Appropriation of Divine Life*, 24–25.
39. Cyril, *On the Unity of Christ*, trans. McGuckin, 59. Meyendorff argues that because Cyril's christological conceptions were so tied to the soteriological issue of participation in God's life, this was a key issue in his rejection of Nestorius's views. See Meyendorff, *Byzantine Theology*, 32.

Truly to understand Cyril's conception of deification then, we must see the key insights of his single-subject Christology that are so integrally interconnected with his conceptions of salvation. Because Cyril's christological views were articulated against the backdrop of the controversy with Nestorius, it is important briefly to examine these concepts within the context of that debate and against the Nestorian view he sought to refute.[40] This is important not simply to locate his views in historical context, but also to understand the key paradigmatic differences between Cyril and Nestorius. Their respective Christologies functioned in truly different soteriological paradigms. As we will see in later chapters, those divergent patterns of redemption and ways in which the one person and two natures of Christ are seen in relationship to one another continue to influence modern theology, including ongoing discussion about the teleology of human life. If we are to understand the importance of Cyril's insights, we must see them as they develop in conversation with Nestorius and his alternative christological and soteriological paradigm.

The Debate with Nestorius

When Nestorius delivered a series of lectures in 429 pronouncing that Mary could not properly be called the Mother of God, the very real differences between two divergent conceptions of Christology and soteriology were placed on a collision course. In Cyril's emphatic responses to Nestorius's public squeamishness about calling Mary

40. McGuckin argues that after Nicaea, the key issue facing fifth-century theologians was a clear articulation of how a single-subjectivity (union) of Christ could be reconciled with the affirmation of two natures. The dilemma was to avoid a conception of two subjects, one human, one divine, while also avoiding a single subject conception that would, in asserting Jesus' humanity, evacuate his divinity or vice versa, or create a *tertium quid*. See John McGuckin, *Saint Cyril and the Christological Controversy: Its History, Theology and Texts* (Crestwood, N.Y.: St. Vladimir's Seminary Press, 2004), 178–179.

"Theotokos," Nestorius believed he heard Cyril advocating an Apollinarian mixture of divine and human that erased Jesus' true humanity and impinged upon the divine impassibility. Cyril, on the other hand, believed that affirming Mary as Theotokos was critical for any authentic conception of the real union of divine and human in the incarnation and the salvation of humanity made possible by it.

With these debates between Nestorius and Cyril, John McGuckin argues that several key issues regarding Christology had come to a head: the need for a consensus on terms for discussing and defining the issues; the conception of the way divine and human were related in Christ, as well as what it meant to be human; and the concept of Christ's personal identity or what McGuckin terms the "active subject referent" of the Incarnate Christ.[41] In addition, and perhaps most importantly, there were real differences in the framework within which Cyril and Nestorius viewed the incarnation and the economy of salvation. We will look at each in turn to ensure that we have grasped the critical issues necessary to understanding Cyril's Christology and soteriology.

Critical Issues in the Debate

In order to better understand the differences between Cyril and Nestorius, we must examine their theological frameworks, which include Nestorius's conception of the prosopic union, Cyril's conception of the hypostatic union, the two theologians understanding and use of the common language and concepts available for these descriptions, their understandings of what constitutes human being, and how they view the relationship of humanity to divinity in Christ. All of these issues play a role in

41. McGuckin, *Saint Cyril*, 194.

understanding the conflict that emerged between the two men and their views of Jesus and his soteriological work.

Nestorius: Prosopic Union

As we begin an exploration of Nestorius, it is crucial to note that his conceptions grew out of the soil of Theodore of Mopsuestia's theology. To understand Nestorius, one must understand Theodore and the soteriological background for his Christology. Thus, a brief examination of Theodore is necessary, not only to understand Nestorius's and Cyril's disagreements, but also because Theodore's concepts have not disappeared totally from the landscape of modern theology, as we will see in subsequent chapters.

Theodore believed that humans were created in the image of God and thus became the place where all other creatures came into contact with God.[42] As Frederick McLeod explains, for Theodore humans, beginning with Adam as created in the image of God, are the bond uniting the material and spiritual worlds. Adam is the head of mortal life and is an image of the invisible God. He provides a visible manifestation of God's image, mediating God so that creatures can love and worship God through the free exercise of obedience.[43] It is critical to note that this concept of image is tied to the necessity for humans to live freely according to God's will.[44] However, sin and

---

42. Frederick McLeod, *The Image of God in the Antiochene Tradition* (Washington, D.C.: The Catholic University of America Press, 1999), 64. For a discussion of the importance of human freedom and obedience in Theodore, see Richard A. Norris, *Manhood and Christ*, (Oxford: Clarendon Press, 1963) especially 209–210, 233–238.

43. Frederick McLeod, *The Roles of Christ's Humanity in Salvation: Insights from Theodore of Mopsuestia* (Washington, D.C.: Catholic University of America Press, 2005), 11–12, 60–62, 104–106.

44. See Norris, *Manhood and Christ*, 173–189 for an extensive discussion of the role of Theodore's anthropology, especially his concept of free will, in his christological conceptions. See also, 209–210, 233–238.

death have broken that relationship and image. As a result, humans can no longer serve as the bond between creation and God.[45]

Because Adam freely chose to sin, in order to overcome this sin Christ must freely choose to not sin through his own free human will. While aided by the Spirit through all temptations, nonetheless, Christ's human will freely chose to be obedient to God's will.[46] So if Christ is not completely human with a completely free human will, he cannot fulfill his role as image, mediator, and bond between creatures and God.[47] It is because Christ lives a sinless life through obedience that he is not subject to death. It is thus Christ's obedient humanity that overcomes sin and death as he unites his human will with God's will and alters the cosmic effects of Adam's disobedience and sin. [48] Donald Fairbairn argues that for Theodore, humanity actually plays the most active role in salvation as it strives through obedience to live into conformity to God's intention.[49]

45. McLeod, *The Image of God*, 67. See also Donald Fairbairn, "The One Person Who Is Jesus Christ: A Patristic Perspective" in *Jesus in Trinitarian Perspective*, ed. Fred Sanders and Klaus Issler (Nashville: B&H, 2007) 96, who argues that Theodore's soteriology places the primary accent on humanity's efforts to exercise obedience to the example Christ sets, but does not really see the Spirit as indwelling or enabling a real participation in God's life via the incarnation.

46. McLeod, *The Roles of Christ's Humanity in Salvation*, 63. See also Fairbairn, "The One Person," 93–94, and Norris, *Manhood and Christ*, 192–195.

47. See McLeod's arguments through *The Roles of Christ's Humanity in Salvation*, especially 118–120 and *The Image of God*, 137. See also Paul B. Clayton, *The Christology of Theodoret of Cyrus: Antiochene Christology from the Council of Ephesus (431) to the Council of Chalcedon (451)* (New York: Oxford University Press, 2007) for his exploration of the importance of the humanity and its free will in the Antiochene tradition represented by Theodore, Nestorius, and Theodoret, 94, 134, 284–285.

48. McLeod, *The Roles of Christ's Humanity in Salvation*, 62–65. See also McLeod, *The Image of God*, 246–247. Because Christ's humanity and the complete obedience of his human will play a critical role in Theodore's conception of salvation, he carefully guards the humanity in his conception of the prosopic union. This insistence on the importance of Jesus' human obedience to God's will is part of the reason why Theodore so adamantly opposed those who said that the Word was also the subject of Christ's human actions. Theodore believed that this severed the unity of Jesus' human obedience to God's will. In his view, the Word was the source of energy for Christ's human acts, the responsibility and locus for his human actions emanated from his humanity's free will as he chose to be faithful and obedient to God's will. See McLeod, *The Image of God*, 188–190, 241. See also Norris, *Manhood and Christ*, 205–207, 237–238 for a discussion of the importance of Christ's obedient humanity for Theodore.

49. Fairbairn, "The One Person," 93–94

In addition to this critical role played by Christ's human will, McLeod argues that it is important to see Theodore's conception of "nature."[50] Coming from a tradition of scriptural interpretation and exegesis that was historical and literal, rather than abstract or allegorical, Theodore did not deal in universals or abstractions regarding "nature." Every truly existing nature must have both its own *hypostasis* and its own *prosopon*.[51] In other words, for every nature to be real it must be a concrete, individual existence (*hypostasis*) of a more abstract reality and it must have an externally visible appearance or manifestation (*prosopon*) by which its concrete inward characteristics or *hypostasis* are made outwardly known. Every nature must have both in order to be real.[52] So in Christ, if he is to be affirmed as fully human and fully divine, there must be two *hypostases* and two *prosopa*. The divine and human natures are concrete, existent natures that are the agents of their own individual actions.[53] So, for Theodore, only divine attributes can be directly predicated of the Word and only human attributes can be directly predicated of the assumed man. Thus, he could not assert that Mary is the Mother of God without some qualification that she was not the mother of the divine *nature*.[54] For Theodore, these two *hypostases* and two *prosopa* come together in an "exact union" in which they are

50. See Francis A. Sullivan, *The Christology of Theodore of Mopsuestia* (Rome: Analectia Gregoriana, 1956) 204–219. Sullivan argues that Theodore simply does not make a distinction between the abstract concept that the Word assumed human nature and the concrete idea that the Word became a particular, individual man.

51. See McLeod, *The Roles of Christ's Humanity in Salvation*, 150–151. See also Clayton, *The Christology of Theodoret of Cyrus,* 70–74, 99 for a discussion of Theodoret, Theodore's successor among the Antiochenes and a leading spokesperson during the Nestorian conflict and aftermath. Clayton argues that the Antiochene tradition as seen in Theodore and Theodoret does not have a conceptual paradigm to understand Cyril's insistence that Christ is the Word of God, the sole subject of the incarnation. Instead, there are only two possibilities: either the human becomes absorbed by the divine and thus cannot fulfill its salvific role, or the humanity fuses with the divine into a *tertium quid* that is still not really or fully human.

52. See McLeod's discussion in *The Roles of Christ's Humanity in Salvation*, 140–145.

53. See Norris, *Manhood and Christ,* 200–202.

revealed in one common *prosopon* of Christ, who visibly acts in divine and human ways and thus reveals that he is both. McLeod explains that Theodore moves from the outward manifestation to the inward reality.[55] The fact that Christ visibly acts in both human and divine ways reveals that he is both human and divine. But if he is both, then the two natures must each have their own *hypostasis* and *prosopon*. While the Word gives power to the humanity for activity, it never overpowers or replaces the humanity's own *hypostasis*.[56] Theodore is adamant that the *hypostasis* of Christ's humanity is always united with the *hypostasis* of the divine Word—even on the cross.[57] However, for Theodore, since each nature must have its own *hypostasis* and *prosopon*, the term *hypostatic union* would mean that Christ's human nature had been absorbed into the divine and now only the divine nature existed.[58] Francis Sullivan argues that the real issue behind Theodore's theology was a rejection of Arianism and a fear of Apollinarianism, coupled with an inability to distinguish between nature and person. Theodore insisted that human and divine activities must be attributed at the level of each respective *nature* and could not see that there was another option—the option chosen by Cyril and the Alexandrians to attribute human and divine activities to the single *person* of the Incarnate Word, without violating the proper nature of either God or humanity.[59]

---

54. See Clayton, *The Christology of Theodoret*, 15–52 and Sullivan, *The Christology of Theodore,* 286–288 for a basic summary and scholarly analysis of the Antiochene position and their difficulties with the conception of Theotokos.

55. McLeod, *The Roles of Christ's Humanity in Salvation*, 150–151.

56. McLeod, *The Roles of Christ's Humanity in Salvation*, 155. See also Clayton, *The Christology of Theodoret*, 62–63, 70–73 for the way Theodore uses these terms, and Sullivan, *The Christology of Theodore,* 203–214, 223–232.

57. McLeod, *The Roles of Christ's Humanity in Salvation*, 153–157.

58. See Clayton, *The Christology of Theodoret*, 73, and McLeod, *The Image of God*, 132–134. In addition, to say that the divine nature has been united to the human nature hypostatically would be saying that the divine nature has now limited itself to one spatial location, and God could never be so limited.

Given Theodore's conceptual framework and his understanding of nature, Christ's unity was best expressed as a *prosopic union*—one common *prosopon* in which Christ is visible on earth. Each nature, divine and human, has its own *prosopon*, but each functions in free and visible ways through the one visible *prosopon* of Christ common to both.[60] The two natures and wills function independently as *hypostatic* natures and yet come together in such a way that they are visible as one.[61] Christ's one *prosopon,* acting in both divine and human ways, reveals that he has both a divine *prosopon* and *hypostasis* and a human *prosopon* and *hypostasis*.[62] We can see one Christ, but this one Christ with one *prosopon* acts in both human and divine ways. Seeing this, we then know that Christ has both a human and a divine *hypostasis* and *prosopon* because every nature must have both in order to be real. The divine and human *prosopa* are distinct and separate as human and divine, but they act together in a complete outwardly visible unity.[63] Theodore uses *prosopon* as a descriptive, not a metaphysical term, as McLeod notes. It does not define the kind of union but rather the way in which the two natures act together in such unity as to manifest one visible Jesus.[64] While Theodore is adamant that the Word and human are to be thought of as one in the prosopic union, he still maintains the existence of two sons, one the (divine) Son by nature and the other a (human) son by God's grace, who function as one in a common *prosopon*.[65] Even in the presence

59. Sullivan, *The Christology of Theodore*, 286–287.
60. See Sullivan, *The Christology of Theodore*, 260–284, 287–288 for a detailed analysis of Theodore's conception of the one *prosopon*, and Clayton, *The Christology of Theodoret*, especially 72–73 for a thorough discussion of the Antiochene conception of prosopon and the prosopic union. See also McLeod, *The Image of God*, 133.
61. See Norris, *Manhood and Christ*, 201, 216 and McLeod, *The Image of God*, 147.
62. McLeod, *The Roles of Christ's Humanity in Salvation*, 166. See also Sullivan, *The Christology of Theodore,* 227–228.
63. See McLeod, *The Roles of Christ's Humanity in Salvation*, 166–167 for an extensive discussion.
64. McLeod, *The Image of God*, 165. See also Norris, *Manhood and Christ*, 276–277.

of Christ's one common *prosopon*, one must still discern between the characteristics, words and action that pertain to the human and those that belong to the divine.[66]

Theodore thus argues for a basically functional unity and offers this functional, existential explanation of how the two natures act as one because, Sullivan and McLeod argue, he simply has no way to conceive of a more ontological union.[67] A substantial union for Theodore only can be between two realities of the same substance. For him a substantive union meant that one or the other substance was altered.[68] Since Theodore excluded a substantial or ontological union because he believed such a union would necessarily blur or obliterate the distinction between divine and human. He sought a union at the level of grace and a harmony of wills and activity. Richard Norris argues that for Theodore, there could be "a single source (though not a single subject) of all that Christ is and does."[69]

This strong emphasis on the distinctiveness of the two natures, combined with Theodore's view that the center of divine and human

65. See Clayton, *The Christology of Theodoret*, 57, McLeod, *The Image of God*, 161 and Sullivan, *The Christology of Theodore*, 276–288. For Theodore, the term "God" was used only to refer to the Father. Theodore was unwilling to affirm that Christ is God in this way. See *The Roles of Christ's Humanity in Salvation*, 249 for McLeod's discussion.

66. McLeod, *The Roles of Christ's Humanity in Salvation*, 200. See also McLeod, *The Image of God*, 153. Theodore's conception of the prosopic union does allow for a form of *communicatio idiomatum in concreto*, in which the interchange of predicates regarding humanity and divinity happens in the one *prosopon*, not at the level of natures. See George Kalantzis, "Is there Room for Two?: Cyril's Single Subjectivity and the Prosopic Union," *St. Vladimir's Theological Quarterly* 52, no. 1 2008: 95–110. See also Sullivan, *The Christology of Theodore*, 276–288 for a discussion of Theodore's understanding of the one prosopon and communication of idioms.

67. See Sullivan, *The Christology of Theodore*, 276–288 and McLeod, *The Image of God*, 242–243. See also, McLeod, *The Roles of Christ's Humanity in Salvation*, 176–204. See also Clayton, *The Christology of Theodoret*, 56, 176, 189–191 for a discussion of his agreement with Sullivan that the Antiochenes inability to distinguish between nature and person is rooted in their fight against Arianism—with their inability to distinguish between nature and person, the Antiochenes were driven to a two-subject Christology.

68. McLeod, *The Roles of Christ's Humanity in Salvation*, 178, McLeod, *The Image of God*, 139, and Sullivan, *The Christology of Theodore*, 236.

69. Norris, *Manhood and Christ*, 228, cited in McLeod, *The Roles of Christ's Humanity in Salvation*, 193.

activities lay in the distinctive natures themselves, led to trouble in the christological debates with Cyril when Nestorius tried to use Theodore's model. While Cyril used *hypostasis* to mean the *subject* of unity and attribution, arguing that the Word is the common subject of all Jesus' sayings and actions, for Theodore and Nestorius the centers for divine and human activities are in the existing *natures*.[70] Because of the way the Antiochenes understood *physis* as a concrete, existing reality, they looked upon nature as the subject responsible for actions.[71]

Different Concepts, Different Language

In the christological debates with Cyril, Nestorius pressed beyond Theodore's use of *prosopon* as a descriptive and functional conception, employing it in a more metaphysical sense.[72] In addition, the terms *physis* and *hypostasis*, which played a critical role in the conversation between the two sides, were in flux. In his extensive discussion of the issue, McGuckin notes that Cyril often used the ancient conception of *physis,* meaning the concrete, existing reality of an individual thing, and Nestorius the more current meaning denoting the nature of the thing itself, while in the case of *hypostasis*, Cyril used the more modern meaning conveying the concrete reality of an individual and Nestorius the more ancient conception meaning the nature or

---

70. McLeod, *The Roles of Christ's Humanity in Salvation*, 157–158. See also Clayton, *The Christology of Theodoret,* especially 72–73, 283–286 for a review and comparison of Theodoret and Theodore where he finds this same emphasis on the natures as the center of activities.

71. McLeod, *The Image of God*, 241. In addition, for them a human person is characterized by function, not by metaphysics. See McLeod, *The Roles of Christ's Humanity in Salvation*, 157–158.

72. At the time, McGuckin explains, there were four terms available to express this idea of union: "*Ousia*: essence, substance, being, genus or nature. *Physis*: nature, make-up of a thing. (In earlier Christian thought the concrete reality or existent.) *Hypostasis*: the actual concrete reality of a thing, the underlying essence, (in earlier Christian thought the synonym of physis). *Prosopon*: the observable character, defining properties, manifestation of a reality." *Saint Cyril*, 138.

makeup of the thing itself. In addition, during the course of the controversy, each tended to use the terms in different ways, and this inconsistency added to the confusion and difficulty.[73]

In the Alexandrian school, *physis* was used to mean the physical existent—a concrete individual reality. Cyril uses the term to mean both the basic elements of a thing and to convey the idea of an individual existent or subject. Cyril's dual use of the term made it difficult for Nestorius and others to understand what he meant by *mia physis* or "the single *physis* of the Incarnated Word."[74] But for Cyril, the whole point of Christology is to insist on the fact of union, not to spend time talking about the distinction of two things—human and divine—whose differences were already obvious.[75] So the key was to say "The one enfleshed nature of God the Word"[76]—the adjective "enfleshed" qualifies "the word nature, not the personal pronoun Logos," McGuckin explains.[77] By this, Cyril meant one concrete individual *subject* of the Incarnate Word, but Nestorius took this to mean one physical composite of the Word as a mixture of the divine and human, creating a hybrid.[78]

At the time, the word *hypostasis* meant making a generic or abstract thing concrete and real. While the term *physis* carried some of this

---

73. In addition, McGuckin argues that many modern studies translate the two key terms *prosopon* (preferred by Nestorius) and *hypostasis* (preferred by Cyril) into one word "person" when the two terms were not synonyms, and in the fifth century neither term meant what the modern term "person" means. See *Saint Cyril*, 138–140. See also Donald Fairbairn "The One Person," who argues that one of Cyril's most significant contributions "is that one must not treat a nature as if it were a person." 108.

74. Cyril, *Second Letter to Nestorius*, in *Cyril of Alexandria, Select Letters* (Oxford Early Christian Studies) trans. Lionel Wickham (Oxford: Oxford University Press, 1983), 10, and McGuckin, *Saint Cyril*, 140.

75. See Cyril, *Third Letter to Nestorius*, in *Cyril of Alexandria*, trans. Wickham 19–23.

76. McGuckin, *Saint Cyril*, 208.

77. McGuckin, *Saint Cyril*, 208.

78. McGuckin, *Saint Cyril*, 140. See also Fairbairn, "The One Person," 99, who notes that Cyril uses *physis* to denote the single subject of the incarnation, as well as Sullivan, *The Christology of Theodore*, 281–288.

connotation, gradually *hypostasis* became the preferred term for this notion in which an abstract entity became a concrete, individual entity.[79] Conversely then, anything that was a real existent had to be hypostatized, and it was here that the real difference between Cyril and Nestorius came into play.

Cyril asserted that if Christ was to be truly one individual then he could have just one hypostatic reality, whereas, like Theodore, Nestorius argued that every *ousia*, or genus, had to have its own *hypostasis*.[80] For Cyril *hypostasis* was the term that carried the meaning of subject center, and for Nestorius the term meant the physical basis of a genus. McGuckin explains that Cyril used the concept of the *hypostatic union* to mean "it was a single individual subject (the *hypostasis*: God the Word) who realized the union of two different realities (divinity and humanity) by standing as the sole personal subject of both."[81] Cyril, drawing upon the conception of *hypostasis* used in the Nicene-established Trinitarian language, used the term *hypostasis* to refer to the Word of God, second person of the Trinity, enfleshed in the incarnation.[82]

However, Nestorius, using the older meaning of *hypostasis*, heard Cyril's hypostatic union as meaning a material, hybrid union of divine and human, and argued that Cyril's conception rendered the humanity of Christ null since it deprived it of an actual, separate *hypostasis*.[83] For Nestorius, such a union in the incarnation would

---

79. McGuckin, *Saint Cyril*, 141. This usage can be seen in the trinitarian debates of the previous century with the definition that God was one *ousia* expressed in three hypostases.

80. See McGuckin's discussion, 149–150. See also Cyril, *Third Letter to Nestorius*, trans. Wickham, in *Cyril of Alexandria*, 23. See also Grillmeier, *Christ in Christian Tradition*, Vol. 1: From the Apostolic Age to Chalcedon (451), 2nd edition, trans. John Bowden (Atlanta: John Knox, 1975) 433–439.

81. McGuckin, *Saint Cyril*, 141–142. See Cyril, *Second Letter to Nestorius* trans. Wickham, in *Cyril of Alexandria*, 19–23.

82. See Thomas Weinandy, *Does God Suffer?* (Notre Dame: University of Notre Dame Press, 2000) and McGuckin, *Saint Cyril*, 149–150.

83. McGuckin, *Saint Cyril*, 142–143. See also Grillmeier, *Christ in Christian Tradition*, 433–439.

mean that the divine Logos became subject to the demands of the flesh and its suffering, destroying both divine impassibility and God's free act of entering into solidarity with humans.[84] Rather than *hypostasis*, Nestorius preferred Theodore's term *prosopon*, an external form of a *physis* made visible to external observation in a concrete form.[85]

In addition, Nestorius, following Theodore, was adamant about his conception that God did not take to God's self another, human nature (Cyril's position) but rather took up a human *prosopon* into an intimate union based on God's love and grace.[86] For Nestorius, the oneness of Christ was not compromised by being comprised of two natures. He proposed "a conjunction by interrelation," founded on the divine freedom of love rather than at the level of any necessity of nature. He argued that such a grounding of the union in the depth of God's love and grace made it superior and more ontologically stable than any union posed in terms of the natures, as McGuckin notes.[87]

---

84. McGuckin, *Saint Cyril,* 151. See also Clayton, *The Theology of Theodoret,* especially 285–286, for an extensive review of this aspect of Antiochene thought.

85. McGuckin, *Saint Cyril,* 143–144, 151–159. For Nestorius, each *ousia* (genus) is defined by it *physis* (proper nature) and every nature that is real is observable in its own *prosopon.* *Saint Cyril,* 144. But McGuckin argues that the problem is that he used the same technical term *prosopa* to deal with both the concepts of "differentiation and convergence." *Saint Cyril,* 156. While his intent was not to expound a "two sons" theory, nonetheless, the implications of Nestorius's use of language and the ways in which it could be interpreted in the common life of believers was problematic because it was not read as truly securing the unity of subject in Christ. Additionally, in Nestorius's schema, precision of language became crucial: for instance one could not properly say "Jesus raised Lazarus from the dead," because this was clearly not a human but a divine act of the Logos. Similarly one could not properly say, "the Logos died on the cross" because clearly the divine Logos cannot die, only the human Jesus. Thus, attempts as *communicatio idiomatum* were regarded by Nestorius as suspicious and inexact grammatical usages that were to be avoided. See McGuckin's discussion, 153.

86. McGuckin, *Saint Cyril,* 143, 162. See also Clayton, *The Christology of Theodoret,* 105–134, 141–152 for an extensive discussion of Theodoret's works, which Clayton argues are in harmony with Theodore and Nestorius. See Sullivan, *The Christology of Theodore,* 252–276 for a discussion of Theodore's concept of the union based on grace.

87. McGuckin, *Saint Cyril,* 162, 169–170. Unfortunately, Nestorius seemed unable to find language that could adequately communicate his concept. McGuckin explains three factors that weakened his argument: his rigid use of technical christological language; the inflexibility of the term *prosopon* he used to describe the union, which he tried to use to indicate both the

Nestorius struggled to posit a union parallel to that of Cyril, but his understanding of God's transcendence, immutability, and impassibility could not allow him to get there. McLeod quotes Leonard Hodgson to describe Nestorius's conundrum: "Nestorius is throughout perfectly consistent, and his theory a brilliant attempt to solve the problem on the basis of a principle which renders all solution impossible."[88] Pressed by Cyril on the issue, "Nestorius fell into a metaphysical maze that had no exit," McLeod argues.[89]

Cyril, of course, objected, arguing that Nestorius's conception simply did not account for the ontological reality of the union. If the union was based on grace or will it could be lost or rejected and this would be unthinkable.[90] Further, Nestorius's insistence on semantic exactness fed Cyril's suspicion that Nestorius viewed the unity of Christ as only a kind of language game as opposed to something ontologically real.[91]

Cyril: Hypostatic Union— The One Subject of the Incarnation

Certainly the differences in language did not help the situation. But the real clash went deeper than any rhetorical nuance—it was grounded in different soteriological paradigms. For Cyril, the

individual *prosopa* of divine and human as well as the one prosopic union; and his efforts to be overly precise with religious language, which appeared as a denigration of common piety and worship practices.

88. McLeod, *The Image of God*, 181, n. 77, citing Leonard Hodgson in *Nestorius: The Bazaar of Heracleides*, ed. Godfrey Driver, trans. Leonard Hodgson (Oxford: Clarendon, 1925), xxxv.

89. McLeod, *The Image of God*, 243.

90. Cyril, *On the Unity of Christ*, trans. McGuckin, 71.

91. McGuckin, *Saint Cyril*, 173. For a discussion of the continuing development of Cyril's concept of union by theologians in the next century, see Brian Daley's "Nature and the 'Mode of Union': Late Patristic Models for the Personal Unity of Christ" in *The Incarnation,* ed. Stephen T. Davis, Daniel Kendall, and Gerald O'Collins (Oxford: Oxford University Press, 2004), 196. Daley argues that even though the language moved in a more relational direction around the mode of existence, the union remains substantial and ontological for these theologians.

ontological reality of the hypostatic union is the basis for the entire economy of salvation. Cyril's model of salvation is a three-step process of creation, fall, and restoration, in which the acts of creation and salvation are seen as Trinitarian acts. In addition to an emphasis on the single subjectivity of Christ, Cyril also has a strong role for the Holy Spirit in the pattern of redemption.

In Cyril's account, in which he follows the pattern of redemption that was primary in the early church, humanity was created in the image of God and Adam received the inbreathing of the Holy Spirit. Meyendorff notes that it is important to see in this Greek patristic pattern, outlined by Cyril, the intent for humans to live by graced participation in the life of God, and that only in this participative relationship are they truly human.[92] Humans were also given free will and commandments to preserve this gift of life in the Holy Spirit, but disobeyed. This results in a gradual loss of the divine likeness as sin darkens the likeness and causes it to fade and degrade over time. Finally, when sin becomes dominant, human nature becomes devoid of this grace and the Spirit no longer dwells within it.[93] Jesus, as the Incarnate Word, enables our reacquisition of the Spirit. The Holy Spirit forms the vital indwelling link between creation and God through the one person of Christ and provides a stable, secure base for the Spirit's indwelling and transforming work in humanity.[94] This is a concept Cyril inherited from Athanasius and developed into a major

---

92. Meyendorff, *Byzantine Theology*, 139.

93. See Cyril, *The Commentary on John*, John 1:32-33 in Pusey, Vol. 1, 141. See also Keating, *The Appropriation of Divine Life*, 24–26. Cyril outlines this conceptual framework of the history of salvation in his earliest writing, *The Adoration in Spirit and in Truth*. See Russell, *Cyril of Alexandria*, 13, citing Cyril in PG 68, 145Bff. Russell notes that in these earliest of writings, Cyril's chief theological characteristics are already evident—among them his soteriological emphases. "It is these that determine his christology, just as his christology shapes his trinitarian theology." Russell, 14.

94. See Anatolios, *Athanasius*, 157–163 for a detailed exposition of this conception in Athanasius. Cyril takes up this theme: See Keating, *The Appropriation of Divine Life*, 24–26 and Cyril, *Commentary on John*, John 1:32-33, Pusey, Vol. 1, 142–143.

emphasis of his soteriology. The movement of the pattern is the gift and indwelling of the Holy Spirit, first given to Adam in creation, lost through the fall, and reappropriated in the Spirit through the Incarnate Word.[95]

Jesus makes it possible for us to recover this divine image, not simply through a remaking of our deformed or corrupt nature, but also by a reappropriation of the divine life through the indwelling of the Holy Spirit.[96] In the incarnation, the divine Son, who lacks nothing in himself, becomes human so that he can receive, as a human, the gift of the Holy Spirit that is crucial for human redemption and renewal.[97] The key here in Cyril's understanding is that, as the Incarnate Word, Jesus sanctifies his own humanity. As Cyril notes,

> Being also Himself by nature holy as God, and granting to the whole creation participation in the Holy Spirit to their continuance and stablishing and sanctification, He is sanctified on our account in the Holy Spirit, no one else sanctifying Him, but rather He Himself working for himself to the sanctification of His own Flesh. For He receives His own Spirit, and partakes of it, in so far as He was Man, yea, and gives it to Himself as God.[98]

From the moment of inception, the Word sanctified the humanity he assumed. The human is from its very inception hypostatized by the Word, giving the humanity of Christ a full, concrete and real humanity.[99] This sanctification is then shared with us through

---

95. Fairbairn, "The One Person," 95–96. See also Lois M. Farag, *St. Cyril of Alexandria, A New Testament Exegete: His Commentary on the Gospel of John* (Piscataway, N.J.: Gorgias, 2007) 109–110.

96. See Anatolios, *Athanasius*, 149–155, 158–163, Keating, *The Appropriation of Divine Life*, 25–28, and Farag, *St. Cyril*, 116, 135, who notes the way in which for Cyril, the incarnation has provided a stable base for the Holy Spirit to take root in humanity.

97. As we have seen, this is a theme in Alexandrian theology. See Anatolios, *Athanasius*, 142–163 for its exposition in Athanasius and Keating for an exposition of the theme in Cyril, *The Appropriation of Divine Life*, 28.

98. Cyril of Alexandria, *Commentary on John,* John 17:18-19, Pusey, Vol. 2, 540.

Jesus' life, death, resurrection, and ascension. Through Christ as the Second Adam, the Spirit returns to humanity through Jesus' baptism at the Jordan and then Christ breathes that Spirit on the disciples at Pentecost.[100] Through the ascension, as Keating explains, Christ intercedes and reigns for us as human, having fully restored human nature.[101]

A key feature of Cyril's Christology is its insistence on the transformation of humanity in Christ. In the incarnation, both divinity and humanity are united without either being diminished, but the Logos infuses the humanity with the glory and power of his own divine nature.[102] While there is no change in the humanity in a way that makes it divine or less than human, there is a transformation of it into something more fully human than it was.[103] It is through the Logos's total assumption of his completely full humanity, and the resulting transformation of the human being itself, that all humanity is therefore transformed and freed from sin and corruption.[104] This

99. McGuckin, *Saint Cyril*, 184. See also Russell's discussion of the soteriological impetus behind Cyril's adamant defense of Mary as Theotokos, in *Cyril of Alexandria*, 35. See also, Frances Young, "Theotokos: Mary and the Pattern of Fall and Redemption in the Theology of Cyril of Alexandria," in *The Theology of St. Cyril of Alexandria: A Critical Appreciation*, ed. Thomas G. Weinandy and Daniel A. Keating (London: T&T Clark, 2003), 55–74.

100. Cyril, *Commentary on John*, John 7:39 in Pusey, Vol. 1, 547–552 and also John 20:22-23 in Pusey, Vol. 2, 671–680.

101. See Keating, *The Appropriation of Divine Life*, 44–45.

102. Cyril argues: ". . . he made his own the flesh which is capable of death so that by means of this which is accustomed to suffer he could assume sufferings for us and because of us, and so liberate us from death and corruption by making his own body alive as God." *Explanations of the Twelve Chapters*, in McGuckin, *Saint Cyril*, 292–293. This conception also has significant implications for the sacrament. If the Logos does not own his own body—if the flesh is merely human flesh rather than flesh infused with the Logos' power—then the flesh received in the Eucharist is mere cannibalism. For the bread to truly be life giving then is must be the flesh of the Logos himself. See also Steven A. McKinion, *Words, Imagery & The Mystery of Christ: A Reconstruction of Cyril of Alexandria's Christology* (Leiden: Brill, 2000), 212.

103. Cyril, *Commentary on John*, John 16:7, in Pusey, Vol. 2, 440–444. See also Meyendorff, *Byzantine Theology*, 163–164 for his discussion of the way in which this sanctification of humanity through the incarnation in no way makes the human less human but rather more fully human precisely because humans are created to be in a participative life with God. In Christ, humans finally become what there were always intended to be. See also Anatolios, *Athanasius*, 157–163 for an exploration of this conception in Athanasius.

soteriological affirmation is the impetus for Cyril's adamant insistence on the hypostatic union as a christological cornerstone.

Within this framework, it is crucial that there be one subject in Christ—the Word who has taken on full humanity in Jesus Christ—because for Cyril, what is not assumed is not redeemed. It is precisely because it is the Word who becomes human, and precisely because it is fully a human being that the Word becomes, that humanity is freed from sin and death and for a transformed life of participation in the life of God. Cyril's insistence on the hypostatic union as a way of securing the single subjectivity of Christ flows from this soteriological conviction.

As we have seen, hypostasis means individual reality for Cyril. When he says hypostatic union, he means there is only one subject in the incarnation—the divine Logos—and that the union of the Logos with humanity is real and true. For Cyril, there are two christological principles at stake in his insistence on the single subjectivity of Christ: Christ is one divine and human individual, completely God and completely human; and the Word truly becomes a fully human person with a body and soul.[105] Russell notes that for Cyril, "hypostatic" denotes actual reality rather than a mere appearance, and a truly substantial existence. The hypostatic union was "real (i.e. ontological rather than moral) and personal (i.e. resulting in a concrete individual who was the single subject of the actions and experiences of Jesus Christ.)"[106] Meyendorff also emphasizes that for

---

104. McKinion, *Words, Imagery & The Mystery of Christ*, 211. See also Farag, *St. Cyril*, 110–117 and Weinandy, "Cyril and the Mystery of the Incarnation" in *St. Cyril of Alexandria*, 26.

105. As McKinion puts it, "The Word has added to his own divine nature a new human nature taken from the Virgin," and as a consequence, "the Word now possesses not only a divine nature, which is his as God, but also a human nature, which is his as a human being." McKinion, *Words, Imagery & The Mystery of Christ*, 203–204. See also, Cyril, *Explanations*, Anathematism 2, in McGuckin, 285.

106. Russell, *Cyril of Alexandria*, 42–43, and Weinandy, "Cyril and the Mystery of the Incarnation," 27.

Cyril, "hypostasis" does not designate nature but personal existence. The Logos is the active subject of all of Jesus' human acts.[107]

While Nestorius distinguished completely the humanity and divinity at the level of nature but perceived them as united in worship in the one *prosopon*, Cyril argued that after the union there was simply no point in such distinctions. As Cyril puts it, "And so our Lord Jesus Christ must not be divided up, as if there was a distinct man and distinct deity. No, we say that Jesus Christ is one and the same even though we recognize the difference of natures and keep them unconfused with each other."[108]

In the incarnation, the divine and human work in continual seamless unity with one another, so there is no instance of a solely divine or solely human act in Christ's life. Every word and action of the incarnate Jesus is, as McGuckin explains, "an act of God enfleshed within history."[109] In addition, because the Logos possesses his own body, all the sayings and actions of Christ—hungering, weariness, suffering and death or working miracles—belong to this one individual who is the Word of God incarnate.[110] In Cyril's conception of the *communicatio idiomatum*, anything that is predicated of the divine also can be predicated of the humanity and vice versa because the predication is not at the level of "nature" but rather all predicates are applied to the one subject, the Word Incarnate.[111] For Cyril, once the union has taken place, there is no real point in

---

107. Meyendorff, *Byzantine Theology*, 154–155.

108. Cyril, *Scholia on the Incarnation*, trans. McGuckin in *Saint Cyril*, 307.

109. McGuckin, *Saint Cyril*, 200.

110. Cyril, *On the Unity of Christ*, trans. McGuckin, 76–77. McGuckin argues that a difficulty modern readers have with Cyril's conceptual framework is understanding his insistence that the divine knowledge is self-limited in the incarnation. While in his divinity Jesus knows all, he nonetheless in the incarnation mediates that knowledge through human mental limitations. For modernity, personality is defined as "subjective intellectual consciousness," but for Cyril this was simply one of the functions of personhood rather than a defining factor. The one person of the Logos is not the result of Jesus' human consciousness—the Word is the origin of it. See *Saint Cyril*, 134.

continuing to speak of or regard them as two—to talk unceasingly about the two distinctions leads to the suspicion that one does not really believe in a real union.

Cyril was convinced of the necessity of a single subject in the incarnate Jesus, and he consistently argued that there is only one creative, acting subject in the incarnation—the divine Logos—who has made a human nature his own.[112] Human nature in itself is passible. But in its union with the divine in the incarnation that human nature becomes the vehicle of God's impassible power. Because Cyril so strongly believed that the purpose of the incarnation was to give new life to humanity and truly transform it, this affirmation of the union was crucial. The union of these two realities is a salvific act that is life giving and transformational for human beings.[113] The incarnation is a unique ontological reality. The union must have ontological depth—not in the sense of mixing the two natures, but in affirming the profound reality of the eternal Son of God as a human being. For Cyril, the term Theotokos "encapsulated the entire plan of salvation," Russell argues.[114]

---

111. See Russell, *Cyril of Alexandria*, 43 for a discussion of the way this differs from Nestorius's conceptual understanding. See also Meyendorff, *Byzantine Theology*, 154–155 for his discussion of the importance of this conception to Cyril and the Byzantine theological tradition.

112. Cyril, *Scholia*, in McGuckin, *Saint Cyril*, 317; and McGuckin, *Saint Cyril*, 183.

113. Cyril, *Third Letter to Nestorius*, Wickham's translation in *Cyril of Alexandria*, 23; and *Scholia*, McGuckin's translation in McGuckin, *Saint Cyril*, 304–305. See also McGuckin, *Saint Cyril*, 185.

114. Russell, *Cyril of Alexandria*, 44. From Nestorius on, Cyril's concept of union as securing the single subjectivity of Christ has been the subject of debate and misunderstanding, particularly when attempts have been made to reduce Cyril's complex thought patterns into formulas. McGuckin argues that Cyril's Christology is primarily discursive, and attempts to use sections of his work as a formula are misleading. Cyril and his contemporaries are struggling to use existing grammatical terms to perform in new ways christologically. See McGuckin, *Saint Cyril*, 194. In addition, Richard Norris also argues that Cyril has been misunderstood in modernity because scholars have tried to fit his christological conceptions into physical models, when in fact Cyril's model is linguistic, focusing on grammatical or logical relations among certain groups of words. See Richard A. Norris, "Christological Models in Cyril of Alexandria," *Studia Patristica*, Vol. 13, 1975, 255–268. See also Sarah Coakley's critique of Norris' approach as imposing a post-Kantian and post-liberal linguistic framework on Cyril and Chalcedon in

What Does It Mean to Be Human
and How Does Humanity Relate to Divinity in Jesus?

There is one more issue we must explore, and that is the conception of humanity and the way in which divine and human relate in Jesus. A common reading of the differences between Alexandrian and Antiochene Christology has focused on Alexandrian conceptions emphasizing the divinity (often to the detriment of the humanity) and the Antiochene position seeking to emphasize and preserve the humanity.[115] However, as we shall see, this oversimplifies and even somewhat obscures the real difference between the two, which is whether there is a real union of human and divine in which the Son of God is the sole acting subject of the fully human and fully divine Jesus. We turn our attention next to exploring this theme in Nestorius and Cyril, for it contains a key element in Cyril's conception of deification.

For Nestorius, as we have seen, Jesus must experience the full range of human emotions and subjectivity because it is Jesus' freely exercised human obedience that is salvific. We have also explored how Nestorius's conceptual framework requires a human subject in addition to a divine one in order to accomplish this. Because human emotions and actions must be predicated of the human *nature*,

---

"What Does Chalcedon Solve and What Does It Not? Some Reflections on the Status and Meaning of the Chalcedonian 'Definition' in *The Incarnation*, 146–152.

115. See Fairbairn's helpful exposition of the ways in which the differences between Alexandrian and Antiochene positions have been seen by scholars. He identifies three common explanations for the christological controversy: 1) political and personal rivalries that complicated theological understandings and obscured how close the two positions actually were, 2) a significant theological difference about whether the beginning point for Christology is the unity of the person or the duality of the natures in preserving the full humanity of Jesus, 3) a deep-seated issue about the central affirmation that in the incarnation God is personally present in human history. Fairbairn persuasively argues that the last of these three options is actually the driving force in the controversy—not an emphasis on divinity or humanity per se, but rather on the presence of God in the Incarnate Christ in the world. See *Grace and Christology in the Early Church*, 6–11.

Nestorius has no way to attribute them to a single subject without impinging on either the humanity or the divinity. The divine and human in Christ are represented by "two distinct, unchanged and unconfused natures" that remain in their respective divine and human spheres throughout his life. The two natures exist side by side and are neither confused nor limited by the other, McGuckin notes.[116] However, Nestorius was then left with the need to explain how his conception of the distinctiveness of the natures could be unified in Christ in a way that avoided a duality of subjects. His approach was to attempt to conceive unity in a more exacting and technical theological language, as we have seen in the previous section.

On the other hand, Cyril has often been accused of overshadowing the humanity of Jesus with his divinity and of making the humanity a mere instrument of the divine.[117] Often, concerns about Cyril's understanding of Christ's humanity have focused on whether he believed that Christ was fully human with a rational soul.[118] As Cyril

116. McGuckin, *Saint Cyril,* 133–135. See also Sullivan, *The Christology of Theodore,* 259–284 and Clayton, *The Christology of Theodoret,* 261, 267–268, 284–286 for his argument that this feature of Antiochene thought continued in Theodoret throughout the Nestorian controversy, and then through Chalcedon and its aftermath.

117. Norris has also argued that Cyril's thought pattern does not really fit into the "physical models" so often ascribed to him in an attempt to force his thought into either a "Logos/Flesh" or a "Logos/Man" model. While Cyril uses physical language, he consistently notes that it is inadequate in itself and returns to the linguistic form of the divine Logos made flesh. See Norris, "Christological Models," 267. In addition, Cyril's repeated use of the terms "ineffable" and "incomprehensible" are ways of saying that these physical terms are not explanations of the incarnation, but are merely images that remind us that "to speak of Jesus Christ is to speak of one subject in two distinct ways—to insist that he be described and understood both in the way that we can describe and understand God and in the way that we normally describe and understand man." Norris, "Christological Models," 267.McKinion points out that Cyril is not attempting to technically describe the "how" of the incarnation. Rather he uses images such as a body/soul analogy to help his readers better understand *what* had happened. He is using the images to reinforce the sense of union as "real and genuine" as different from what he saw as merely external union by way of divine favor or good will, and to drive home that there is one single subject in Christ. See McKinion, *Words, Imagery & The Mystery of Christ,* 77–78. See also Cyril in *Scholia* and *First Letter to Successus,* trans. McGuckin, in *Saint Cyril:* Scholia, 294-335; Successus, 352-358.

118. See Aloys Grillmeier, *Christ in Christian Tradition, Vol. I: From the Apostolic age to Chalcedon (451),* trans. John Bowden (Atlanta: John Knox, 1975), 416–418, 443–450, 473–483 for his

became more aware of the ways in which his christological language could be construed as Apollinarian, he began to emphasize more strongly his belief that Christ had a human mind and soul.[119]

For Cyril, the Logos did become a complete human, which means he had both a human body and rational soul, and lived a completely human life, though without sin.[120] Through a series of images (body and soul, the burning bush, the ark) Cyril argues that Christ can truly be one person, a single subject, both fully divine and fully human without either the humanity or divinity being diminished. "We declare that there was no mingling, or confusion, or blending of his essence with the flesh, but we say that the Word ineffably united to flesh endowed with a rational soul in a manner which is beyond the mind's grasp."[121]

Steven McKinion and John Meyendorff argue that the humanity of Christ actually has an important place in Cyril's Christology because of his soteriological convictions that what is not assumed is not redeemed, and his belief that the Logos, in becoming human, elevates and redeems humanity.[122] God truly becomes a human being. The incarnation is not a mere juxtaposition of divine and human because, as McKinion puts it, "The Word must die as a human being in

---

discussion of Cyril's Christology. See also McKinion, *Words, Imagery & The Mystery of Christ,* 149–155.

119. See Russell, *Cyril of Alexandria,* 41 for a discussion of the way in which this developed. Cyril continued to refine his language throughout the debate with Nestorius and its aftermath as he became aware of the differences in language and conceptual frameworks between him and the Antiochenes and the ways in which this led to a misunderstanding of his thought, particularly as being Apollinarian.

120. Cyril, *Third Letter to Nestorius,* trans. Wickham, in *Cyril of Alexandria,* 23 and McKinion, *Words, Imagery & The Mystery of Christ* 170–171. See also Farag, *St. Cyril,* 112.

121. Cyril, *Explanations of the Twelve Chapters,* Anathematism 1, trans. McGuckin, in *Saint Cyril,* 284. See also McKinion, *Words, Imagery & The Mystery of Christ* 172.

122. McKinion, *Words, Imagery & The Mystery of Christ,* 175 and Meyendorff, *Byzantine Theology,* 152–153, 159–164. See also Anatolios, *Athanasius,* 71–73, 80–83, 138–143 and Farag's study in *St. Cyril,* 77 for the ways in which Cyril is echoing Athanasius's insistence on the full humanity of Christ as a key soteriological aspect of the incarnation and 86–87 for her exposition of this critical theme in Cyril, particularly in his Commentary on John.

order to save as God."[123] For Cyril, the incarnation truly transformed human nature as the Word recreated that nature in his own humanity.[124]

In Cyril's conception, Christ's human nature does not act independently, but is rather what McGuckin terms "the manner of action" of the divine Logos, who is responsible for all words and acts of the incarnate Jesus.[125] It is important to note that for Cyril, the fully human Christ was not a human person, but rather a divine person who chose to live in the human condition. Nonetheless, "he made the things of the flesh his own so that the suffering could be said to be his."[126] Cyril in *Scholia on the Incarnation* says,

> [H]e through whom God the Father made the world was truly made man. He did not, as some think, come in a man so that we might consider him a man who had God indwelling him. If they hold this to be the case, and rely on it as true, then surely the saying of the blessed evangelist John appears pointless: 'and the Word was made flesh' (John 1:14). If he did not become flesh, what was the point of the Incarnation? Or why did he say that he had become flesh? The meaning of the term 'incarnation' signifies that he became like us, though even so he remained above us, and indeed above all the creation.[127]

123. McKinion, *Words, Imagery & The Mystery of Christ*, 182. See Cyril, *Third Letter to Nestorius*, trans. Wickham, *Cyril of Alexandria*, 19–25. See also Meyendorff, *Byzantine Theology*, 156–157, 159–161 for a discussion of the importance and role of Christ's humanity.

124. See Cyril, *Commentary on John*, John 12:27-28, Pusey, Vol. 2, 150–155 and John 17:18-19, in Pusey, Vol. 2, 536–543. See also Russell, *Cyril of Alexandria*, 45. Russell notes that this was the part of Cyril's conception that Nestorius "with his emphasis on the moral rather than ontological character of the union of the natures, found least acceptable." See also Farag's exposition of Cyril's thought in *St. Cyril*, 86–87.

125. McGuckin, *Saint Cyril*, 186 and Meyendorff, *Byzantine Theology*, 152, 157, 159, 163–164. See Cyril, *First Letter to Succensus*, trans. McGuckin, in *Saint Cyril*, 353 for Cyril's insistence that the Logos is the Son both before and after the incarnation. See also Meyendorff, *Byzantine Theology*, 154–156, for a discussion of the centrality of this concept in Cyril's theological tradition.

126. Cyril, *Letter to the Monks*, trans. McGuckin, in *Saint Cyril*, 260.

127. Cyril, *Scholia*, trans. McGuckin, in *Saint Cyril*, 312.

John O'Keefe argues that for Cyril, "The man we meet in the Gospels and in prayer is none other than the incarnate presence of the second person of the Trinity; no competing subjects, such as a separate human subject, vie for control of Jesus."[128]

Despite the often-reiterated criticism that Cyril's Christology fails to give due to the full humanity of Jesus, the opposite is true. For Cyril, Keating argues, Christ's humanity is crucial and is at once both representative and corporate as well as concrete and individual.[129] It is the divine Word who has fully taken on this full, concrete humanity and, as Second Adam, his humanity becomes representative for the whole race. In taking on all of the particularities of a concrete human life, he brings about, in his own humanity, a new human nature in which we participate through the Holy Spirit. Keating notes that for Cyril "the universal sense of this new human nature is, crucially, contained *within* the concrete, individual humanity Christ has assumed and transformed."[130] Given Cyril's strong conception of the single subjectivity of Christ, he affirms that Christ personally experiences real human suffering and temptation and at the same time overcomes them from within, and he provides this as a model for all of humanity who can now overcome these difficulties through the indwelling power of God.[131] While sin was not possible for Jesus, his mastery of the human passions by bringing them into submission to God's will, transforms human nature within himself.

128. John J. O'Keefe "Impassible Suffering? Divine Passion and Fifth-Century Christology," *Journal of Theological Studies* 58 (1997) 39–60, quote 48.

129. Keating, *The Appropriation of Divine Life*, 49. See also Meyendorff, *Byzantine Theology*, 154–156, 159, 163–164 for his discussion of this two-fold aspect of Jesus' humanity.

130. Keating, *The Appropriation of Divine Life*, 50 and Meyendorff, *Byzantine Theology*, 154–159, 163–164 for his discussion of this theme. See Cyril, *Commentary on John*, John 1:14 in Pusey, Vol. 1, 109–111.

131. Keating, *The Appropriation of Divine Life*, 127. See Cyril, *Commentary on John*, John 11:33–34, in Pusey, Vol. 2, 122 and John 12:28–30 in Pusey, Vol. 2, 150–155.

Christ's assumption of full humanity is thus necessary in order for him to save humanity and provide the pattern for human life.[132]

For Cyril, Keating and Farag note, the purposes of the incarnation were to recapitulate all things in Christ, to overcome sin and defeat death, and to make us his "sons" or children through the Spirit's regeneration.[133] It is precisely through the taking on of full humanity that the Son defeats sin and death in the flesh and transforms it, sanctifying the flesh. Moving back to the creation story, Cyril notes that humans originally participated in God's incorruption. They did not possess this of their own nature, but only through participation in the Spirit. Through disobedience that Spirit was lost and humanity became corruptible and subject to destruction. Christ, the fully divine Word who takes on full humanity, makes that participation once again possible. As Cyril puts it:

> "It was not otherwise possible for man, forasmuch as he was of a nature that was perishing, to escape death, save by recovering that ancient grace, partaking once more in God who holds all things together in being and preserves them in life through the Son in the Spirit. Therefore He has become partaker of blood and flesh, i.e. He has become man, being by nature Life, and begotten of the Life that is by nature, i.e., of God the Father, to wit. . . uniting Himself with the flesh that by the law of its own nature was perishing, He might bring it back unto His own life and make it through Himself partaker of God the Father. . . . And He wears our nature, remoulding it to his own Life. And He himself is also Himself in us, for we have all been made partakers of Him, and have Him in ourselves through the Spirit; for this cause we have both, being made 'partakers of the divine nature' (2 Pet. 1:4), and are entitled sons, after this sort having in us also the Father Himself through the Son."[134]

132. Keating, *The Appropriation of Divine Life*, 124–126. See Cyril, *Commentary on John*, John 17:4-5, Pusey, Vol. 2, 491–497.

133. Keating, *The Appropriation of Divine Life*, 163, and Farag, *St. Cyril*, 111. See this in Cyril, *Commentary on John*, John 14:20 in Pusey, Vol. 2, 316–322. See Russell, *Cyril of Alexandria*, 19, for a discussion of Cyril's use of three aspects of recapitulation: moral overcoming of sin, physical defeat of death, and spiritually becoming sons of God.

134. Cyril's *Commentary on John*, John 14:20 from Pusey, Vol. 2, 320. See also Keating, *The Appropriation of Divine Life*, 165.

The real humanity that the Logos becomes is thus crucial for Cyril's soteriology. The Logos is now enfleshed, having willingly taken on all the conditions of bodily existence in the flesh *in order* to use them in salvific ways. For Cyril, the Word did not simply "assume" or "occupy" a human body, he actually took on a real human life with all that means. The Logos now expresses divinity through this humanity, and this flesh of Christ becomes life giving for humanity.[135] The divinity of the Logos deifies his human body and moves out from this source to restore all of humanity. In the miracle and ineffable mystery of the hypostatic union, humanity is infused with the life-giving power of the Word. This does not mean that it becomes "divine" or less human, but rather it becomes truly and fully human in Christ and provides the way for all of humanity to be transformed.

Summary of Cyril's Christology

As McGuckin notes, there are three foundational concepts of Cyril's christological doctrine that must be kept in mind. First, there is only one "single-subject referent" and this subject—the "what"—is the eternal Word of God. Second, to understand the "how" of the incarnation requires first understanding the reason for it. One must begin with the "why," and the "why" is the salvific redemption and deification of humanity. In the incarnation, by taking on human flesh, the Logos achieves the regeneration of the human race at the ontological level. To questions of both the "why" and "how" of the incarnation, Cyril's answer was "as an economy of salvation." Third, explaining the "how" has to connect the "why" and the "what."

---

135. Cyril, *Scholia,* trans. McGuckin, *Saint Cyril,* 298 and Cyril, *On the Unity of Christ,* trans. McGuckin 131–133. See also McGuckin, *Saint Cyril,* 186.

For Cyril, only one available word could adequately speak of the "how"—*henosis* or hypostatic union.[136]

Cyril repeatedly called attention to the ineffable paradox and mystery at the heart of the incarnation: the divine Logos had truly become human. To deny full divinity and impassibility to the Logos is to destroy the economy of salvation because only God can destroy death and bring life. And to deny the full humanity of the incarnation is also to destroy the economy of salvation because it is only if the fullness of humanity is taken on by the Logos that it can be redeemed and deified.

Cyril's point was that the incarnation was a completely unique ontological event. The Logos did not replace a human fetus with its own hypostatic reality in Mary's womb, because this human fetus never existed independently of God's act, which alone was responsible for the inception. McGuckin notes that Cyril insisted that Christ is entirely human, but he is not a man. He is God made man—God enfleshed.[137]

Further, it is *in* this one person, fully divine and fully human—through his life, death, and resurrection—that humanity is transformed, and through that event of this person we are freed from sin and death and actually given a share of life in the life of God. Jesus Christ, the Incarnate One, is both agent and recipient of this transformation, as Anatolios and Keating have pointed out.[138] He cannot be less than fully divine because his divinity is the agent

---

136. See McGuckin's discussion of these three concepts, *Saint Cyril*, 184, 194–195. See Cyril, *Third Letter to Nestorius*, trans. Wickham, *Cyril of Alexandria*, 19–25; and *On The Unity of Christ*, 107–113.

137. See McGuckin's discussion, *Saint Cyril*, 215–216. See also Meyendorff's discussion, *Byzantine Theology*, 154–155.

138. See Anatolios, *Athanasius*, 147, 155, 157–161 and Keating, "Divinization in Cyril: The Appropriation of Divine Life," in *Saint Cyril of Alexandria*, 159. See also Frances Young's discussion of Cyril's *Commentary on Isaiah* in "Theotokos" in *Saint Cyril of Alexandria*, 66–67, particularly her note of the crucial role of Mary's receptivity in the pattern of redemption Cyril sets forth.

and he cannot be less than fully human, because his humanity is the recipient and becomes the stable grounding for the indwelling of the Spirit. He both divinely gives it and humanly receives it in perfect fullness and constant obedience as the Second Adam—for the transformation of all humanity and all creation.

Given this exploration of Cyril's theology, we can see that, as Thomas Weinandy notes, the heart of the argument between Nestorius and Cyril was not that they were using different words to describe the same concepts, but rather that they had different concepts of the incarnation altogether. Weinandy argues that Nestorius conceived of the two natures as separate before the incarnation and this consistently led him to think that the two natures were joined together rather than being truly united in Christ. His initial approach led to the difficulty that "having mentally separated them prior to the joining, he could not possibly conceive them as becoming ontologically one without destroying them in the process." This difficulty led him to believe that Cyril's conception resulted in a *tertium quid*.[139]

On the other hand, Cyril realized the implications of Nicaea's statement that God directly creates everything in the universe. If this were so, then God also could have directly created this real, substantial union between Christ's two natures.[140] God has the power to do this without becoming less than God or without a threat to God's transcendence or to humanity. Cyril remarks that, "indeed the mystery of Christ runs the risk of being disbelieved precisely because it is so incredibly wonderful."[141]

---

139. Weinandy, *Does God Suffer?* 181. See also Clayton, *The Christology of Theodoret*, 15, 46–47, 56–67, 142–149, 284–285.for his exposition of the differences between the conceptual frameworks of Cyril and Nestorius.

140. McLeod, *The Image of God*, 181. See also Anatolios, *Athanasius*, 22–25, 36–37, 50–51, for an exploration of this connection between the incarnation and God as creator in Irenaeus and Athanasius.

141. Cyril, *On the Unity of Christ*, trans. McGuckin, 61.

During the Arian controversy, the Alexandrians had come to understand the Word as the subject of Christ's human actions, but they distinguished between a predication of attributes to the divine nature itself and the divine nature in the economic plan of salvation. This allowed them to affirm that while the Word does not suffer in His divine nature, he can be said to suffer in the economy.[142] To put it simply, Cyril grasped the difference between nature and person. Nestorius used the term *hypostasis* to mean a "complete, existing nature that functions as the subject of its own actions."[143] For Theodore and Nestorius, *hypostasis* refers to a true, existing *nature* and each nature must have its own *hypostasis*. Because Christ has two natures, he therefore also must have two *hypostases*.[144] For Cyril, on the other hand, *hypostasis* signified the single subject of the person of Christ as a real, existing *individual,* to whom all divine and human attributes and acts could be assigned.

Weinandy sums up Cyril's position well by saying, "Jesus is one ontological entity and the one ontological entity that Jesus is, is the one person of the divine Son of God existing as a complete and authentic man."[145] Jesus *is* the divine Son existing as a human, as one being, fully human and fully divine. The concrete reality of the human Jesus is truly the Word of God. It is within this one person that the two natures come into union. Weinandy argues that Cyril distinguishes "between the person (the who) and the person's

142. See Sullivan, *The Christology of Theodore*, 161–165 for an exposition of this insight. See also McLeod, *The Roles of Christ's Humanity in Salvation*, 159, and Anatolios, *Athanasius*, 80–83, 134–138, 140–147 for an extensive discussion of Athanasius's understanding and use of the concept of predication.

143. McLeod, *The Image of Christ*, 144.

144. Kalantzis, "Is there Room for Two?" See also McLeod, *The Image of God*, 144, and *The Roles of Christ's Humanity in Salvation*, 152–153.

145. Weinandy, *Does God Suffer?* 174. See also Paul Gavrilyuk, "Theopatheia: Nestorius's main charge against Cyril of Alexandria," *Scottish Journal of Theology* 56, no. 2 (2003): 198 for his argument that "Cyril insisted that is was not a man indwelt by God, but God the Word incarnate who was the subject of all statements about Christ."

nature (the manner of the who's existence)" and clarifies that Jesus is "one and the same person, who existed eternally as God, who now exists as man." So for Cyril, Weinandy notes, "the incarnation does not involve the changing, mixing, or confusing of natures . . . but rather the person of the Word taking on a new mode or manner of existence" as a human being.[146]

In Cyril's understanding of the incarnational union, God, through union with the human, can now experience historical, bodily reality within the economy God has chosen to enter.[147] In similar fashion, the human nature, via the incarnation, is enhanced in such a way that its original condition is transformed by this unique reality.[148] As McGuckin puts it, "the union is about interchange and transformation . . . for the purpose of transfiguration and regeneration."[149]

In reading Cyril's Christology and his conceptions of deification, two common misunderstandings seem to prevail. Critics assume either that Cyril's understanding swallows up humanity into divinity, or they assume conversely that humanity impinges on the divine and threatens the divine impassibility. Both of these views simply fail to see Cyril's key insights and the basic understanding of the union that underlies his Christology and a vision of human life that flows from it.

The person of Christ is the place where the divine and human meet. This union forms the basis and creates the possibility for humans to participate in God's life, while also setting the boundaries

---

146. Weinandy, *Does God Suffer?* 197. See also footnote 46, pg. 196.
147. Cyril, *Scholia*, trans. McGuckin, *Saint Cyril*, 298; Cyril, *On the Unity of Christ*, trans. McGuckin, 102–113. See also McGuckin, *Saint Cyril*, 201.
148. Cyril, *Scholia*, trans. McGuckin, *Saint Cyril*, 304–305. See also Wilkin, *Judaism and the Early Christian Mind*, 110, 115–117, 120, 192–196, 219–221. See also McGuckin, *Saint Cyril*, 201, and Anatolios, *Athanasius*, 146–161 for a discussion of the importance for all humanity of this transformative power of Jesus' humanity in the incarnation. Cyril takes up this emphasis.
149. McGuckin, *Saint Cyril*, 204.

of that participation.[150] Cyril notes that Christ becomes a "common frontier" of divinity and humanity and holds together within his one person these two natures that are otherwise so radically different.[151] Christ makes this connection not only within his person, but he is also the only source for our transformation and participation in God's life.[152] The incarnation for Cyril brings about an exchange of attributes in which Christ "receives in himself the things particular to us and gives back the things that are of himself."[153] We are lifted up to a "new level of being," Russell notes, precisely because the Word has deified—transformed—the humanity he has taken on in the incarnation. "Cyril's single subject Christology is the necessary presupposition for his transformational spirituality."[154]

Partakers of the Divine Nature:
Ontological Transformation and Moral Response

As we have seen, a key feature of Cyril's Christology is its insistence on the transformation of humanity, and this contributes to his insistence on the union of the human and divine in the one person of Christ. In the incarnation, both divinity and humanity are united without either being diminished, but the Logos infuses the humanity with the glory and power of his own divine nature.[155] This view

---

150. See Keating's discussion, *The Appropriation of Divine Life*, 177.

151. Cyril, *Commentary on John*, John 10:15, trans. Keating from P. E. Pusey, *Sancti patris nostril Cyrilli Achiepiscopi Alexandrini in d. Joannis Evangelium*, 3 vols. (Oxford: Clarendon, 1872) 232–233 in Keating, *The Appropriation of Divine Life*, 178.

152. Keating, *The Appropriation of Divine Life*, 179. See also Anatolios, *Athanasius*, 150–161 for a discussion of the transformational effect of the incarnation on human being and its emphasis in Alexandrian thought.

153. Cyril, *Commentary on John*, John 20:17, trans. Keating from Pusey, Vol. 2, Keating's translation 122–123 in Keating, *The Appropriation of Divine Life*, 179.

154. Russell, *Cyril of Alexandria*, 45–46, quote 45.

155. Cyril argues: ". . . he made his own the flesh which is capable of death so that by means of this which is accustomed to suffer he could assume sufferings for us and because of us, and so

contributed to Cyril's adamant rejection of Nestorius's Christology, which Cyril viewed as positing an extrinsic union of humanity with the Word. Russell argues that "such a Christology could not recapitulate the whole of humanity in his person and transform it by divine power. Indeed, in Nestorius's Antiochene tradition there was no place for the deification of the Christian. Without a single-subject Christology salvation must be seen primarily in moral and exemplarist terms."[156] For Cyril, and the Alexandrian tradition he inherited from Athanasius, salvation is the transformation of human life as a participation in God's life. This *is* God's intention for human life.

Within this conceptual framework then, deification is the process by which humanity is restored to incorruption and through which humans participate in the divine life, both now and in eternal life. In the tradition Cyril inherited, deification involves growth in knowledge and love of God, illumination by God, and participation in the sacraments, which infuse the believer with grace and life.[157] However, Keating explains that Cyril uses the word "participation" far more than "deification," using three guiding premises that provide an analogical framework for his conception. This framework, which we have also seen in Athanasius, is designed to uphold the distinction between divine and human while also providing for a real participation of humanity in the divine life that results in transformation and moral response. Those premises as summarized by Keating are: 1) as human beings who participate, we are distinct in kind from the divine in which we participate; 2) we receive the qualities in which we participate only partially and in an external

---

liberate us from death and corruption by making his own body alive as God." *Explanations of the Twelve Chapters*, in McGuckin, *Saint Cyril*, 292–293.

156. Russell, *The Doctrine of Deification*, 199.

157. Williams, *The Ground of Union*, 30.

way, while that in which we participate possesses those qualities in an intrinsic and fully complete way; and 3) as those who participate, we can lose that which we have by participation, while that in which we participate possesses those qualities by nature and can never lose them.[158] Thus, this concept of participation defines both the analogical depth and breadth of the participation and also its boundaries and limits.[159]

Our participation in Christ is not such that our human natures in any way become co-mingled with the divine nature at the level of essence. As Cyril puts it, "Therefore the Son does not change the least thing belonging to the created order into the nature of his own deity (for that would be impossible), but there is imprinted in some way in those who have become partakers of the divine nature through participating in the Holy Spirit a spiritual likeness to him and the beauty of the ineffable deity illuminates the souls of the saints."[160]

Cyril takes over the Alexandrian exchange formula, but he is careful to say that even in this exchange Christ remains Son by nature and we are participants only through grace in the Spirit. The future glory in which we will participate through the resurrection, as well as our present participation in the divine life through the Holy Spirit, does not remove human beings' finite creatureliness. Even in this participation we remain completely human beings.[161] For Cyril to say that we are "partakers of the divine nature" does not mean the "frontier" that separates human and divine is ever transgressed in the sense of losing the distinction.[162]

---

158. See Keating, *The Appropriation of Divine Life*, 162, and Anatolios, *Athanasius*, 50–51, 56, 82–84, 104–109, 124. See also Cyril, *Commentary on John*, John 1:9-13, trans. Russell from Pusey, Vol. 1, in *Cyril of Alexandria*, 100–101.

159. Keating, *The Appropriation of Divine Life*, 162.

160. Cyril, *Against Nestorius*, trans. Russell, from texts by Eduard Schwartz in ACO I, 1, 6, 60.16-20, in *Cyril of Alexandria*, 163. See also Keating's discussion, *The Appropriation of Divine Life*, 181.

161. See Keating, *The Appropriation of Divine Life*, 176–177 and Russell, *The Doctrine of Deification*, 199.

This theme is repeated over and over again in Cyril's work, from his earliest commentaries through his writings to Nestorius and beyond. In his Commentary on John 1:12, Cyril says, "For having become partakers of him through the Holy Spirit, we were sealed with his likeness, and we mount up to the archetypal form of the image, according to which the divine Scripture says that we were made . . . Therefore we mount up to a dignity above our nature on account of Christ, but we also will be sons of God, not according to him identically, but through grace in imitation of him."[163] In his Commentary on Isaiah, Cyril notes, "it is the property of human nature not to possess any trace of the heavenly graces of its own will, or, as it were, by its own nature . . . Rather, it was enriched from outside and by acquisition, that is, from God, with that which transcends its own nature."[164]

Cyril is clear: Christ is a Son by nature, one in essence with the Father and Spirit, while we are partakers of his Sonship by participation through the gift of grace. As Cyril notes, "We, therefore, ascend to a dignity that transcends our nature on account of Christ, but we shall not also be sons of God ourselves in exactly the same way as he is, only in relation to him through grace by imitation. For he is a true Son who has his existence from the Father, while we are sons who have been adopted out of his love for us, and are recipients by grace . . ."[165]

With these boundaries firmly in place, Cyril understands that, through the incarnation, humans do participate in the divine life and are thus transformed and empowered by the Spirit for new life. But it

---

162. Russell, *The Doctrine of Deification,* 201–202.

163. Cyril, *Commentary on John,* John 1:12, trans. Keating from Pusey, Vol. 1, 133, in Keating, *The Appropriation of Divine Life,* 183.

164. Cyril, *Commentary on Isaiah,* trans. Russell, from Migne, *Isaiah 2.4,* PG 70, in *Cyril of Alexandria,* 83.

165. Cyril, *Commentary on John,* John 1:9–13, trans. Russell from Pusey, Vol. 1, in *Cyril of Alexandria,* 101.

is in the incarnation, and only in the Incarnate Word, that the divide between divine and human is overcome. Here that divide is truly *overcome*. The divine life of the Word infuses the humanity of the incarnate with life-giving power, overcoming the sin and death of the flesh that came with Adam and the Fall and empowering humans to participate in and imitate Christ's pattern of life. We become truly and fully human in this process.

Ontological Transformation

Cyril's conception of the incarnation emphasizes the one subject of the Word who has taken on full humanity and infused it with life-giving power without in any way destroying or confusing the divine and human. This understanding of the incarnation is directly tied to his soteriological conviction that God's intent through Christ is the ontological transformation of humanity through participation in the divine life in the power of the Spirit. We are given, solely as a gift of grace, a participation in Christ's being—not in essence but by grace.[166]

For Cyril, it is the union of divine and human, the Word's ownership of his humanity that makes it possible for Christ to overcome *in himself*, sin and the power of death, while giving humanity a share, through grace, in his life and power for newness of life. Here we see the way in which Cyril's single subject Christology is vital to his soteriology of deification. It is only because the Word truly is united with his humanity, without collapsing the distinction between divine and human, that it is possible for Christ to refashion humanity itself and infuse it with life-giving power. In Christ, God

---

166. See Cyril, Commentary on John, 17:22-23, Pusey, Vol. 2, 553–556. See also Keating, *The Appropriation of Divine Life*, 158–164, 185–187; and Frances Young, "Theotokos," 66 for her exposition of Cyril's emphasis on this gift of grace from outside of human nature.

makes it possible that "giving up the life that originally belonged to us, we should be transformed into another, and the very elements of our being be changed into newness of life well-pleasing to God."[167] Cyril's account of this transformation is a completely Trinitarian account in which we receive the gift of partaking in the divine life from the Father, through the Son, and in the Holy Spirit. Christ partook of our nature so that we might participate in his life.[168]

When Nestorius had difficulty with this concept, Cyril was amazed, asking, "What is strange or somehow impossible to believe about the Word of God the Father, who is Life by nature, rendering the flesh united to him capable of endowing with life?"[169] For Cyril, the Word *is* life itself and in the Word's hypostatic union with his own humanity, he infuses his life into all of humanity through participation.

Cyril argues in the *Commentary on John:*

> Moreover, the human qualities were active in Christ in a profitable way, not that having been set in motion they should prevail and develop further, as is the case with us, but that having been set in motion they should be brought up short by the power of the Word, nature having first been transformed in Christ into a better and more divine state. For it was in this way and in no other that the mode of healing passed over into ourselves too.[170]

Or again, as he put it in his *Commentary on Isaiah*, "For human nature blossomed again in him, acquiring incorruption, and life, and a new evangelical mode of existence."[171]

---

167. Cyril, *Commentary on John*, John 16:7 in Pusey, Vol. 2, 443.

168. Keating, *The Appropriation of Divine Life*, 173, 203–204. See also Farag, *St. Cyril*, for her discussion of this strong Trinitarian pattern in Cyril's thought.

169. Cyril, *Against Nestorius*, trans. Russell (from Schwartz's critical edition in ACO I, 1, 6) in *Cyril of Alexandria*, 168.

170. Cyril, *Commentary on John*, John 12:27, trans. Russell (from Pusey, Vol. 2) in *Cyril of Alexandria*, 120.

For Cyril, human nature truly has been renewed ontologically through participation by grace in Christ. In his commentary on John 17:18-19, Cyril notes that Christ asks

> that human nature be renewed and refashioned, as it were, to its original image, through participation in the Spirit, so that by having put on that first grace, and having been raised up to conformity with him, we may be found better and already more powerful than the sin which reigns in this world, and may attend only to the love of God, entirely devoted by the desire for every good thing whatever; and having our minds stronger than the love of the flesh, may keep the beauty of the image implanted in ourselves unspoiled.[172]

This leads Cyril to a consideration of freedom and human will, and of faith and obedience. Keating notes that there is a distinction in Cyril between full liberty and free will. Full liberty is lost with the fall and can be reestablished only by Christ, while free will remains intact after the fall and humans retain their ability to cooperate with grace.[173] In the incarnation, Christ fully gives and receives divine grace and freely offers himself, living in human obedience without sin.[174] Christ thus receives and responds to the grace and will of God with complete and perfect receptivity and obedience.[175]

The Alexandrian school had longed viewed the terms used to express deification—adoption, salvation, sanctification, renewal, and so on—as referring to the sacramental effects of Baptism. However, Russell argues that Cyril refines and completes this inherited conception and integrates it with the moral aspects of deification.[176]

---

171. Cyril, *Commentary on Isaiah*, trans. Russell (from Migne, PG 70, Isaiah 2.4, 309B–316B) in Russell's *Cyril of Alexandria*, 82

172. Cyril, *Commentary on John* 17:18-19 trans. Keating, (based on Pusey, Vol. 2,) in Keating, *The Appropriation of Divine Life*, 139.

173. Keating, *The Appropriation of Divine Life*, 114, n. 23, citing Marie-Odile Boulnois's work in "Liberte, origine du mal et prescience divine, 75 selon Cyrille d'Alexandrie," *Revue des Etudes Augustiniennes*, 46 (2000): 61–82.

174. Anatolios, *Athanasius*, 156–161 for a helpful exposition of this giving and receiving.

175. Keating, *The Appropriation of Divine Life*, 140–142.

Through Baptism, we receive the new birth in the Spirit and become partakers in the divine life, not merely through an external sign of grace but through a real indwelling of the Spirit in humanity. In the incarnation, Jesus in his full and perfect humanity receives the Spirit and provides a stable base, securing the Spirit's transforming power for all of humanity.[177] Cyril notes that the "Holy Spirit changes the disposition of those in whom He is, and in Whom He dwells, and molds them into newness of life."[178] Through the Eucharist, we participate in new life through the power of the Holy Spirit and through the infusion of participation through the flesh of Christ. [179] Christ's flesh has this ability to give life—not by any special property of its own physical nature, but rather through its unique union with the Word.[180]

Yet, Cyril's emphasis on the physical partaking of the sacrament should not be overstated in a way that fails to see the importance of his pneumatological emphasis on the indwelling of the Spirit.[181] Russell, like Keating, notes that along with a sense of ontological participation through the Eucharist, there is also a moral progress in participation made possible by the Spirit.[182]

Transformed "being" leads to transformed "doing." Our new life of participation in the divine life through Christ in the power of

---

176. Russell, *The Doctrine of Deification*, 185.

177. See Cyril, Commentary on John, John 1:32-33, Pusey, Vol. 1, 134–147. See also Keating, *The Appropriation of Divine Life*, 102, and Anatolios, *Athanasius*, 156–161.

178. Cyril, *Commentary on John*, John 16:7, Pusey, Vol. 2, 443.

179. Cyril, *Commentary on John*, John 6:35, Pusey, Vol. 1, 373–374 and Keating, *The Appropriation of Divine Life*, 64–68.

180. Cyril, Commentary on John, 6: 51, Pusey, Vol. 1, 410–411 and John 6:53-54, Pusey, Vol. 1, 419–420. See also Keating, *The Appropriation of Divine Life*, 69. Cyril argues that the incarnation of the Word and Christ's resurrection have universal impact—all will be resurrected because Christ, by his union with humanity, has given every human life. However, true fullness of life comes only to those who have truly received Christ by faith. See Keating, *The Appropriation of Divine Life*, 70.

181. Keating, *The Appropriation of Divine Life*, 103.

182. Russell, *The Doctrine of Deification*, 202.

the Spirit leads to transformation of our human being as we are united with the life-giving power of the Word. This ontological re-creation calls forth and makes possible a moral response lived in a true imitation of Christ that is also empowered by the Spirit, beginning now and progressing to and through the resurrection and the age to come. Marie-Odile Boulnois argues that this movement toward a Christ-formed pattern of life is the Spirit's primary role in the economy of salvation for Cyril.[183]

Moral Response

The transformative power of participation in Christ is an ontological re-creation of our being that truly overcomes the power of sin and death. That transformation, while not yet completely fulfilled, is not merely an eschatological hope for Cyril. Rather the transformative power of our graced unity with Christ makes possible a change in our living and the moral pattern of our life, here and now. It is crucial to realize that for Cyril, ontological transformation is always coupled with a moral response by humanity.[184] Keating argues, "human response and the moral life are not merely tacked on to a theological account that begins and ends with divine action through the Word. Though divine initiative possesses both temporal and theological priority, human response is essential to Cyril's narrative account of salvation."[185]

The Word's unique union with humanity in the incarnation means Christ's humanity has what Keating calls "certain qualities that exceed

183. Marie-Odile Boulnois, "The Mystery of the Trinity according to Cyril of Alexandria: The Deployment of the Triad and Its Recapitulation into the Unity of Divinity" in *St. Cyril of Alexandria*, ed. Weinandy and Keating, 92.
184. See Meyendorff, *Byzantine Theology*, 138–140 for a discussion of this dynamic between being and doing between receipt of grace and response in the Alexandrian tradition.
185. Keating, *The Appropriation of Divine Life*, 140.

our humanity."[186] This makes it possible for Christ to transform humanity and to serve as a pattern for human life as he receives the divine life through the Spirit and lives in the divine image.[187] In concert with Athanasius, Cyril emphasizes that the Incarnate Word both divinely gives and humanly receives redemption and transformation.[188] The whole span of Jesus' human life is one in which human nature is being progressively sanctified, which is made possible because Christ takes that humanity to himself and transforms it.[189]

For Cyril, as Frances Young has argued, Christ is truly the most human of all humanity precisely because he is perfectly receptive to God's grace and will.[190] Yet Keating argues that this is not merely a passive receptivity, but rather Christ's response is active obedience.[191] It is the Word's receptivity, obedience, and voluntary self-giving to become human and to suffer the cross that become the pattern for our life and obedience.[192] As Cyril notes, "for the Only-begotten is never forced against his will. Rather, it was of his own accord, out of his

186. Keating, *The Appropriation of Divine Life*, 186. See also Anatolios, *Athanasius*, 150–155, and Meyendorff, *Byzantine Theology*, 151–153 for discussions of the ways in which Christ's humanity is fully human in a way that overcomes death and sin and transforms human being into its truly human and therefore perfectly receptive and responsive form.

187. See Cyril, *Commentary on John*, trans. Russell in *Cyril of Alexandria*, 126–128 for a discussion of the role of the Spirit in our participation in the divine life. See also Keating, *The Appropriation of Divine Life*, 187, 188.

188. Keating, *The Appropriation of Divine Life,* 189. See also Anatolios, *Athanasius*, 155–159 for an account of the presence of this theme in Athanasius.

189. See Cyril, *Commentary on John*, John 17:18-23, Pusey, Vol. 2, 537–543 and John 17:25, Pusey, Vol. 2, 560–563. See also Keating, *The Appropriation of Divine Life*, 188–191. See also Robert Wilkin, *Judaism and the Early Christian Mind: A Study of Cyril of Alexandria's Exegesis and Theology* (New Haven and London: Yale University Press, 1971) 93–200 for his discussion of the ways in which Cyril talks of a the renewal of humanity in Christ as resulting in a new dimension of human being and life that was not present in Adam.

190. Frances Young, "A Reconsideration of Alexandrian Christology," *Journal of Ecclesiastical History*, 22 (1971): 113–114, cited in Keating, *The Appropriation of Divine Life*, 142.

191. Keating, *The Appropriation of Divine Life*, 142, drawing upon the work of Young, "A Reconsideration of Alexandrian Christology," 113–114. See also Anatolios, *Athanasius*, 58–61, 66–67 for a discussion of active receptivity.

192. Cyril, *Commentary on John*, trans. Russell in *Cyril of Alexandria*, 112–114. See also 120–121, 126.

love for us, that he accepted the self-emptying and persevered with it."[193]

Using the vine and branches imagery from John, Cyril argues that this is a model for human union with Christ. This union is "reciprocal though unequal" in that Christ is the primary actor, the vine who grafts us onto himself and then nourishes us through the Holy Spirit and the Eucharist. However, we must also act by holding on to Christ and bearing fruit in love, which is necessary for remaining connected to the vine. We preserve the gift of the Spirit indwelling in us by obediently living as Christ commands in love and faithfulness.[194]

While the incarnation makes it possible for us to become partakers of the divine nature, we must respond with obedience by faithfully following Christ if this participation is to be made actual in our lives. For Cyril, true freedom comes through new life in Christ, which is received by faith and put to work in our present life. Keating sums it up this way: While we cannot do anything without God's gift of grace through Christ, that gift also makes it possible for us to cooperate with it through holy living.[195] While faith is first and obedient acts follow, Cyril denies any separation of faith and acts, or of divine initiative and human response. The virtues are gifts from God, but they require our co-operation to be fully effective.[196]

To convey this synergy, Cyril uses the imagery of a painter who uses many hues and shades. "For just as those who are skilled in delineating forms in pictures cannot by one color attain to perfect beauty in their painting, but rather use various and many kinds of hues, so also the God of all, who is the Giver and Teacher of spiritual beauty, adorns our souls with that manifold virtue which consists

193. Cyril, *Commentary on John*, trans. Russell in *Cyril of Alexandria*, 126.
194. Keating, *The Appropriation of Divine Life*, 135. See Cyril, Commentary on John, John 15:1-17, Pusey, Vol. 2, 364–411.
195. Keating, *The Appropriation of Divine Life*, 116–118.
196. Keating, *The Appropriation of Divine Life*, 137–138.

in all saint-like excellence of living, in order to complete in us his likeness. For in his rational creatures the best and most excellent beauty is the likeness of God, which is wrought in us by the exact vision of God, and by virtue perfected by active exertion."[197] While God paints our lives with this multiplicity of beauty, that beauty is perfected in our living. It is a gift, but the gift bears fruit as we actively respond to God's grace.[198]

The Christological Relationship between Nature and Grace

For Cyril, the relationship between nature and grace, between what humans are by nature and what we are by grace, is not one of opposition or dichotomy, though Cyril would not have used those terms. This will be a key point in our consideration of Barth and Balthasar, for Barth denies the concept that grace perfects nature, while Balthasar embraces it. Cyril's conception is one in which grace and nature are in an analogical and noncompetitive relationship with one another, because in the incarnation, the divine and human are not in competitive relationship in the one person. The relationship between grace and nature is analogically grounded and yet kept distinct in the incarnation as a Trinitarian act.[199]

The gift of being, which for Cyril includes rationality, is what we are by nature as humans and cannot be lost, Keating explains. But the Spirit's indwelling is a gift of grace, whose reception depends on

197. Cyril, *Homilies on Luke*. 14:12-14, trans. R. Payne Smith from *A Commentary upon the Gospel according to S. Luke by S. Cyril, Patriarch of Alexandria* (New York: Studion, 1984), 413 in Keating, *The Appropriation of Divine Life*, 137.

198. Keating, *The Appropriation of Divine Life*, 137. See also Keating's footnote 56, in which he notes that A. M. Bermejo, in *The Indwelling of the Holy Spirit according to Cyril of Alexandria* (Ona: Facultad de Teologia, 1963), 74–75, argues that Cyril makes a significant development by bringing the ontological concept of the image of God within us together with the concept of progress in living in the image of God through a moral pattern of life.

199. See Keating's discussion, *The Appropriation of Divine Life*, 201.

the free exercise of our will and can be lost. For Cyril, at creation these were distinct but one. It is only with the fall that the two are divided.[200] Through the incarnation, Christ's life, death, and resurrection make possible the forgiveness of sin and the overcoming of death, redeeming these effects of the fall. When the Spirit returns to the human race through Christ, the Spirit now finds a secure human dwelling in the Incarnate Word and humanity in the full image of God is re-established. As Cyril puts it in the *Commentary on John*, Christ has received the Spirit, "in order to preserve for human nature the grace which was lost, by receiving this grace as a man, and in order to make it take root in us again. . . . so that the Spirit might grow accustomed to dwell in us, without having the occasion to withdraw."[201] When Christ breathes the Spirit on the disciples, Christ restores humanity to its original and supernaturally gifted being, but now that image receives what Keating terms an "unshakeable stability" in Christ that cannot be undone.[202]

The Trinitarian framework and pneumatological emphasis of Cyril's Christology must not be overlooked.[203] The incarnation is the way in which the triune God gives new life to humanity through the secure indwelling of the Holy Spirit and participation in Christ's life-giving flesh via the sacraments. Because Cyril is so confident in the life-giving power of God through Christ in the Holy Spirit, he has confident expectations of the ways in which human life is truly transformed here and now, as well as eternally.[204] Williams notes

---

200. Keating, *The Appropriation of Divine Life*, 201.

201. Cyril, *Commentary on John* 1:32-33, in Pusey, Vol. 1, p 184.

202. Keating, *The Appropriation of Divine Life*, 201. See also Anatolios, *Athanasius*, 155–161 for Athanasius's discussion of the way in which the incarnation secures the indwelling of the Spirit for humanity.

203. See Boulnois, "The Mystery of the Trinity," 75–111 and Keating, *The Appropriation of Divine Life*, 204. See also Russell for a discussion of the Spirit's role in participation. Russell notes that in the *Commentary on John*, "not only does the Spirit transmit knowledge of the divine nature as in the earlier texts, but participation in the divine nature as well," In *Cyril of Alexandria*, 25.

that, for Cyril, deification is a present reality in the lives of believers. "Redemption becomes an uninterrupted process" that begins in this life and is perfected in the resurrection.[205]

Keating argues that with his account, Cyril "overturns any strict dichotomy between the natural and supernatural."[206] Rather, humans were created to receive God's supernatural grace and the gift of the indwelling Spirit and thereby to share in the divine life. Keating also argues that his conception of the relationship between nature and grace may be one of the most significant areas of Cyril's thought.[207] Justification and sanctification intricately and intimately relate with both God's action for us and God's action in us—a process that involves our active receipt and response to the gift of grace. While the grace of God precedes every act of human response, nonetheless that human response must be offered if the gift is to be truly appropriated.

Summary

The concept of deification or participation in the life of God has deeply Christian roots. The concept is developed against an understanding of humanity as created in the image and likeness of God, with the image being an imprint on human nature through grace and the likeness being those qualities of human freedom and moral action that participate in likeness to God through the Spirit. Through the fall, death and sin enter creation and destroy humanity's

---

204. Keating, *The Appropriation of Divine Life*, 203–204. See also Brian E. Daley, "The Fullness of the Saving God: Cyril of Alexandria on the Holy Spirit," in *St. Cyril of Alexandria*, ed. Weinandy and Keating, 131, who notes that for Cyril, the Holy Spirit is the primary way God is at work *in* humanity.

205. Williams, *The Ground of Union*, 30.

206. Keating, *The Appropriation of Divine Life*, 202.

207. Keating, *The Appropriation of Divine Life*, 201.

likeness to God, though the image of God is never completely eradicated. In the Alexandrian tradition, through the christological exchange formula, Christ is understood to become human in order to recover the loss to humanity incurred through Adam, and to recreate in humanity the image and likeness of God. As this concept of deification or participation developed, a series of "rules" developed to keep in place the necessary distinction between humanity and divinity. Out of this background, Cyril developed a fully Trinitarian account of deification. Cyril's conception is strongly pneumatological and stresses the two-fold ontological and moral aspects of deification as an ongoing dynamic and transformational process made possible by the gracious gift of Jesus Christ.

Cyril's theology provides an account of human participation in the life of God that both preserves the distinction between divinity and humanity, and also allows for a real and dynamic sense of transformation in human life, both now and eternally. Through the Holy Spirit, humans are changed ontologically by the incarnation, being made more fully human and empowered to live now in ways that truly participate in the life of God. Transformation, deification, and participation in the life of God begin in the present and extend into the eternal life of God, in which humanity has been called to participate—not out of any inherent capacity or goodness, but simply and solely by the gracious love and grace of God in Jesus Christ.

In Cyril's christological and soteriological understandings, deification plays a critical role because it expresses God's gracious purpose and intention for humanity. In Cyril's conception, deification does not mean that humanity becomes divine. It rather becomes more fully and truly human, not due to any inherent capacity within humanity but because of the wondrous love of God who personally takes on humanity in the one incarnate person of Jesus Christ to save and transform human beings and bring them in to a participation in God's very life. This participation begins to be lived out in the present, as transformed by God's gracious power. Liberated from sin and death, humanity is freed and empowered to begin living the new reality made possible by the wondrous exchange.

2

Barth

Elected for Covenant-Partnership with God

In Jesus Christ . . . our human essence is given a glory and exalted to a dignity and clothed with a majesty which the Son who assumed it and existed in it has in common with the Father and the Holy Ghost—the glory and dignity and majesty of the divine nature.[1]

The spoil of divine mercy, the result of the act of atonement is exalted man: new in the power of the divine exaltation . . . the first-born of a new humanity . . .[2]

God became man in order that man may not become God, but come to God.[3]

—Karl Barth, *Church Dogmatics* 4.2

1. Karl Barth, *Church Dogmatics*, Vol. 4.2, *The Doctrine of Reconciliation*, ed. G. W. Bromiley and T. F. Torrance (Edinburgh: T&T Clark, 1958), 100.
2. Barth, *Church Dogmatics*, 4.2, 103
3. Barth, *Church Dogmatics*, 4.2, 105–106.

For Karl Barth, the relationship between God and humanity is a covenant relationship, initiated wholly by God, who determines God's self to be God in fellowship with humanity and who elects humanity to that covenant fellowship. God's freedom is freedom to love the human beings that God has elected to covenant partnership, and to save those human beings from the consequences of their own disobedience and failure to keep that covenant. Through Christ, who is both the subject and object of election, humans have truly been freed to be God's partners in fellowship, freed for wholehearted, inward, and outward obedience to God.

Because this overarching concept of election in which Jesus is both subject and object, both judge and judged, is so central to his christological views, Barth's insistence on the single subject of Christ in the hypostatic union is a key note in his christological compositions. Barth articulates Cyril of Alexandria's emphatic affirmation of the one subject of Christ as well or better than any twentieth-century theologian, recovering this emphasis at a time when Cyril was still the bad boy of early church theology and a favorite whipping boy of theologians and historians of an array of theological positions.[4] Barth is insistent and eloquent that in Christ, God acts to restore humans to fellowship with God, to set them on their feet as God's covenant partners, to exalt them to life with God.

In Barth we have a proponent of single-subject Christology every bit as ardent and eloquent as Cyril, and yet one who emphatically

---

4. Both Cyril's personal character and his theology had often come under attack: personally as the power hungry and often alleged murderer of the female philosopher Hypatia, and theologically for importing unbiblical allegory and metaphysics into Christology. Norman Russell, in *Cyril of Alexandria*, vii, sums up the reception of Cyril in much of the nineteenth and early twentieth centuries by saying, "In the English-speaking world our perception of him, moreover, has been colored by [Edward] Gibbon's damning portrait of him in the forty-seventh chapter of the *Decline and Fall of the Roman Empire*, where he is represented as the murderer of Hypatia and the bully of the Council of Ephesus. His writings, described by Gibbons as 'works of allegory and metaphysics, whose remains, in seven verbose folios, now peaceably slumber by the side of their rivals' are little read."

rejects any concept he believes to espouse deification. What accounts for Barth's substantive agreement with Cyril's emphasis on the one person of the incarnation and his rejection of what Cyril holds to be the purpose of the incarnation—the deification of humanity? What results from Barth's rejection? Does Barth simply misunderstand what is meant by "deification," reading it through the lens of his old teacher Adolf von Harnack?[5] Does he reject what he thinks that term means (that humanity as such becomes divine), while in reality affirming something similar to Cyril's vision of human life in Christ under a different name? Or does he truly reject a Cyrillian concept of deification altogether and, if so, why does he think it necessary to do so? Is it possible to truly hold Cyril's single-subject Christology without his conception of deification? What does Barth offer in place of Cyril's concept of deification, and does his concept offer a teleological pattern that provides an alternative to the nihilistic loss of hope, meaning and purpose for human life as compelling as Cyril's pattern?

These are the questions that will occupy us in our exploration of Barth. After a brief look at the concept of election that forms the basis of Barth's whole christological framework and an overview of the dialectical style that Barth uses, we will examine his treatment of themes that are key to concepts of participation or deification: creation and fall, nature and grace. We will then turn to a close examination of Barth's Christology, with particular attention to his conceptions of the hypostatic union and the two natures, the relationship between divine and human, and the soteriological pattern he establishes within his doctrine of election. Then we will consider Barth's rejection of deification, exploring what he actually

---

5. Harnack viewed deification as the importation of pagan Greek conceptions in Christianity, resulting in a view that human nature actually became divine, with an erasure of distinction between divine and human.

rejects and why, before examining his vision of human life in Christ and highlighting issues that will have to be addressed as we look toward a comparison with Cyril and Hans Urs von Balthasar in our final chapter. Our purpose in this chapter is to focus on understanding Barth's christological and soteriological pattern of thought—particularly as it relates to a vision for human life as a participation in God's life—in preparation for that fuller analysis and comparison.

The Structure of Barth's Thought: Election and Dialectics

To understand Barth's Christology, it is important to keep in mind the key themes that underlie the structure of his massive theological explorations. The first theme to consider is Barth's use of the dialectics that characterize his work and how this use of dialectics relates to his conception and use of analogy.[6] There is significant disagreement in the field of Barthian scholarship about this very issue, which is complicated by the sheer volume of Barth's work and the complexities of his thought. In addition, the very term "dialectics" is a subject of critical debate in theological and philosophical circles. However, for the purposes of this discussion, we will focus on Barth's understanding and use of dialectics as a strategy to highlight the "antithesis" between divine and human, the absolute free sovereignty of God and creation's complete dependence upon the God who created and sustains it, the complete initiative of God's supernatural grace flowing toward creatures with no synergistic ability to cooperate in their own salvation.

---

6. See Bruce L. McCormack, *Karl Barth's Critically Realistic Dialectical Theology: Its Genesis and Development 1909–1936* (Oxford: Oxford University Press, 1995) for a thorough discussion of Barth and his dialectical method.

From the perspective of scholars such as Bruce McCormack, the accent is on Barth's dialectics rather than on analogical relationship. Barth sees a constant dialectic between God and creature. Without Christ there is an unbridgeable chasm between the two. Second, this interplay of antithesis between God and creature is important to see if one is to understand the importance of revelation for Barth. Revelation is wholly God's activity and God must be at work through grace for that revelation to be perceived and received. There is no inherent natural capacity to know or receive God in human nature per se—it is wholly an act of divine grace. God speaks and reveals God's self as a gracious gift in God's absolute freedom to love. Humans receive this gift. This dialectical pattern of Barth's thought has led some scholars to characterize Barth's theology as grace versus nature or grace disrupting nature, with humanity conceived as a merely passive recipient of an alien grace.[7]

However, other scholars argue that while Barth uses a dialectic style, his thinking shifted toward more analogical patterns as his theology matured. Balthasar himself began this trend among Barth scholars, arguing that in developing the *analogia fidei*, Barth developed an implicit analogy of being, though he did not carry through this insight as fully as he might have. (At this point, it's also important to note Barth's categorical rejection of what he believed to be the Roman Catholic notion of the *analogia entis*, the analogy of being. Barth saw this concept as positing an inherent capacity in human nature for knowing God. But more importantly, he believed it created a category of "being" that was ultimately larger than God

---

7. Kenneth Oakes notes this characterization of Barth in "The Question of Nature and Grace in Karl Barth: Humanity as Creature and as Covenant-Partner," *Modern Theology*, 24: 4 (October 2007): 595–616, where he cites the criticisms represented by John Milbank, in his *The Suspended Middle: Henri de Lubac and the Debate Concerning the Supernatural* (Grand Rapids: Eerdmans, 2005), as well as by John R. Betz, "Beyond the Sublime: The Aesthetics of the Analogy of Being," *Modern Theology* 21, no. 3 (July 2005): 367–411 and 22, no. 1 (January 2006): 1–50.

in God's self, and blurred the distinction between God and creatures. God and creature become merely different gradations of this larger category of "being."[8] Barth does develop an *analogia fidei*—the analogy between the Word and human words operating at the level of faith—but he continually rejected any analogy of being.)

Carrying forward this analogical aspect of Barth's work, Kenneth Oakes has recently argued that within the doctrine of election, Barth develops an account of grace and creaturely response that is much more analogically patterned and that gives attention to the capacities of human receipt of, and active response to, God's revelation and election of humanity as covenant partners.[9] Working with Barth's conception of creation as the "exterior basis of the covenant" and covenant as "the interior basis of creation,"[10] Oakes argues that Barth preserves both the distinction between God and creation, while also allowing for an analogical relationship between the two. In Barth's covenant conception, Oakes argues, creation is, from its inception, created to both receive and respond to God's Word and revelation. There is an inherent openness to God.[11] John Webster also identifies

8. While most scholars agree about Barth's adamant rejection of the *analogia entis*, they disagree over Barth's understanding and use of an analogical framework in his theological conceptions. Hans Urs von Balthasar argues that Barth's thought shifted over time and that he came to embrace a more analogical pattern—not the *analogia entis*, but an *analogia fidei*. See Hans Urs von Balthasar, *The Theology of Karl Barth: Exposition and Interpretation*, trans. Edward T. Oakes (San Francisco: Ignatius, 1992). On the other hand, Bruce McCormack argues that while Barth used the term analogia fidei, it represented no major shift in his thought. He continued to use a critically realistic dialectical model throughout his work, though this became much more christocentric over time. This area of dialectics and analogy deserves careful attention in Barth's Christology, particularly regarding its effect on his conception of how humans are affected by the incarnation and the way in which they "participate" in Christ. For a discussion of Barth's dialectics and his use of analogy, see McCormack, *Karl Barth's Critically Realistic Dialectical Theology*.

9. Oakes, "The Question of Nature and Grace in Karl Barth," 595–616.

10. See Barth, *Church Dogmatics* 3.1, *The Doctrine of Creation*, ed. G. W. Bromiley and T. F. Torrance (Edinburgh: T&T Clark, 1958) 94–228 for Barth's use of these terms and an extensive discussion of their meaning.

11. Oakes, "The Question of Nature and Grace in Karl Barth," 601–606. Christologically, the challenge then becomes to move from the specific humanity of Jesus to humanity as a whole. Barth's christological discussion aims to achieve this by highlighting the similarities within

two basic themes in the *Dogmatics* and Barth's conception of the relationship between divine and human: humans truly act in corresponding ways that respond to God's initiative and in the process the divine and human can never be collapsed together or held rigidly separate.[12] "Barth seeks to construct an account of the relation of God and humanity which refuses the antithetical alternatives of autonomy and heteronomy, preferring to think of a set of analogical relations between the action of God and human acts."[13]

Whether one believes Barth to be primarily either a dialectical or an analogical thinker, two priorities are clear: God has elected humanity to covenant partnership and fellowship, and at the same time, a clear distinction, an antithesis, must be maintained between divine and human. These similarities and dissimilarities between God and humanity are brought into harmony only through the concrete person of Jesus Christ, who is the elect one. God's full revelation, or unveiling, occurred through the veil of creatureliness in the humanity of Jesus of Nazareth, in whom the relationship between divine and human rises above antithesis.

Jesus as the Elect One (within Barth's concept of election) is thus a key theme that is crucial for Barth's Christology. God freely decides to be God in covenant fellowship with humans. God chooses to be this God and no other and God's freedom from necessity allows God to determine God's own being in this way. While Barth affirms that God is complete in God's self and does not of necessity need to be in relationship with humanity to complete anything lacking in God's self, nonetheless for Barth, God does not choose to be God

an always greater dissimilarity—which Oakes argues is an analogical, not a dialectical move. Further, he argues that Barth is making an ontological claim in his discussion of these similarities and dissimilarities.

12. John Webster, *Barth's Ethics of Reconciliation* (Cambridge: Cambridge University Press, 1995), 117.

13. Webster, *Barth's Ethics of Reconciliation*, 211.

without humanity.[14] Rather, from eternity, God freely determines God's own being to be God in relationship with humankind and to elect them to fellowship with him.[15] Thus "God with us" in Jesus can be seen only against the backdrop of God's covenant with Israel—a covenant of grace in which God elects to be present to and to act in saving ways in Israel's history.[16] The doctrine of election remains key for Barth, though he radically revises the traditional Reformed understanding by arguing that Jesus is the only truly elect one and all humans can participate in his election. Within this concept of election, Barth argues that the act of atonement in Jesus is not God's reaction to the state of the world as if something completely new has been introduced, but rather it is the culmination of God's ongoing faithfulness to humans from the time of creation.[17] God *is* the atonement and reconciliation, and through Jesus, the sin of humans is "met, refuted, and removed" forever.[18] "As a history which took place

14. Webster argues that there are three elements of Barth's argument in the Dogmatics that must be kept in mind in reading any part: 1) The work is a lengthy treatment of the affirmation "God is." 2) Within this affirmation, it is also a statement of the covenant between God and creation and means that God also deals with humanity. 3) This makes ethics an integral part of Barth's work of covenant theology and Christology. Webster, *Barth's Ethics of Reconciliation*, 2–5. Adam Neder notes the centrality of Barth's conception of the covenant of election as an important foundation for Barth's christological conceptions and his framework for human participation in Christ. See Adam Neder, *Participation in Christ: An Entry into Karl Barth's Church Dogmatics* (Louisville: Westminster John Knox, 2009).

15. Bruce McCormack, and more recently Paul Dafydd Jones, argues for a more radical interpretation of Barth's concept, arguing that by reformulating the doctrine of election, Barth actually reformulated his doctrine of God, in which this decision by God to be in fellowship with humans actually constitutes God's being as Trinity—God simply does not elect to be God without humanity. This interpretation is a subject of debate among Barthian scholars, and we will visit McCormack's and Jones's arguments throughout this chapter. See McCormack, *Orthodox and Modern: Studies in the Theology of Karl Barth* (Grand Rapids: Baker Academic, 2008) and Paul Dafydd Jones, *The Humanity of Christ: Christology in Karl Barth's Church Dogmatics* (London: T&T Clark, 2008).

16. Barth, *Church Dogmatics*, 4.1, *The Doctrine of Reconciliation*, ed. G. W. Bromiley and T. F. Torrance (Edinburgh: T&T Clark, 1956), 34–35.

17. Barth, *Church Dogmatics*, 4.1, 36–37.

18. Barth, *Church Dogmatics*, 4.1, 48. Thus for Barth, the incarnation is not solely in response to human sin because the atonement is a "necessary happening" that reveals the fullness of God, rather than an evolutionary result of some ongoing creative process such as one sees in

in time, the true humanity of Jesus Christ is, therefore, the execution and revelation, not merely of *a* but of *the* purpose of the will of God, which is not limited or determined by any other, and therefore by any other happening in the creaturely sphere, but is itself the sum of all divine purposes and therefore that which limits and determines all other occurrence."[19]

Thus, we see another key emphasis for Barth: the incarnation is wholly God's initiative, a gracious gift with no "cause, or merit, or co-operation on the part of the creature."[20] Jesus is not the natural evolution of humanity from some kind of innate possibility but is a complete eruption of God into history, in which God the Son is the subject, acting to take human being into a union with him.[21] Barth is insistent that Jesus not be treated as simply an abstract sign of some general event. Rather, Jesus is the unique event in himself, the central point in the entire reconciliation history, present and future.[22] The incarnation, crucifixion, and resurrection are all seen as one event. Who Jesus is never gets separated from what Jesus does, which is to reconcile humans to God.

Further, Barth is firm in grounding the event of the incarnation in the Trinitarian life of God and in the eternal will and purposes of God. Here, Barth insists that Jesus defines any understanding of who God is, rather than abstract conceptions of God defining Jesus, and Jesus reveals that this kenotic descent and humility is what it means to be God.[23] In exploring this kenotic self-emptying, Barth is adamant that God is not conflicted within God's own being. God does not contradict God's self, and sin and death do not enter God's

---

Schleiermacher. "It is for the sake of Christ that creation takes place" (4.1, 50) and through Christ, that creation is reconciled with God as a gift of total grace. See pages 48–51.

19. Barth, *Church Dogmatics*, 4.2. 31.
20. Barth, *Church Dogmatics*, 4.2, 45.
21. Barth, *Church Dogmatics*, 4.2, 45–46.
22. Barth, *Church Dogmatics*, 4.1, 122–123.
23. Barth, *Church Dogmatics*, 4.1, 179–185; see also 52–53; 66–68.

self. While God gives God's self completely, "God gives Himself, but He does not give Himself away."[24] While dialectic plays a strong role in Barth's theology, he insists that God is never the victim of a dialectic within God's own self, but instead always acts in freedom as the one He has determined to be in covenant with humanity.[25]

Encompassed by the Covenant:
Barth's Views of Creation and Fall, Nature and Grace

In his treatment of creation within the covenant of election initiated by God, Barth argues that the *imago dei* can be seen properly only in light of Jesus Christ. Humans truly have their own created nature, but this is always grounded in Christ and, as Balthasar puts it, "nature is also pointed *toward* grace." Creation is the "presupposition" of the incarnation.[26] Barth's oft repeated maxim that creation is the external basis of the covenant and the covenant is the internal basis of creation is the driving paradigm of his thought here. Balthasar argues that in Barth's early writing (*Epistle to the Romans, Prolegomena*) humanity is seen as completely immanent and separate from God, existing in a constant dialectic confrontation with a completely "alien" grace.[27]

---

24. Barth, *Church Dogmatics*, 4.1, 183–185, quote 185. See also McCormack, *Karl Barth's Critically Realistic Dialectical Theology*, 356, who argues that for Barth, the Father exists above contradiction "and the Son exists in contradiction and overcomes it," which would seem to read Barth through a Hegelian lens, though McCormack denies this.

25. Barth, *Church Dogmatics*, 4.1, 194–201. Yet, Barth argues we must affirm "the offensive fact that there is in God Himself an above and below, a *prius* and *posterus*, a superiority and a subordination." 4.1, 200–201. Despite Barth's attempts to uphold Nicaea and Chalcedon, it is difficult not to see subordinationism in this outworking of the conception of prior and posterior, origin and consequence, but it is important to remember that Barth is trying to stay true to the scriptural accounts and that he is referring more to the missions than the persons here. While Barth is trying to maintain both divinity and humanity in Christology here, the kenotic language of his position and the implications for Trinitarian conceptions in this final stage of his argument are somewhat troubling.

26. See Balthasar, *The Theology of Karl Barth*, 126. See Barth's extensive discussion in *Church Dogmatics*, Vol. 3.2 *The Doctrine of Creation*, ed. G. W. Bromiley and T. F. Torrance (Edinburgh: T&T Clark, 1960) especially 219–220.

However, as his theology developed, Barth came to see humans solely in terms of their covenant relationship to God within the conceptual framework of election. In other words, if Christ is the Elect One, then humans are chosen to be in relationship with God. Balthasar argues that Barth came to see that creation, that is nature, is "the presupposition for grace."[28]

However, Keith Johnson argues that, contrary to Balthasar's reading, Barth actually rejects and revises what he sees as the traditional Catholic understanding that redemption is based on God's initial act of grace in creation, an understanding in which grace perfects nature.[29] Instead, Barth turns things around and asserts that God's decision of election and redemption "is the presupposition of creation."[30] In other words, creation exists to fulfill the covenant. Johnson notes that for Barth there simply is no prior relationship between God and creation outside of the covenant of election.[31] Paul Jones agrees, arguing that "creation does not move towards Christ; now it *begins* with Christ."[32] According to Johnson, Balthasar misinterpreted Barth's move by seeing it as congruent with the Catholic view, in which creation and human nature are acts of grace that sin affects but does not completely destroy. Human nature is seen to have some inherent relationship to God by virtue of its

27. Balthasar, *The Theology of Karl Barth,* 127.

28. Barth, *Church Dogmatics,* 3.2, 1–25, 33–34 and Balthasar, *The Theology of Karl Barth,* 127, 165.

29. See Keith L. Johnson, *Karl Barth and the Analogia Entis* (London: T&T Clark, 2010), especially 83–121; 193. Johnson argues that Barth does not reject the *analogia entis* because he believes it posits a larger category of being that contains God and creature, but because he sees it as relying on the mistaken belief that humans' experience of God resides within human nature as nature—even with the proviso that that nature must be perfected by grace. For Barth this experience or knowledge simply cannot reside in human nature itself in any way. Johnson, 98–100.

30. Johnson, *Karl Barth and the Analogia Entis,* 202.

31. Johnson, *Karl Barth and the Analogia Entis,* 204–205. See also Neder, *Participation in Christ,* 16–20, 30–35.

32. See Paul Dafydd Jones, *The Humanity of Christ: Christology in Karl Barth's Church Dogmatics* (London: T&T Clark, 2008), 87.

createdness.[33] Johnson argues that, for Barth, sin destroys any inherent human capacity to know God, and humans are determined at every point by sin. However, in the covenant of election through Christ, sin is not the primary word nor is it determinative of humanity. God's election of humans as covenant partners is.[34] Johnson explains that in Barth's view, creatures do not have any "nature" outside of Jesus' humanity. Rather, they participate in Jesus' humanity. Outside of God's act in Jesus, humans simply do not exist.[35]

Turning to an exposition of the fall and the sin and evil that mark creation, Barth argues that while God creates the world by pulling it from chaos, God does not thereby take away creation's affinities to chaos. While human nature is good in itself and creation is not itself chaotic, it is subject to chaos without God's continual intervention.[36] Sin, humans' willful disobedience, allows the inbreaking of that chaos and sin is an "alien" intrusion into God's intended creation.[37] Human nature and freedom are really understood only in the light of who Jesus is as he is perfectly obedient. True freedom is this surrender. True freedom is only freedom for obedience—all other forms of freedom are a perversion.[38] As Barth puts it,

> When man sins, he does that which God has forbidden and does not will. The possibility of doing this is not something which he has from God. That he can put this possibility into effect does not belong, as is often said, to his freedom as a rational creature. What kind of reason is it which includes this possibility! What kind of a freedom which on the

---

33. Johnson, *Karl Barth and the Analogia Entis,* 207.

34. See Barth, *Church Dogmatics,* 3.2, 28–42, and Johnson, *Karl Barth and the Analogia Entis.*

35. Johnson, *Karl Barth and the Analogia Entis,* 207–211.

36. Barth, *Church Dogmatics,* 3.1, 102–110; *Church Dogmatics* 4.1, 139–140; Balthasar, *The Theology of Karl Barth,* 229, 357.

37. Barth, *Church Dogmatics,* 4.1, 139.

38. Barth, *Church Dogmatics,* 3.2, 196–297. See also Balthasar, *The Theology of Karl Barth,* 128–129, 236–238.

one hand is a freedom for God and obedient to Him, and on the other a freedom for nothingness and disobedience to God![39]

Evil thus is not simply a consequence or deficiency of humans' creaturely finitude. It is that to which God eternally says "No." So, for Barth, it is not accurate to say that "evil is nothing"—it is "something"—but its only being is from God's no. It is humans who give evil a kind of being against God's no and judgment.[40] Thus for Barth, the fall is human rejection and refusal to live in the intended relationship of obedience to God. In this process of disobedience and refusal, humans estrange themselves from the nature God gave them, and the one who sins "becomes someone other than himself . . . his nature is altered in all its elements when he commits sin." But, he continues, "It is also true that his nature, he himself, is not destroyed and does not disappear when he becomes someone other than himself and his nature is altered. . . . Even when he does evil, he is still himself, the good creature of God."[41] Sin thus arises out of what God has not willed. However, even here, God fulfills the covenant, taking on the responsibility for this contradiction and resolving it with his yes in Christ.

Within this framework, Barth calls sin an "ontological impossibility."[42] Unlike in Hegelian dialectic, sin does not inevitably flow from creation, and reconciliation is not a synthesis of creation and sin, but rather the very antithesis of sin. God is wholeheartedly against sin.[43] God has no part in it, did not create it, and it has no

---

39. Barth, *Church Dogmatics,* 4.1, 409.

40. Barth, *Church Dogmatics,* 4.1, 139–145, 408–409; see *Church Dogmatics,* 3.3, 289–368 for Barth's discussion of evil and nothingness. See also *Church Dogmatics,* Vol. 4.3.1, *The Doctrine of Reconciliation,* ed. G. W. Bromiley and T. F. Torrance (Edinburgh: T&T Clark, 1961), 177–180, and Balthasar, *The Theology of Karl Barth,* 230.

41. Barth, *Church Dogmatics,* 4.1, 406 (quote). See also *Church Dogmatics,* 3.2, 26–28, 32–34. Neder notes that sin is humanity's failing to act as the humans they are created to be as God's covenant partners in Christ. See also Neder, *Participation in Christ,* 36.

42. Barth, *Church Dogmatics,* 3.2, 146.

possibility in him or in itself. In fact, sin is so significant that only God himself can interrupt it with Godself. "God Himself is affected and disturbed and harmed by it. His own cause, His purpose for man and the world, is disrupted and arrested; His own glory is called in question. He himself finds Himself assaulted by it in His being as God, and He hazards no less than His being as God to encounter it."[44]

For Barth there is a real covenantal bond between God and creature and while this cannot be completely broken by sin, the actual relationship can be perverted. However, the realities of the covenant partnership between God and creatures in Christ, Kenneth Oakes notes, both "precede and limit whatever effects sin has upon our nature."[45] For Barth, it is humans' refusal to see and obey the Word of revelation that makes them total sinners. So for Barth, sin truly exists only in relation to redemption and human awareness of it.[46] We only see our sin in the light of our redemption in Jesus. While sin masks human knowledge of truth and corrupts our obedience, it cannot change humanity's fundamental reality as creatures who are created and elected to be God's covenant-partners.[47] "Even his sin cannot alter this fact. Sin means that he is lost to himself, but not to his Creator. . . . It does not mean that the being of man as such has been changed or replaced by a different being."[48] Barth continues, "the corruption of man cannot make evil by nature the good work of God."[49] Barth can argue this because who humans

43. Barth, *Church Dogmatics*, 4.1, 80, footnote.

44. Barth, *Church Dogmatics*, 4.2, 400–401.

45. See Barth, *Church Dogmatics*, 3.2, 25–54, 132–144. See also Kenneth Oakes's discussion in "The Question of Nature and Grace in Karl Barth," 611. However, Johnson argues that for Barth, sin destroys any inherent capacity to know God—this knowledge comes only by the sheer miracle of God's gracious self-revelation. Johnson, *Karl Barth and the Analogia Entis*, 108.

46. Barth, *Church Dogmatics*, 4.1, 358, 413. See also Balthasar, *The Theology of Karl Barth*, 157; 186, 206.

47. Barth, *Church Dogmatics*, 3.2, 30–32. See also Kenneth Oakes, "The Question of Nature and Grace in Karl Barth" for a helpful exposition of Barth's theology here, 610–611.

48. Barth, *Church Dogmatics*, 3.2, 197.

49. Barth, *Church Dogmatics*, 3.2, 274.

are is not ultimately rooted in any "nature" they possess in themselves, but in their participation in Jesus' humanity within the covenant.[50]

Because human nature is rooted in the grace of Jesus Christ, the incarnation liberates human nature and exalts it to its intended orientation.[51] Yet Barth is clear. While the ground of human nature is grace, this is not an essential, inherent component that becomes infused into creatureliness itself, but rather into its telos that always lies outside of human nature in its history with God.[52] Barth's conception of grace is always supernatural. It is always a gift from completely outside ourselves, ontologically grounded in Jesus.[53]

50. See Johnson's discussion *Karl Barth and the Analogia Entis*, 207–211.

51. See Barth's discussion throughout Church *Dogmatics,* 4.2. See also Balthasar, *The Theology of Karl Barth,* 140–141.

52. See Barth's discussion throughout *Church Dogmatics,* 3.1 and 3.2. See also John Webster, *Barth,* second ed. (New York: Continuum, 2004), 27, 61, 77–83, 100.

53. Barth, *Church Dogmatics,* 4.1, 44–45, 86–87. In addition, Balthasar notes this aspect of Barth's conception in *The Theology of Karl Barth,* 197. To understand Barth's concept of the relationship between nature and grace, it is important to remember that he is writing as a Reformed Protestant theologian with a particular view of, and reaction to, what he believes to be the Roman Catholic understanding of nature and grace. In Roman Catholicism historically nature was viewed as ordered to grace. This was never to deny the sheer gratuity of God's grace, but nature was not seen as opposed to grace—rather it was ordered to it and perfected by it. This was often expressed as creation, humankind, being ordered to a supernatural end, the beatific vision, life with God. While humanity had no inherent capacity in and of itself to achieve this end, it was graced with an ability to participate in it through the free gift of God. Even with the fall, nature was not so corrupted as to have no capacity to see and respond to grace—but this capacity itself was seen as a gift of grace. During the Reformation, any number of the reformers reacted against what they saw as scholastic Catholicism's conception of an inherent capacity within human being itself (apart from grace) that made it possible to move toward God and to live in accordance with God's will. In response, a number of the Reformers argued that there is *no* inherent capacity in human beings themselves as any secure foundation for grace or for movement toward God. This same issue could be seen in disagreements over justification itself. For the Catholics, operating with a sense of infused grace, both justification and sanctification took place through Baptism as God infused the grace of the Spirit, making the baptized righteous with God and enabling them to live out that righteousness through life in the church, participation in the sacraments and moral living. (See the essay by Anthony Lane, "Two-fold Righteousness: A Key to the Doctrine of Justification?" in *Justification: What's at Stake in the Current Debates,* ed. Mark Husbands and Daniel J. Treier (Downers Grove, Ill.: Intervarsity, 2004) for a helpful discussion here. The Reformers insisted on a forensic understanding of justification—it was the imputation of Christ's alien righteousness that saved—there is nothing inherent in the human being, there is no "infusion" of grace, we never cease to be sinners even while at the same time being justified. See also the essays of Bruce McCormack, Simon Gathercole, Henri A. Blocher, and

Barth is constantly concerned to preserve both the distinction between nature and grace and the sheer gratuity of God's gracious revelation in Jesus Christ. For him, there can be no full, inherent capacity in nature to receive grace. Grace is wholly other. It comes to us completely from outside ourselves. Similarly, Barth's *analogia fidei* argues that there is nothing in human beings that prepares them to receive God's revelation and grace in Christ. Humans do not even know who they are until they look at Jesus. So there is no inherent capacity in nature itself to see, hear, understand, or respond. Rather, not only is revelation itself a gift of grace, but even our human ability to receive or respond to that revelation is a gift of grace that comes from completely outside ourselves. Barth reacted strongly to any hint of "pure nature" or to any conception of what he defined as natural theology, which for him was an argument that there were structures in the created world or in human reason that could lead to knowledge of God or to receipt of God's grace. His response was always "nein!" In Barth, grace is seen more as that which confronts and overrules nature. Grace does not perfect nature. Rather, the relationship of grace to nature is one of miracle and of death and resurrection.[54] Barth's concept of the relationship between nature and grace means

Carl Trueman in *Justification in Perspective: Historical Developments and Contemporary Challenges,* ed. Bruce L. McCormack(Grand Rapids: Baker Academic, 2006) for a helpful analysis of these issues. Grace and nature are seen to be in opposition or at least in dialectic tension in this Protestant understanding. It's important to remember that Barth is situated within this Reformed Protestant tradition and its rejection and fear of "inherent" capacities or grace. See also Neder, *Participation in Christ*, 48–50, who argues that Barth's primary argument with what he views as the Roman Catholic understanding of grace is opposition to the idea of dividing grace at all, or seeing it as an "offer or impetus" that relies on human response to become effective.

54. There is ongoing debate, about the relationship of nature and grace in Barth, with some Barthian scholars arguing that while Barth wanted to safeguard against particular forms of natural theology, he did have space in his thought for a more analogous relationship between nature and grace than is sometimes seen. See for instance, Kenneth Oakes, Balthasar, and Hauerwas.

that the two are always in confrontation and tension—at least this side of the *eschaton*.

The Hypostatic Union:
The Person of the Son as the Single Subject

Our exploration of Barth's concept of covenant and election—and of the relationship within that covenant between divine and human, and between nature and grace—positions us to move into a more focused discussion of his Christology. In all of his christological discussions, Barth is firm in his upholding the Chalcedonian framework that Jesus is one—without division or distinction, both God and man—not a third alternative between God and creature nor a mixture of the two. Indeed, a strong single-subject Christology is critical to Barth's soteriological edifice, given Barth's key convictions that Jesus is both subject and object of election, who in himself is both judge and judged and thereby removes sin and death for humanity. So Barth affirms that in the incarnation, in the hypostatic union, both God and human is "on both sides a real being together."[55] This being together involves no confusion or mixture. "It is not that in Him a changed God who loses His deity becomes and is a changed man who loses his humanity, but the one unchangeable true God becomes and is unchangeably true man. . . . God assumed a being as man into His being as God. He has therefore taken up a being as man into unity with His being as God . . ."[56] Barth insists, "the Incarnation *is* God in his mode of being *as* the Son."[57] The Son is voluntarily sent by the Father and becomes human, in the eternal love of the Holy

---

55. Barth, *Church Dogmatics,* 4.2, 40.
56. Barth, *Church Dogmatics,* 4.2, 40–41.
57. Barth, *Church Dogmatics,* 4.2, 43, my emphasis.

Spirit, through whom the love of the inner life of God is shared with creation.[58]

Throughout his christological discussions of the hypostatic union, Barth is emphatic about the single subjectivity of Christ. The unity of divinity and humanity occurs only and exclusively in Jesus as the second person of the Trinity. The humanity is not an "autonomous principle" alongside the divinity, nor is there a "Being" that is a larger category than the unity of the divine and human in the person of Jesus.[59] "It is not that divine and human creaturely essence are found and united in Him simply and directly, but that He who is 'by nature God' with the Father and the Holy Spirit took human essence to Himself and united it with His divine nature."[60] Further, the second person of the Trinity's unity with human flesh is irrevocable.[61] However, in his discussions of Jesus' humanity, Barth is careful with his use of the term human "nature." Nature cannot be understood in any generic or abstract way. Rather, God assumes into unity with himself not "humanity" in general, but the concrete existence of this one man in a specific form and in this specific man is that which is human in all.[62] In his customary pattern, Barth insists on moving from the particularity of Jesus' humanity to all of humanity, not the other way around.

In this part of Barth's discussion, one can hear echoes of Cyril's insistence on the single subjectivity of Christ as a soteriological concern. In Cyril's conception, Christ's human nature does not act independently, but is rather "the manner of action" of the divine Logos, who is responsible for all words and acts of the incarnate Jesus.[63] The Logos is now enfleshed, having willingly taken on all

58. Barth, *Church Dogmatics*, 4.2, 42–43.
59. Barth, *Church Dogmatics*, 4.2, 46–-47.
60. Barth, *Church Dogmatics*, 4.2, 47.
61. Barth, *Church Dogmatics*, 4.2, 47.
62. Barth, *Church Dogmatics*, 4.2, 48.

the conditions of bodily existence in the flesh *in order* to use them in salvific ways. For Cyril, the Word did not simply "assume" or "occupy" a human body, he actually took on a real human life with all that means. The Logos now expresses divinity through humanity, and this humanity of Christ becomes life giving to all humans.[64] Both divinity and humanity must be fully affirmed but within this one acting subject, who is the person of the Word.

In this area of single subjectivity, Barth's work with the concepts of *anhypostasis* and *enhypostasis* becomes critical for his understanding.[65] In his discussion of the *anhypostasis*, Barth insists that, "As a man, therefore, He exists directly in and with the one God in the mode of existence of His eternal Son and Logos—not otherwise or apart from this mode."[66] The Word does not assume a human being who existed independently before the incarnation. Rather, Jesus' humanity has always, from the moment of conception, been the humanity of the Word. Barth notes that while some theologians have argued that this single subjectivity evacuates the full humanity of Jesus, "it is hard to see how the full truth of the humanity of Jesus Christ is qualified or even destroyed by the fact that as distinct from us He is also a real man only as the Son of God, so that there can be no question of a peculiar and autonomous existence of his humanity."[67] In the incarnate Jesus, the humanity and divinity do not exist "side-by-side or even within one another."[68] Rather, there is only the one Son, and the humanity and divinity are united in this one person of the Son.

63. John McGuckin, *Saint Cyril and the Christological Controversy: Its History, Theology, and* Texts (Crestwood, N.Y: St. Vladimir's Seminary Press, 204), 186. See Cyril, *First Letter to Succensus*, trans. McGuckin, in *Saint Cyril*, 353 for Cyril's insistence that the Logos is the Son both before and after the incarnation.

64. Cyril, *Scholia*, trans. McGuckin, *Saint Cyril*, 298 and Cyril, *On the Unity of Christ*, trans. McGuckin 131–133. See also McGuckin, *Saint Cyril*, 186.

65. See Bruce McCormack's discussion *Karl Barth's Critically Realistic Dialectical Theology*, 327–328.

66. Barth, *Church Dogmatics* 4.2, 49.

67. Barth, *Church Dogmatics*, 4.2, 49 footnote.

68. Barth, *Church Dogmatics* 4.2, 50.

Again, this becomes a critical affirmation for Barth's soteriological argument that Jesus is both subject and object of election. Only if Jesus is one subject, one person, can he be both judge and judged, the one who can and does completely atone for humanity.

From this point, Barth turns his attention to general schemas of union that have been proposed to understand the hypostatic union, ultimately arguing that no such schema is adequate—the hypostatic union can only be understood in terms of itself because it is the unique event of God taking on humanity. For Barth, none of these analogical conceptions really work in understanding the hypostatic union, because the fact that the existence of God in his Son became the existence of the humanity of Jesus is completely unique and calls us to "dispense with formal analogies altogether."[69] For Barth, "not even in the being of the triune God is there any analogy for the fact that He does actually do it." For Barth this would imply a necessity for the incarnation and he is adamant about preserving it as a free act of God.[70]

How then are we to think of the union? For Barth it is only in the reality and event of the particularity of the incarnation. "The statement that Jesus Christ is the One who is of divine and human essence dares to unite that which by definition cannot be united."[71] Yet, "this Subject, the one Jesus Christ, demands this statement, not as a statement about the possibility of uniting that which cannot be united, but as a statement about the uniting of that which is otherwise

---

69. Barth, *Church Dogmatics*, 4.2, 57. The incarnation is not an instance of a larger category of divine/human principle. While Barth will concede that analogies do have their proper place, for instance in understanding the relationship between heaven and earth or the covenant, he argues that when it comes to Christ himself, analogies simply have no place because he is the place where all other analogies are based. There is no neutral space from which to observe the incarnation because Christ defines every space.

70. Barth, *Church Dogmatics* 4.2, 59.

71. Barth, *Church Dogmatics*, 4.2, 61.

quite distinct and antithetical as it has actually taken place and been achieved in Him."[72]

Barth makes a strong case for the single-subject Christology, in many ways reminiscent of Cyril. For Cyril, this strong affirmation of the union of divine and human in the one person of Christ means that we can then extend this analogically to include the relationship of all of humanity to God as humans are drawn into a participation in God's life. While the distinction between divine and human remains, the divide has been bridged. However, as we will see, Barth is more hesitant in extending incarnational union into an analogical pattern for human salvation.

The Two Natures

As Barth moves to a discussion of the two natures, we see his soteriological argument again taking shape through his insistence that the two natures be viewed within the context of the single-subject Christology he has so carefully set out. He argues that these discussions cannot take place within abstract or philosophical notions of either divinity or humanity because there simply are no such generic categories. We can only know what is human and divine from looking at Jesus Christ.[73] Barth notes that the classical tradition speaks of the two natures only *a posteriori* to the actuality of Jesus Christ. The two natures do not derive from any *a priori* abstract conceptions of divinity and humanity, but only from the concrete reality of the one person of Jesus Christ.[74] Thus, any statement about the two natures or the hypostatic union is best understood only in

---

72. Barth, *Church Dogmatics*, 4.2, 61.
73. Barth, *Church Dogmatics* 4.2, 26–27.
74. Barth, *Church Dogmatics*, 4.2, 62.

obedience to the person of Jesus Christ as this concrete reality that has actually occurred.

Barth begins by making clear that the discussion of the two natures can take place only within the context of the incarnational union. Within this understanding, Christ "does not exist as the Son of God without also participating as such in human essence," nor does he "exist as the Son of Man without participating as such in the essence of the Son of God and therefore in divine essence. On both sides, there is a true and genuine participation" and this two-sided participation—the union of the two natures—comes from and exists only in and from him.[75] There is a "real and strict and complete and indestructible union" in which no element of the human is unaffected or excluded from existence in the Son and no divine element is unaffected or excluded from existence in the human.[76] "The unification of divine and human essence in Him, the One, and therefore His being as very God and very man, rests absolutely on the unity achieved by the Son of God in the act of God."[77] Thus, it is more accurate to speak not of a unity but of a union in which divinity and humanity are united but in which both still retain their distinction without confusion. Further, as Neder argues, "the divine and human natures *are* in the union and communion of Jesus Christ's divine and human actions."[78]

Having set this backdrop, Barth's exposition of the two natures comes through his discussion of the two states of Jesus—humiliation and exaltation—framed within the covenant of election. This two-

---

75. Barth, *Church Dogmatics*, 4.2, 62. See George Hunsinger's discussion of Barth's Christology and its Chalcedonian structure in "Karl Barth's Christology" in *The Cambridge Companion to Karl Barth*, ed. John Webster (Cambridge: Cambridge University Press, 2000), 128–139. See also Hunsinger, *Disruptive Grace: Studies in the Theology of Karl Barth* (Grand Rapids: Eerdmans, 2000).

76. Barth, *Church Dogmatics*, 4.2, 64.

77. Barth, *Church Dogmatics*, 4.2, 63.

78. Neder, *Participation in Christ*, note 25 to Chapter 5, 113.

fold salvific movement—the divine Son's journey into the far country so that all of humanity might be brought home to God through him through the eternal election of God's grace—characterizes Barth's Christology.[79]

Barth works to reframe these two "states" in a manner that better captures the event of God's action in Christ. He criticizes the older Reformed and Lutheran discussions of the hypostatic union and the two natures as static and separated from the "event" of Christ. He believes that somehow they considered his person and his works in separate categories.[80] Barth thus understands these classical Protestant conceptions as one of "static" being and he reacts by arguing, "How can a being be interpreted as an act, or an act as a being? How can God or man, or both in their unity in Jesus Christ be understood as history?"[81] Thus, Barth seeks to give this "older" Christology a different form that can more adequately account for its event and history and that redefines being in terms of act and decision.[82]

---

79. Working with John 1:14, Barth says, "If we put the accent on 'flesh,' we make it a statement about God. We say—and in itself this constitutes the whole of what is said—that without ceasing to be true God, in the full possession and exercise of his true deity, God went into the far country by becoming man in His second person of mode of being as the Son—the far country not only of human creatureliness but also of human corruption and perdition. But if we put the accent on 'Word,' we make it a statement about man. We say—and again this constitutes the whole of what is said – that without ceasing to be man, but assumed and accepted in his creatureliness and corruption by the Son of God, man—this one Son of Man—returned home to where He belonged, to His place a true man, to fellowship with God, to relationship with His fellows, to the ordering of His inward and outward existence, to the fullness of His time for which He was made, to the presence and enjoyment of the salvation for which He was destined. The atonement as it took place in Jesus Christ is the one inclusive event of this going out of the Son of God and coming in of the Son of Man." See Barth, *Church Dogmatics*, 4.2, 20–21. See also page 31.

80. Barth, *Church Dogmatics*, 4.2, 105–106, footnote. "What was seen between these two poles was a kind of great phenomenon with its own definite structure, and the ensuing doctrine of the person of Christ a kind of great phenomenology of the relationship between the Logos and its two natures, or between the two natures themselves, as created by that *unitio* and presupposed in the work of Jesus Christ, but itself static, immobile and at rest. A dynamic movement was found both before and after, in the form of an event of divine-human existence and actuality, but here itself there ruled the great calm of a timeless and non-actual being and its truth."

81. Barth, *Church Dogmatics*, 4.2, 108.

With these criticisms in hand, Barth follows the definition of Chalcedon in arguing that it is as necessary to assert the full humanity of Jesus as it is to assert the full divinity. However, he again sounds a cautionary note in these discussions. First, while affirming Jesus' full humanity, Barth is adamant that "God is always God even in His humiliation. . . . He humbled himself, but He did not do it by ceasing to be who He is."[83] In the incarnation, God does not evacuate deity to change into a man. If this were the case then there would be no salvific power in the incarnation. No, Barth insists that God "is always the One He is, that he becomes and is man as God, and without ceasing to be God. . . . the one thing God cannot do is cease to be God."[84] And if God had somehow changed God's self into a human being, he would not be a true human being, truly like us.[85]

Moving to the humanity of Jesus, Barth takes on a lengthy exposition of what is means to say that Jesus is truly human. Again, Jesus' full humanity is critical to Barth's soteriological conviction. If he is not fully human and fully divine in one person, Jesus cannot be both subject and object of election—he cannot assume humanity's judgment and overcome sin and death. So Barth affirms that Jesus, the Son of God, truly lived a historical life in all of its finite dimensions. Jesus took on humanity with all that means: human nature that has been corrupted and is subject to death through sin. Though Barth will assert with all of classical theology that Jesus himself did not sin, he nonetheless took on a human nature that was subject to the consequences of sin and death.[86]

82. McCormack argues that Barth is moving away from problematic "substantialist" conceptions of being associated with Chalcedon and towards an "actualized" account, in which being is defined as action and decision. See McCormack, *Orthodox and Modern*, especially 201–234. Jones too reads Barth in this manner. See Jones, *The Humanity of Christ*. See also Neder, *Participation in Christ*, 60–61.

83. Barth, *Church Dogmatics,* 4.1, 179–180.

84. Barth, *Church Dogmatics,* 4.2, 40.

85. Barth, *Church Dogmatics,* 4.2, 40.

Barth is also adamant that Jesus does not exist as an afterthought or as a change of God's mind in response to human sin. He is rather the eternally elect one. "The humanity of Jesus Christ is not a secondary moment in the Christ event. It is not something which happens later, and later again will pass and disappear. It is not merely for the purpose of mediation. Like his deity it is integral to the whole event."[87] In speaking of Jesus' humanity, Barth says,

"We cannot conceive ourselves and the world without first conceiving

---

86. Barth, *Church Dogmatics,* 4.2, 25.
87. Barth, *Church Dogmatics,* 4.2, 35. Significant debate has taken place over Barth's conception of the relationship between the immanent and economic Trinity and his treatment of the *Logos asarkos* in light of his doctrine of election. Bruce McCormack has argued that in light of his doctrine of election, Barth in effect revised his entire doctrine of God—although Barth himself did not carry forth the necessary revisions. See McCormack, *Orthodox and Modern,* especially 183–233. McCormack argues that after *Church Dogmatics* 2.2, Barth has essentially denied the *Logos asarkos* any separate being after the decision for election and that, in making Jesus both the subject and object of election, Barth must essentially agree with McCormack's statement that "the Second Person of the Trinity has a name, and his name is 'Jesus Christ.' " (*Orthodox and Modern,* 223–224) McCormack argues that Barth's doctrine of election necessarily makes the immanent and economic Trinity identical in content. Even more, McCormack argues that in saying that God determines to be the electing God and no other, that Barth has essentially made election constitutive of the Trinity itself. (190–192) In other words, as a result of God's determination to be the electing God, God then constitutes God's self as Trinity to carry out this election. George Hunsinger has replied to McCormack's thesis with a staunch defense of Barth's distinction between the immanent and economic Trinity, as well as Barth's upholding of the *Logos asarkos.* See Hunsinger, "Election and the Trinity: Twenty-five Theses on the Theology of Karl Barth," *Modern Theology* 24, no. 2 (April 2008): 179–198. Hunsinger argues that throughout his career, Barth is consistent in upholding the distinction between immanent and economic, that God is complete and fully relational in God's self as Father, Son, and Holy Spirit and that God has no need of creation. Barth does reconfigure the doctrine of the election in large measure because of concern that the Calvinistic concept of election led to abstract speculation about a God back behind the economy of salvation whose will could not be truly known or trusted. Barth argues that election must be grounded in the revelation of God in Jesus Christ and can only be read from this event. So Barth is wary of any abstract, speculative concept of God, and this includes his uneasiness with speculative talk about the *Logos asarkos* (see Barth's discussion in *Church Dogmatics,* 4.1, 52, footnote). Barth does argue that we must not try to conceive of the Logos in itself, because "the eternal Son of the Father is not just the eternal Logos, but as such, as very God from all eternity, he is also the very God and very man he will become in time." (*Church Dogmatics,* 4.1, 66. See also 52–53, 66-68.) But Hunsinger argues that his uneasiness does not lead him to collapse the distinction between immanent and economic Trinity or to read God as being wholly "constituted" by God's economic activity. Barth understands that is it crucial to uphold the being of the eternal Son in the immanent Trinity apart from the Son's economic activity in salvation history.

this man with God as the witness of the gracious purposes with which God willed and created ourselves and the world and in which we may exist in it and with it. It is not the world and ourselves, ourselves and the world, who are first elected and willed by God and come into being—and then at a later stage and place this man. But He was and is there first, the One whom God has elected and willed, who is there in being."[88]

Here we see the heart of Barth's Christology and soteriology: within God's election of grace, the Son of Man is elected by the eternal Son of God and in Jesus Christ, and within the hypostatic union, the humanity is elected to a fellowship with God and an exaltation to a participation in the divine life.[89] Barth argues that for God, the fellowship of humans with God is as important as God's fellowship with humans.[90] Neder argues that Jesus' humanity is crucial in Barth's thought because that humanity freely acts in perfect obedience to the divine covenantal command of God and thereby becomes the way all humans participate in exaltation to fellowship with God.[91]

Recently, Paul Jones has argued that the humanity of Christ plays a critical and central role in Barth's Christology within his concept of election.[92] Jones argues that throughout Barth's christological discussions, he is concerned to explicate and guard Christ's full human "agential complexity." While God, through Christ's divinity, is clearly the initiator of all salvific events, Christ's humanity plays a critical, active role in humanly enacting and realizing his identity as the elected human. Jesus' humanity exercises an active response and is not simply "united to," but actually "*unites with*" the divine Son.[93]

---

88. Barth, *Church Dogmatics,* 4.2, 32–33, quote 33.

89. Barth, *Church Dogmatics,* 4.2, 34.

90. Barth, *Church Dogmatics,* 4.2, 36.

91. Neder, Participation in Christ, 30–39, 67–69, 73.

92. See Jones argument throughout *The Humanity of Christ.*

93. Jones, *The Humanity of Christ,* 110. See Jones' discussion, especially 103–110, 125–126, 130–146, 154, 174–176, 191–192. Jones carries this line of thought to the extent that, like McCormack, he argues that for Barth, when God establishes this indirect identity between

The Relationship of Divine and Human:
The Communication of Idioms

Related to his insistence on the single subjectivity of the person of Christ, and a proper understanding of the two natures, is Barth's argument for a careful understanding of the communication of idioms between the two natures. He sets out the relationship between divine and human through a lengthy discussion, beginning by arguing that any sound conception of the *communicatio idiomatum* rests on a firm understanding of the hypostatic union, "the union made by God in the hypostasis (the mode of existence) of the Son."[94]

How then do these two natures relate to and communicate with one another in the single subject of Jesus?[95] For Barth, the *communicatio idiomatum* is crucial because we must be able to say, "The Son of God suffers—the final extreme is also and primarily true of Him—He was crucified, dead, and buried." This has to be said "not of a 'man' called Jesus . . . but of the Son of God who is of one essence with the Father and the Holy Ghost."[96]

the divine Son and the human Jesus, Jesus' humanity "transforms Godself eternally; Christ's concrete existence becomes eternally constitutive of God's second way of being." (248. See also 88–102) Interestingly, Jones makes the argument that Barth is actually taking Cyril's emphasis on the one person and radicalizes it by pressing this union back into the divine Son's being. (See Jones, 213–215) While I agree that Barth is at pains to safeguard the integrity of Jesus' humanity, he is also careful to guard God's immanent Trinitarian life as well. Barth does allow a qualified internal mutability to God in that God chooses to be "affected" by the event of the incarnation, but this is different than saying God's immanent being is constituted by union with humanity, a suggestion that would not have sat well with Cyril. This argument is reminiscent of McCormack's argument that Barth denies the *Logos asarkos*, addressed previously in this chapter.

94. Barth, *Church Dogmatics*, 4.2, 51, footnote.
95. Barth, *Church Dogmatics*, 4.2, 73. Barth distinguishes between the *communicatio idiomatum* (which he defines as the mutual impartation of human and divine essence with one another in Jesus Christ), the *communicatio gratiarum* (the address to human essence by the divine in grace), and the *communicatio operationum* (the "common actualization" of divine and human essence in Christ, in which the divine gives and the human receives.)
96. Barth, *Church Dogmatics*, 4.2, 74.

In a discussion of the *communicatio*, Barth also reacts to classical conceptions of impassibility and immutability, which he thinks have contributed to problematic conceptions of how the natures are united, how they communicate, and what, if any, effect each has on the other—and by extension the rest of creation. Barth argues that all historic Christology succumbed to the Greek conception of immutability and impassibility, with the effect that God is made "the prisoner of his own Godhead."[97] The nineteenth-century kenoticists tried to overcome this problematic conception of immutability with the concept of an equally "intolerable mutability" which simply indicated that they themselves were still imprisoned in this Greek system of thought. This results in an "unchristian conception of a God whose Godhead is supposed not to be affected at all by its union with humanity."[98]

> If we shake off the spell, and try to think of the Godhead of God in biblical rather than pagan terms, we shall have to reckon, not with a mutability of God, but with the kind of immutability which does not prevent Him from humbling Himself and therefore doing what he willed to do and actually did do in Jesus Christ, i.e., electing and determining in Jesus Christ to exist in divine and human essence in the one Son of God and Son of Man. . . . Even in the constancy (or, as we may calmly say, the immutability of His divine essence) He does this and can do it (new and surprising and alien though it may be to human eyes blinded by their own pride) not only without violation but in supreme exercise and affirmation of His divine essence.[99]

97. Barth, *Church Dogmatics*, 4.2, 85, footnote. This is a sweeping criticism in which Barth does not specify at whom the criticism is directed—he seems to be reading through Harnack's conviction that all of historical Christian thought succumbed to Greek paganism. But as we've seen in Chapter 2, this is certainly not true, and does not reflect Cyril's pattern of thought. However, as we'll see in later sections, this caricatured read of the tradition does contribute to Barth's rejection of deification.

98. Barth, *Church Dogmatics*, 4.2, 85, footnote.

99. Barth, *Church Dogmatics*, 4.2, 85. See also the footnote.

Barth's reading of the classical conceptions becomes part of his criticism of the traditional understandings of the *communicatio idiomatum*. Barth takes issue with any understanding of the *communicatio* that deifies the humanity in a one-way communication of the divine to the human. And, he also takes issue with developments from nineteenth-century kenoticism that humanized the divine nature.[100] He sees these nineteenth-century developments as emanating from the Lutheran understanding of the *communicatio* in which communication was not just from divine to human, but also from human to divine. Barth argues that we can make neither of these moves. Rather, we must look at Christ, and Christ alone, as an event of divine giving and human receiving—any other conception compromises either the true divinity or the true humanity.[101]

In contrast to what he understands as the Lutheran view, Barth affirms the *communicatio gratiae,* in which from eternity, "God elects and determines Himself to be the God of man. And this undoubtedly means . . . that He elects and determines Himself for humiliation."[102] Because this is God's self-determination, God does not need to change in the event of the incarnation. From this standpoint, Barth argues that we cannot maintain that the participation of the two natures is merely one-sided, with humanity participating in the divine but with no corresponding participation of the divine in the human. There is rather a mutual participation.[103] Jones argues that for Barth, Jesus' "human essence must take up and enact . . . the identity God proposes."[104] Further, "it can even be said that Christ's humanity fulfils, and therefore in some sense completes, the divinely established event of the incarnation, given that Christ's human essence wills,

100. Barth, *Church Dogmatics*, 4.2, 79.
101. Barth, *Church Dogmatics*, 4.2, 79.
102. Barth, *Church Dogmatics*, 4.2, 84.
103. Barth, *Church Dogmatics*, 4.2, 87.
104. Jones, *The Humanity of Christ*, 143.

constantly, to exist as the human essence that lives in unity with the Son."[105]

Further, Barth argues that Jesus "exists as man as in the mode of existence of the Son" . . . "his existence as man is identical with the existence of God in His Son."[106] This conception of the union does justice to the freedom of God to love and to enter the human condition, and it does not alter or diminish the humanity but rather exalts humanity to its truth—to its freedom for obedience. It is not a superhuman freedom but a true human freedom. Jesus is sinless, but not at the level of essence. He completely shares in human essence and that exists in a fallen state. If he did not completely share that essence he would not be truly like us and able to redeem us.[107] "If the Word became flesh, if God became man, He necessarily existed as a man in human history, and trod a human way, and on this way had human wants, was subject to human temptation and influences, shared only a relative knowledge and capacity, and learned and suffered and died as a man."[108] Jesus completely bore our sinful condition without committing sin himself. He did not "repeat or affirm" our sin, but lived through it. So, it was not that Jesus could not sin, but that he did not. This concept operates not at the level of essence, but existence and obedience. Yet, in his human existence, Jesus received the ongoing "Yes" of the Father and the power of the Holy Spirit at each step of the journey—he is not superhuman but perfectly obedient.[109] Therefore, it is also not necessary that we sin and misuse our freedom. Jesus is not unlike us. He simply used his

---

105. Jones, *The Humanity of Christ*, 143.
106. Barth, *Church Dogmatics*, 4.2, 90. This position is similar to von Balthasar's argument, which he attributes to an extension of the thought of Maximus the Confessor.
107. Barth, *Church Dogmatics*, 4.2, 92–93.
108. Barth, *Church Dogmatics*, 4.2, 95, footnote.
109. Barth, *Church Dogmatics*, 4.2, 92–95.

human freedom as God intends, in perfect obedience and gratitude to God.

Barth then uses a discussion of the *communicatio operationum* to examine the common actualization of the divine and human in Christ. Barth affirms with the Reformed tradition that "neither the divine nor the human nature as such, nor their union, is the active subject," but rather the union is the one subject Jesus Christ, "active in and through both natures."[110] Through this historical, concrete person of Jesus Christ we truly do see God's glory as Jesus' human essence bears and serves divine power and authority.[111] There is true identity of action between the human and divine. "The speaking and the acting, the suffering and striving, the praying and helping, the succumbing and conquering have all to be in human terms."[112] Further, when the Son became man, he did so for eternity. After the Incarnation, God maintains his human essence eternally. This is how fully God becomes human in Jesus Christ. Thus, Jesus cannot be loved or worshipped except in human flesh. It is only through God in humanity that we can know and love Him. Yet it is not humanity alone. In and of itself, "the humanity of Jesus Christ is a predicate without a subject."[113]

Barth argues that the natures cannot be separated or divided—while they are distinct, they are united "not merely in appearance but in fact," fully and completely.[114] Just as no generic concept of humanity can be applied to the incarnation, so also no generic concept of divinity will suffice either. Rather "He, the divine Subject, carries and determines the divine essence, and not conversely."[115] We do not say

---

110. Barth, *Church Dogmatics*, 4.2, 105, footnote.
111. Barth, *Church Dogmatics*, 4.2, 97–98.
112. Barth, *Church Dogmatics*, 4.2, 97–99, quote on 99.
113. Barth, *Church Dogmatics*, 4.2, 100–102, quote 102, footnote.
114. Barth, *Church Dogmatics*, 4.2, 64–65, quote 64, footnote.
115. Barth, *Church Dogmatics*, 4.2, 65.

the "Godhead" became flesh, but rather the Word, the second person of the Trinity, became flesh. For Barth the two natures depend completely on the one subject of Jesus Christ.[116] The two natures "are not united in the Son of God, who is of divine essence and assumed human, like two planks lashed or glued together . . . as if each retained its separate identity in this union and the two remained mutually alien in a neutral proximity."[117] Rather it is a true union of divine and human in which neither is interchangeable and the union itself is not reversible. It is the Son of God, not either his divine or human essence, but the Son himself who is the acting subject in the event of the incarnation.[118]

A number of theologians have weighed in about Barth's construal of the two natures and their relationship to one another. While some, like George Hunsinger, argue for a Chalcedonian-structured reading of Barth's conception, others have recently emphasized the more radical edges of his thought. At issue is how Jesus' humanity is seen, both in terms of its own fullness and agency and in terms of its relationship to the eternal Son, and by implication, the immanent Trinitarian life. The issues are made challenging by Barth's efforts to convey both the single subjectivity of Jesus, while also holding on to a firm distinction—even confrontation—between the two natures. Scholars have offered a variety of ways to view Barth's conceptions.

Reading Barth within a basic Chalcedonian structure, Hunsinger has noted that even while affirming the single subject, Barth is at pains to keep the divinity and humanity intact and to hold the two in constant tension with one another.[119] For Barth there is an

116. Barth, *Church Dogmatics*, 4.2, 66. See also 104 for Barth's discussion of this common actualization—the *communication operationum*—as a difference in emphasis between Lutheran and Reformed understandings. The Lutherans underlined and stressed the cooperation of two natures in the one person. The Reformed stressed the unity of the one person as the subject of the two natures that cooperated yet remained distinct.
117. Barth, *Church Dogmatics*, 4.2, 70.
118. Barth, *Church Dogmatics*, 4.2, 70–71.

underlying antithesis at stake in saying that Jesus is completely human and completely divine. There is no unifying principle that can explain how Jesus can be one person subsisting in two natures. Such a principle is not possible, nor is it necessary, because it is the freedom of God that makes the impossibility of the incarnation possible.[120]

However, Hunsinger argues that failure to understand Barth's strategy of juxtaposition to keep divine and human in tension has led to misconceptions regarding his Christology. Barth's conception of the two natures has often been characterized as deficient, but this charge is not reasonable when the complexities of Barth's thought and strategy are considered.[121] Barth says, "In the work of the one Jesus Christ everything is at one and the same time, but distinctly, both divine and human."[122] The relation of divine and human will in Jesus is thus one of a "coordination in difference" and of "mutual participation."[123] As Hunsinger puts it, "when in Christ's person two natures, and thus also two wills or operations, met, they did so not merely analogically or externally, but in a relation of mutual participation, indwelling or koinonia, and thus in a Chalcedonian unity-in-distinction and distinction-in-unity."[124]

In addition, as we have seen, Barth also argues that we cannot maintain that the participation of the divine and human is merely one-sided, with humanity participating in the divine but with no

---

119. George Hunsinger, "Karl Barth's Christology," in *The Cambridge Companion to Karl Barth*, 128–139. This dialectic of holding the divine and human apart from one another is seen even in Barth's baptismal theology in which he differentiates between the divine action of Baptism with the Spirit and the human action of Baptism with water.
120. Hunsinger, "Karl Barth's Christology," 129–133.
121. Hunsinger, "Karl Barth's Christology," 133–135.
122. Barth, *Church Dogmatics*, 4.2, 116.
123. Hunsinger, "Karl Barth's Christology," 134, citing Barth in *Church Dogmatics*, 4.2, pages 116 and 117 respectively.
124. Hunsinger, "Karl Barth's Christology," 134, citing Barth in *Church Dogmatics*, 4.2, 126. Neder also notes this conception in Barth's Christology: the two natures are united in the one person through a continual correspondence between divine and human action. Neder, *Participation in Christ*, 34–35.

corresponding participation of the divine in the human. Bruce McCormack notes that this communication is not at the level of "nature," but rather through the person of Christ. McCormack explains that "the predication of the attributes of both natures to the Person of the union is therefore understood by Barth to be 'direct and undialectical.' "[125]

However, Barth argues, even within the one person of Christ, there is the "confrontation" of divine with human, and of human with divine. Each is determined by this confrontation in such a way that the divine remains divine and the human remains human. The human essence of Jesus exists only in its confrontation with the divine Son of God. The relationship of participation between divine and human in Christ is not one of essence or nature but one of a continual confronting event.[126] Further, as mediator, Christ takes the antithesis between humanity and divinity to himself without being overcome by it, and so he triumphs over it. Yet, McCormack argues, "the union of natures was understood to be indirect, mediated through the Person of the union;" this meant that "the antithesis between God and humanity is preserved—even in the union." McCormack argues that for Barth, "the eternal Son is present in history indirectly, never becoming directly identical with the veil of human flesh in which he conceals Himself."[127] While "the Person of the Logos is not dialectically structured, the being of the Mediator (the Person of the Logos in His two natures) *is* dialectically structured. In that

---

125. McCormack, *Karl Barth's Critically Realistic Dialectical Theology*, 365.

126. Barth, *Church Dogmatics*, 4.2, 87–88. See McCormack's discussion of Barth's concept of "unity in differentiation" in which there is no divinization of the human. McCormack argues that the incarnation is for Barth a "dialectical union" that upholds the distinction between humanity and divinity. *Karl Barth's Critically Realistic Dialectical Theology*, 361.

127. McCormack, *Karl Barth's Critically Realistic Dialectical Theology*, 366. Neder argues that this ongoing confrontation in Barth's conception stems from his understanding of the covenantal relationship in which the covenant command of God constantly confronts humanity and calls for the human response of free obedience. See Neder, *Participation in Christ*, 69–70.

the Logos reveals himself in and through the veil of human flesh without becoming directly identical with it, there is a dialectic in the being to be known."[128] However, given Barth's insistence on seeing the relationship between God and creation christologically, the implication of McCormack's view is that, if the relationship is undialectical only in Christ and still dialectical everywhere else, then the relationship of the one person and the two natures in the incarnation cannot be extended to relationship between God and creation *in* Christ. The relationship between God and creation in the one person is not extended to the redeemed relationship between God and creatures after Christ's death and resurrection.

Barth's determination to preserve the distinction between divine and human in the incarnation has also been noted by Trevor Hart. Hart argues that within the conceptual framework of Chalcedon, as Barth works through the dilemma of how God can be truly known in the world without being of the world—without that distinction collapsing—the two natures, one person language of Chalcedon functioned "to insist on the personal presence of God in a particular human life while yet differentiating the content of that life at every tangible point from God's own existence as God . . . God becomes the man Jesus, yet this becoming entails the addition of a human level of existence ('nature') to who and what God eternally is, an existence which remains distinct from his divine 'nature.' "[129] For Barth, this means that humans cannot lay hands on God in God's self. Rather, Hart explains, we see Jesus' "*humanity* which serves as a created veil for the divinity. . . . It is not 'God', but rather God as 'not-God' who is present in the world."[130] God reveals God's self through Jesus'

---

128. McCormack, *Karl Barth's Critically Realistic Dialectical Theology*, 370–371. If this is true, one has to wonder, how are person and being separated without evacuating the person of any real content?

129. Trevor Hart, "Revelation," in *The Cambridge Companion to Karl Barth*, 51. See also Barth, *Church Dogmatics*, 4.2, 51.

life, death, and resurrection, but these are events through the human nature of the incarnation. Hart argues, "the fact remains that the vehicle of revelation, even when it is hypostatically united with God, is not itself God."[131] While Hart does not sufficiently attend to the importance of the *enhypostasis* for Barth in his mature Christology or his insistence on single subjectivity in the one person, it is true that even in his mature work, Barth does speak of the humanity of Jesus as a dwelling for the divine.

Keith Johnson has also noted this aspect of Barth's thought, arguing that Jesus' humanity presents God in his relationship to what is distinct from him—it does not present God in and of himself.[132] Jesus' humanity is not a direct identity with God, but rather corresponds with God in the pattern of relationship that exists between the first and second persons of the Trinity.[133] This is in keeping with Barth's insistence on seeing analogy at the level of *relationship* and *activity*, rather than *being*. Being is the free decision to *act* in correspondence to God's initiative through obedience—both for Jesus and by extension to all of humanity.[134]

Carrying this line of thought further, Jones argues that in Barth's mature Christology, "the *unio hypostatica* is thoroughly actualized and rendered agential, making the cross-attribution of properties readily comprehensible; Christ's human agency is construed in terms of a relationship between grace, gratitude and responsibility; and

---

130. Hart, "Revelation," 52. See Barth, *Church Dogmatics,* Vol. 1.1, *The Doctrine of the Word of God,* ed. G. W. Bromiley and T. F. Torrance (London: T&T Clark, 1936), 166.

131. Hart, "Revelation," 52–53. It should be noted that Hart is drawing on Barth's early work with revelation. Barth's more mature work provides a highly nuanced and more balanced account. Still these notes are present and troubling.

132. Johnson, *Karl Barth and the Analogia Entis,* 214, referencing Barth, *Church Dogmatics,* 3.2, 219-220.

133. Johnson, *Karl Barth and the Analogia Entis,* 214-215.

134. Johnson, *Karl Barth and the Analogia Entis,* 215-218.

reconciliation is framed in terms of the *conjunctive* activity of the divine Son and the assumed human."[135]

Two issues arise with Jones' construal here. The first is that Jones thinks this conjunctive conception of divine and human protects the agential activity of each and actually strengthens Barth's understandings of the hypostatic union. This is because Jones argues for Barth's strong concern for dyothelitism. But Jones also reads this strategy as essentially taking the best of the Alexandrian and the best of the Antiochene conceptions and putting them together. However, as we saw in chapter 1, these two conceptions of the union yield quite different results. Cyril and Nestorius were not merely viewing the same conceptual framework from two differing angles. They had different paradigmatic understandings of the incarnational union. The second issue is that Jones overreads and makes emphatic what Barth leaves as shadings and nuance. Certainly Barth is rightly concerned to protect and keep distinct the divine and human in Jesus and to safeguard the human essence and agency of Jesus. But when one reads Barth through Jones, the agential activity of each nature is emphasized to such a degree that two subjects begin to vie for visibility in the one person. While that nuance is certainly there in Barth, and it is troubling, Barth does not step as far in that direction as Jones' reading of him would argue.

However, Jones' construal of the way in which divine and human act in the one person does highlight the difficult nuances of Barth's thought. Barth clearly intends to stay within the boundaries of the Chalcedonian framework, affirming two natures and one person, with a strong emphasis on the single subject of the incarnation. The two natures are to be seen only in the light of this one person.

---

135. Jones, *The Humanity of Christ*, 147, my emphasis. One again hears notes that Cyril found so troubling in Nestorius – how does one avoid a subtle but nonetheless real shadow of two subjects?

However, issues arise at points in his discussion concerning the way divine and human relate in Jesus. The first is that, despite some passages to the contrary in which Barth says he is moving away from the concept of "nature" to describe Jesus' humanity and divinity, Barth's discussion of the various modes of communication still reverberates with "essence" and "nature." This is related to his continued rejection of what he sees as the traditional (and what he really means here is the Lutheran) view of a two-way *idiomatum* that poses a communication of divine and human *essence*—a rejection he makes primarily because he objects to an infusion of the human by the divine, not because he objects to the divine being affected by the human. While that view may have been something that the "older" Lutherans held, it certainly would not have held true for Cyril, who argued that the communication of idioms was not at the level of nature or essence, but rather at the level of the one person. While Barth echoes this, he still is at such pains to keep human and divine in confrontation with one another that one wonders if his conviction regarding the one person has not sufficiently saturated his conception of the relation between divine and human in Jesus.

Further, Barth continues to draw distinctions between substantialist conceptions of being (which he views as static) and his concept of action as being, which leads him to draw a line between essence and existence in a way that implies a choice must be made between one or the other. This distinction then leads to his hesitation to speak of ontological change or to see that ontology can be coupled with moral existence and acts of obedience in related and complementary ways. Neder would disagree here, arguing that Barth conceives being as action and therefore there is no dichotomy between being and action in Barth's thought. He further argues that Barth's conception of the hypostatic union is one of constant action, a constant "hypostatic uniting."[136] While this may be true, I would argue that Barth's conceptions edge toward seeing the union in functional, extrinsic terms, which is one of the underlying issues that the church found so problematic in Theodore and Nestorius.[137]

One does not have to accept the more radical elements of Jones' thesis to notice the interesting, and even somewhat troubling, nuances in Barth's discussion. On the one hand, Barth pushes against the traditional conceptions of God's immutability, arguing that God is free and therefore can and does humiliate himself to descend into humanity and to be affected by it—though never in a necessary way. On the other hand, he is equally adamant that the humanity of Jesus is not altered, diminished, or enhanced in its communication with the divine. Barth works to hold for a two-way communication of the natures in the one person, while also holding on to an "antithesis" between them. It is difficult ground to traverse.

As we will see, this is part of Barth's rejection of deification and his effort to protect the full humanness of Jesus' humanity. This move is necessary for Barth because in his conceptual framework, Jesus' humanity cannot be "infused" with divine power without evacuating the humanity. In his treatment of the one person and two natures, we have seen Barth emphatically emphasize and uphold the single subject of the incarnation as the one person of Jesus Christ, who is fully divine and fully human. Yet, particularly in his exploration of the two natures through the themes of humiliation and exaltation, one

---

136. See Neder, *Participation in Christ*, note 14 to Chapter 5, 112. Neder notes that Barth's word, translated as conjunction in English carries more of a sense of "hypostatic uniting" in the German.

137. See Frederick McCleod, *The Roles of Christ's Humanity in Salvation: Insights from Theodore of Mopsuestia* (Washington, D.C.: The Catholic University of America Press, 1999), 202–204. See also McGuckin, *St. Cyril*, 166–167. McGuckin describes the underlying paradigm of Nestorius's conceptions by saying, "Replacing the notion of deification of manhood, as too dangerously suggesting some alteration in one or both of the *ousiai*, Nestorius instead pointed to the perfectly free will of the human Jesus, wholly obedient to the will of God (the Logos) and ultimately united with him as the excelling sign and means of salvation." The notes of conjunction, union through action, and obedience sound oddly similar to Barth in places.

senses that Barth is still uneasy about the relationship of human and divine—even in the reconciliation of Jesus. Barth walks the edge of two priorities that vie for position. While he is heavily invested in the covenant fellowship between God and humanity, he never becomes quite comfortable with fully moving away from the antithesis, the conflict and confrontation between divine and human. This may be due primarily to his insistence on upholding the free and loving grace of God, who alone can and does overcome this antithesis, restoring the covenant relationship on behalf of a humanity that is completely dependent upon this gracious favor. Barth consistently rejects and works against formulations that he regards as leading to anthropological reduction and a belief that humans can lay hands on God or develop some inherent capacities, latent within human essence itself, that can reach God. In addition, Barth is truly concerned to preserve the integrity of Jesus' humanity and thus a place for human action in response to God's gracious election. But the continued use of antithesis, confrontation, and conflict in his discussions of the two natures of Jesus sits oddly alongside Barth's adamant insistence on the single subjectivity of Christ and his extolling of a humanity exalted to life as covenant partners with God. The undialectical relationship between divine and human in Christ can never really be extended *through* Christ to the rest of creation in its redeemed relationship with God. In chapter 4, as we compare and analyze Barth and Balthasar with Cyril, we will need to revisit this note in Barth's work and examine whether it has significant effect on his Christology and a compelling soteriological vision of humanity exalted to fellowship with God.

Reconciliation and Exaltation

We turn now to a closer look at Barth's conception of the reconciliation of human beings with God that Jesus achieves in the event of his life, death, and resurrection, and Barth's view of what results from this reconciliation. Again, we see Barth return to the two-fold movement of humiliation and exaltation to describe these events. True divinity, God's true character, consists in this humiliation—that God became human in order that humans might become exalted to a right relationship with God.[138] Barth argues that Jesus' humiliation reveals his divinity as the Son of God and his exaltation as the Son of Man brings about the exaltation of all humanity as they participate in his life, death, and resurrection.[139]

It is the abasement of the Son—his obedience and humility in themselves—that is the divine accusation and condemnation against humans.[140] God in Jesus enters the human condition completely, with all that it means to be human, standing under the divine verdict and judgment, and living with the consequences of sin. Jesus "accepts personal responsibility for all the unfaithfulness, the deceit, the rebellion" of Israel's people.[141] Jesus "not only knew but willed" the crucifixion to happen. It is both and at once "an act of God which is coincident with the free action and suffering of a man." There is a perfect identity of action between divine and human.[142] The Son becomes man in order to judge the world and in that judgment, he becomes the one judged in its place. In this judgment of love and grace, God removes sin not from outside but from within, by being obedient and doing "right at the very place where man had done

138. Barth, *Church Dogmatics*, 4.1, 129–131.
139. Barth, *Church Dogmatics*, 4.2, 19.
140. Barth, *Church Dogmatics*, 4.1, 172–177.
141. Barth, *Church Dogmatics*, 4.1, 172–177.
142. Barth, *Church Dogmatics*, 4.1, 245.

wrong."[143] Again, Barth insists that God has not abdicated divinity, but rather that it is in this act that "God is supremely God," revealed in the passion of the human Jesus who is the eternally begotten Son.[144] Reconciliation is through the perfect obedience and offering of Jesus' self, the taking on of all violence and suffering and defeating it—not the suffering and dying in themselves, but Jesus' bearing the full weight of estrangement from God.[145]

Through this atoning act, Christ has made humans' continued status as sinners impossible. The atonement is an objective event for Barth. Christ has removed the root of sin and, while sins can still be committed, they can no longer count against us in terms of separating us from God.[146] Golgotha is the supremacy and finality of atonement, in which humans in their sinfulness are truly dead, buried, and completely destroyed—they cease to be.[147] A summary of Barth's understanding of the atonement would be: Jesus "took our place as Judge. He took our place as the judged. He was judged in our place. And he acted justly in our place."[148] His complete confidence in the efficacy of this event for all of creation allows Barth to say, "in spite of all that we are, and must be called, without Him, the divine promise that we shall be like Him has already been pronounced. In Him, in His being as man, the reconciliation of the world with God has already taken place, the kingdom of God has already come on earth, the new day has already dawned."[149]

143. Barth, *Church Dogmatics,* 4.1, 222, 232–237, quote 237.
144. Barth, *Church Dogmatics,* 4.1, 246–247.
145. Barth, *Church Dogmatics,* 4.1, 271.
146. Barth, *Church Dogmatics,* 4.1, 75–77.
147. Barth, *Church Dogmatics,* 4.1, 93–95.
148. Barth, *Church Dogmatics,* 4.1, 273.
149. Barth, *Church Dogmatics,* 4.2, 117.

Humanity Exalted, Not Deified

Thus far, we have seen Barth develop a Christology based on the single subject of Jesus Christ, who is the fully divine Son of God, who in humiliation descends into the human condition as a fully human being in order to reconcile humanity with God and exalt humans to fellowship with God as covenant partners. While Barth certainly has particular nuances of his own, this christological emphasis and pattern of soteriology seem remarkably compatible with that of Cyril. In addition, we see that Barth's Christology and his development of the one person and two natures are intimately linked to his soteriology, as they are for Cyril. In order to develop his soteriology around the theme of humiliation and exaltation within the covenant of election—in which Jesus is both subject and object, both the humiliated and the exalted one—Barth must have a strong single-subject Christology. It is also clear, both in his treatment of Christology proper but also throughout the *Dogmatics*, that Barth lays a strong emphasis on human fellowship with God as covenant partners. This is God's intent, and God goes to extraordinary lengths to restore this partnership and to exalt humanity to freedom for obedience in a life with God. Thus, the soteriological aim seems at least similar in pattern and goal to Cyril's.

But when we begin to examine how Barth extends the effects of this reconciliation and the exaltation of Jesus' humanity to all of humanity, differences with Cyril begin to emerge. Barth is adamantly opposed to any attempt to deify the humanity of Christ. The humanity of Jesus is the humanity of all humans, and for Barth such human essence is simply not capable of divinization. He argues that thinking of human essence as capable of divinization results in an abstracting of humanity from the concrete particularity of humanity in Christ, leading to humanism and a wrongly conceived anthropology.[150] Any hint of deifying Jesus' humanity evacuates that humanity of its true humanness and also opens the door to an anthropology that posits an inherent capacity in human nature itself to become deified. If humanity as such can become divine, why do we need Christ? From here, Barth argues, it is only a short distance to Hegel and Feuerbach. Barth argues that if Jesus' humanity is divinized, then there is automatically the deduction that—since the humanity of Jesus is the humanity of all humans—human essence in itself can be divinized. With that comes the possibility of a "high-pitched anthropology" in which Jesus becomes no longer really necessary for humanity to actualize something already latent within it.[151] "If the supreme achievement of Christology, its final word, is the apotheosised flesh of Jesus Christ, omnipotent, omnipresent, and omniscient, deserving of our worship, is it not merely a hard shell which conceals the sweet kernel of the divinity of humanity as a whole and as such, a shell which we can confidently discard and throw away once it has performed this service?"[152]

It's important to note that Barth approaches his discussion of deification through a comparison of the older Lutheran and Reformed traditions, particularly through their understanding of the *communicatio idiomatum* and *genus maiestaticum*.[153] Barth characterizes the Lutheran view as drawing directly on the Greek Alexandrian

---

150. Barth, *Church Dogmatics*, 4.2, 81–82. See Neder, *Participation in Christ*, 65–79 for an extensive discussion of the reasons for Barth's rejection of deification, which include our discussion of Barth's worries that deification turns Jesus' human nature into something other than truly human, that it makes God's grace something that requires human cooperation to be effective, that it relies on a substantialist ontology and that it leads to a receding of the importance of Christ because human transformation becomes rooted in human beings in themselves. Instead Neder argues Barth proposes the exaltation of humanity to a harmony consisting of acts of correspondence to God's decision and will.

151. Barth, *Church Dogmatics*, 4.2, 82–83.

152. Barth, *Church Dogmatics*, 4.2, 82.

153. See McCormack, *Orthodox and Modern*, 32. McCormack argues that in his view Barth comes close to affirming the concept of *genus tapeinoticum* (genus of humiliation) in which all human attributes are properly predicated of the one person with no emptying of any divine attributes.

fathers (though he does not name them or explore them in themselves) and expounding the impartation of divine qualities to the humanity of Jesus with a resulting deification of his humanity.[154] Barth rejects this view, arguing that it abstracts from the event of the one person of Jesus—from the continual event between divine and human that we know and see only in Jesus. In addition, he adds that when the divinizing of the flesh is seen as "the supreme and final" reason for the incarnation—"even to the point of worshipping it—a highly equivocal situation is created."[155]

It becomes clear that Barth sees divinization as the infusion of "distinctive qualities of the divine *nature* to the human" (which he sees as the "Lutheran" view that the human nature receives the actual qualities of the divine nature—a view Barth rejects).[156] Jones notes that what is really at stake here "is the communication of divine attributes to the concrete divine-human person of Jesus Christ."[157] Barth argues that this is not necessary and not permissible. The humanity as the "temple or dwelling" place of the divine is sufficient—we do not have to deify the temple because in doing so we evacuate the true humanity.[158] Rather, the humanity is exalted by the grace of the Son of God dwelling within it. Given this, for Barth, there is no need for any deification—the mere fact that the human essence is totally and exclusively "*determined* by the grace of God" as the dwelling or temple of God is enough. "Is temple or dwelling—a dwelling which is certainly filled with Godhead and totally and exclusively claimed and sanctified, but still a dwelling—not really enough to describe what we have to say of human essence in relation

---

154. Barth's reading of Luther in terms of his focus on *theosis* has been supported recently by the work of the Finnish school of Luther studies, which argues that this was a central focus for Luther.
155. Barth, *Church Dogmatics*, 4.2, 81.
156. Barth, *Church Dogmatics*, 4.2, 88, my emphasis.
157. Jones, *The Humanity of Jesus Christ*, 268.
158. Barth, *Church Dogmatics*, 4.2, 89, footnote.

to Jesus Christ and the history which took place in him? . . . If the human essence of Jesus Christ is deified, can He really be the Mediator between God and us?"[159] McCormack argues that for Barth the conception of deification does not adequately account for the distinction between person and nature. The divine "nature" was not made flesh. The second person was. "Thus, the union of the natures is an indirect union, mediated through the Person in whom both natures are grounded."[160]

God, in the divine essence, is "directed" to and "addressed" to Jesus' human essence and shares in it, but his humanity itself does not receive any "*alien* capacity."[161] Barth argues that Christ's origin in the divine does not alter his human essence itself. "It does not result in any change, diminution, or increase."[162] In addition, if Jesus' human essence is deified, then Barth asks if Jesus can truly be our mediator. Barth seems to assume that if Jesus' humanity is deified then its humanity is evacuated—it becomes no longer human and, if that is the case, then Jesus has not really assumed full humanity. What is not assumed is not redeemed. If Jesus' humanity is not truly and simply human then he cannot really be our mediator and savior.

For Barth, God is capable of the human, but that simply cannot be true in the reverse. He sees any claim to divinization as a claim that humans are inherently capable of divinity *qua* divinity, rather than seeing deification in the sense of analogous participation of the human in the divine. Any conception of divinization or an infused *habitus* also erodes the fullness of Jesus' humanity and moves toward a Docetic view of suffering and death.[163] Jesus must experience truly

---

159. Barth, *Church Dogmatics*, 4.2, See pg. 89, footnote.
160. McCormack, *Karl Barth's Critically Realistic Dialectical Theology*, 364. See also McCormack's discussion of Barth's refusal of deification, page 365, and in *Orthodox and Modern*, 235–260.
161. Barth, *Church Dogmatics*, 4.2, 86, my emphasis.
162. Barth, *Church Dogmatics*, 4.2, 91.
163. Barth, *Church Dogmatics*, 4.2, 94.

human suffering and death in all its historical particularity, and if his humanity has been divinized as Barth understands it, then Jesus' humanity ceases to be fully human and becomes divine. Because Jesus' full humanity and perfect human obedience are so important to Barth's understanding of atonement and reconciliation, we have seen that, as he develops his exposition of exaltation, he takes great care to guard Jesus' humanity from anything that might suggest his humanity has become "divine," that is deified or enhanced in any way that would mean it was no longer fully and simply human. As a result of these conceptions, Barth steadfastly refuses what he understands to be deification and offers instead the exaltation of Jesus' humanity as that which opens up the exaltation of all humanity to life with God.

The Pattern of Exaltation

We have seen that while Barth adamantly insists on a single subject Christology with a fervor that matches Cyril, he also just as adamantly refuses the concept of deification in favor of exaltation. Neder argues that "Barth intends to cut off the sources of all soteriologies which, in one way or another, affirm a cleansing or transformation of human nature through the infusion of divine grace, divine attributes, or the divine nature itself."[164] We now turn to that soteriological pattern of exaltation to see if Barth provides a similarly compelling vision of human life as a participation in God's life, while rejecting what Cyril would understand as deification. Barth sets out a pattern of exaltation in which, through his perfect obedience, Jesus returns to God what all of humanity owes. He is like us in all that we are, but unlike us in what he does—he is perfectly obedient. In Jesus, we see the true and normal form of

---

164. Neder, *Participation in Christ*, 6.

human nature—this is an "authentically human life." Jesus' life is human nature's "normalization."[165] In this area, it is important to realize that for Barth, human being is determined by human action. We are what we do. Human essence is thus a historical event—not an "appropriated state," not a superhuman form of power. Barth argues that God's power and authority are revealed through the event of Jesus' humanity.[166]

The humanity of Jesus always remains completely and only human essence, and is exalted to the full harmony of the Trinitarian life.[167] "In His identity with the Son of God, when He was lifted up into heaven, He was not deified, or assumed into the Godhead (for this was unnecessary for Him as the Son of God and impossible for Him as the Son of Man), but placed as man at the side of God, in direct fellowship with Him, in full participation in His glory."[168] The event of Jesus' life, death, resurrection, and ascension is the enactment of perfect obedience, which is the intended human response to God's love and graciousness. Jesus' exaltation is the empowering of Jesus' human essence to serve God.

This opens a way for all of humanity to be exalted through him.[169] It is important to see the stress Barth places on Jesus' obedient actions as the key salvific and exalting factor in this pattern. For Barth, Jesus' actions are decisive for all humanity. He acts as both God and human in a perfect correspondence of action. This "identity of action" in the event of his life *is* the union of divine and human.[170] Because

165. Barth, *Church Dogmatics*, 4.2, 452.

166. Barth, *Church Dogmatics*, 4.2, 99.

167. Barth, *Church Dogmatics*, 4.2, 72.

168. Barth, *Church Dogmatics*, 4.2, 153.

169. Barth, *Church Dogmatics*, 4.2, 28–30. Neder notes that exaltation for Barth is the freedom humanity receives in Christ that enables them to respond in thankful obedience to the divine command and this is the pattern of divine-human action in correspondence established by Jesus in moment-by-moment action. Neder, *Participation in Christ*, 34–38.

170. Barth, *Church Dogmatics*, 4.2, 98–99. See Neder, *Participation in Christ*, 11–12, 34–35 for an exposition of this theme.

God's being and act are one, and because Barth is determined to do justice to the "event" of God's action in Jesus Christ, he emphasizes the "identity of action" between the divine and human in Jesus as the overriding element of their union in him. The man Jesus of Nazareth perfectly enacts the Trinitarian pattern of the Son's obedience to the Father in the love of the Spirit. Barth also seeks to account for the role of the Holy Spirit in Jesus' life. "As the Son of God, he is obedient man, who is not only filled and impelled by the Spirit, but exists in the activity of the Spirit, establishing His work, incorporating Him in Himself as the capacity to receive the grace of God and its influence in the creaturely world."[171]

Yet, for all his complete identity with humanity, Jesus *is* different from us—or else he becomes simply a uniquely graced man—and Barth must account for this. Barth's response is once again highly nuanced and complex. Barth says that in this event, Jesus' human essence "acquires divine power and authority. It acquires the quality which it lacked to bear and attest this power and authority."[172] Barth argues, "it is human essence, but effectively confronted with the divine, in the character with which it is invested by the fact that God willed to be and became man as well as God, so that without itself becoming divine it is an essence which exists in and with God and is adopted and controlled and sanctified and ruled by Him. This is the exaltation which comes to human essence in the one Jesus Christ."[173] Further, this exaltation is not a mere "improvement" in the current state of humanity but an exaltation of humanity's very essence.[174]

However, this idea of an acquired "quality" sits rather oddly with Barth's adamant rejection of any "enhancement" of Jesus' humanity.

171. Barth, *Church Dogmatics,* 4.2, 167, footnote.
172. Barth, *Church Dogmatics,* 4.2, 99.
173. Barth, *Church Dogmatics,* 4.2, 88.
174. Barth, *Church Dogmatics,* 4.2, 30.

If Jesus' human essence acquires this "quality" of divine power and authority that it lacked, is not that an enhancement of Jesus' humanity? And how does Jesus' humanity acquire this quality? Does it dwell within him through the grace and power of the Spirit and if so, how is that different from the "infused" grace Barth consistently rejects? Barth clearly wants to hold on to the integrity of Christ's human nature by insisting it is not enhanced, but without an analogical conception that human nature can be enhanced or perfected without becoming itself divine Barth has trouble extending the effects of the incarnation to all of humanity.

Barth approaches the issue by using the concept of confrontation again, arguing that as Jesus' humanity is confronted by the divine, it becomes controlled and sanctified by divine power and authority for the obedience that leads to reconciliation and exaltation without becoming changed as human essence. After making note of the divine power acquired by Jesus' humanity through its confrontation with the divine, Barth moves to the role of Jesus' obedience in this movement from humiliation to exaltation. Essentially, Barth argues that Jesus is different from us in that he exercises human obedience perfectly and without sin. While Jesus is completely like us, he is also at the same time completely unlike us because in his human life and history his humanity is exalted.[175] Jesus was "wholly free to do the will of the Father. . . . He was not bound by . . . any power of nature or history, by any destiny, by any orders, by any limits or obstacles."[176]

Again, Barth assures us that this exaltation does not mean any diminution of Jesus' humanity. Rather, because there is no necessity in human nature that wills to sin (even though we in fact do), Jesus' obedience is not a change in human essence but the exaltation to its true end—perfect obedience. The only difference between us

175. Barth, *Church Dogmatics*, 4.2, 28–29.
176. Barth, *Church Dogmatics*, 4.2, 161.

and Christ is that he exercises true human freedom perfectly.[177] It's not a question of Jesus' humanity *being* different. It's a question of him *acting* differently.[178] It is important to remember that for Barth, human essence is not a state. It is an action.[179] Jesus' humanity overcomes our sinfulness not by infusion, but by obedience—by exercising human freedom fully and perfectly and opening up the way for humans to follow this pattern. Yet for Barth, echoing Luther's *simul justus et peccator*, humans never internally possess grace or righteousness. They remain sinners who must constantly receive the imputed, alien righteousness of Christ and exercise the freedom of obedient response.[180] Drawing attention to the importance of this confrontation for Barth, Neder says, "if this confrontation were eliminated, the union could not be an event of discipleship."[181] Neder argues that union in Christ is a continual encounter "between the grace of God and sinful human beings." It never ceases to include confrontation and judgment. So even in exaltation and union with Christ, there remains a distance between Christ and his followers.

177. Barth, *Church Dogmatics,* 4.2, 93.

178. However, this conception raises the issue of what it is that makes Christ able to be perfectly obedient if he is exactly and only just like us. How does Barth account for the difference between Christ and us in this area? Is this the function of the Holy Spirit? How does Barth avoid thinking of Jesus as a uniquely graced human here?

179. Neder notes that it is important to remember that, for Barth, essence is action, not some "static" quality of being. *Participation in Christ,* 13. Katherine Sonderegger has expressed concern that Barth's strong insistence that humans fashion themselves through their own actions causes him trouble christologically. He focuses on Christ's agency to an extent that is detrimental to Christ's nature. In developing the two natures doctrine as action, Christ's divinity and humanity are seen in terms of action rather than "being," and this move is worrisome to feminists concerned with portrayals of human life that focus solely on activity to the neglect of any inward life. "If at any point, a critic is inclined to embrace von Balthasar's claim that Barth has no full theology of the creature, she may be convinced to say so here. Historical being may be creaturely; historical act alone may be far less," she argues. See Sonderegger, "Barth and feminism" in *The Cambridge Companion to Karl Barth,* 266, citing Balthasar, *The Theology of Karl Barth,* part II, chapter 4.

180. Neder, *Participation in Christ,* 48–49.

181. Neder, *Participation in Christ,* 78.

For Barth, Neder says, distance is necessary to guarantee human freedom—otherwise it would be overwhelmed by God's action.[182]

Through their exaltation in Christ, humans are freed for this obedient action in fellowship with God. In a play on the early church's famous exchange formula, Barth writes that, "God became man in order that man may—not become God, but come to God."[183]

Ontological Declaration

Yet, while Barth continually casts the results of exaltation in terms of action, he clearly also wants to articulate that human essence in itself is also given a new ontological status through these events.[184] Of course, this is tricky ground for Barth, given his rejection of any hint of "infused *habitus*" or "enhancement" of Jesus' humanity, and thus an extension of this to all humanity. But Barth does envision an intimate fellowship with God that transforms human life and brings newness and re-creation in Christ. "The spoil of divine mercy, the result of the act of atonement is exalted man: new in the power of the divine exaltation . . . the first-born of a new humanity . . ."[185] In Jesus Christ "our human essence is given a glory and exalted to a dignity and clothed with a majesty which the Son who assumed it and existed in it has in common with the Father and the Holy

---

182. Neder, *Participation in Christ*, 79.

183. Barth, *Church Dogmatics*, 4.2, 106.

184. Keith Johnson argues that Barth reexamined this area of his thought in response to Gottlieb Sohngen's critique that Barth had placed "faith against being" (quoting Sohngen) and had failed to account for the being of the creature at all in his earlier work. Barth talked only about a being that is extrinsic to the creature and thus reduced the relationship between God and humanity to a purely external one. Sohngen argued that a true analogy of being describes human beings who only participate in Christ by faith, but by faith, they do participate in being. See Johnson, *Karl Barth and the Analogia Entis*, 172–198, referencing and quoting Sohngen's argument in "Analogia Fidei: Gottähnlichkeit allein aus Glauben?" *Catholica* 3, no. 3 (1934): 113–136 and "Analogia Fidei: Die Einheit in der Glaubenswissenschft," *Catholica* 3, no. 4 (1934): 176–208.

185. Barth, *Church Dogmatics*, 4.2, 103.

Ghost—the glory and dignity and majesty of the divine nature."[186] It is the act of humiliation of the Son of God that is the exaltation of the Son of Man and in him of human essence. While he makes humanity his own existence, he "does not deify it, but exalts it into the '*consortium divinitatis*' into an inward and indestructible fellowship with His Godhead." [187] Of the human essence, Barth writes, "in its unity of existence with His Son He adopted it into fellowship with His being as God . . ."[188]

The covenant decision of God brings about an "ontological connection" between sinful man and God in Jesus Christ.[189] Jones reminds us that "decision functions as an ontological category" for Barth.[190] This is an "ontological declaration" about our being as humans that applies to all humanity.[191] The decision that has taken place in Christ actually affects our being—a being that Barth argues is "not just an experience that we have, nor a disposition, nor an attitude of the will or emotions, nor a possibility that is available but has still to be realized; but our truest reality, in which we are to see and understand ourselves in truth, for which we are claimed, from which there automatically result certain consequences which

186. Barth, *Church Dogmatics,* 4.2, 100.
187. Barth, *Church Dogmatics,* 4.2, 100–101.
188. Barth, *Church Dogmatics,* 4.2, 100.
189. Barth, *Church Dogmatics,* 4.2, 281.
190. Jones, *The Humanity of Christ,* 109.
191. Barth, *Church Dogmatics,* 4.2, 275. Barth's conception of exaltation is, as expected, related to his conception of election. McCormack argues that Barth does not do away with double predestination. He reframes it to argue that in choosing to be for sinful humanity, God chooses judgment and death for God's self and mercy and life for humans. This means that humanity is exalted through this reversal in Christ. Just as God, in self-determination, chose to be God for us, so too, Jesus in human self-determination chose himself for God and other humans. This becomes the basis for our choosing of God and others as well. Human ontology thus corresponds to the divine covenant ontology. See McCormack, "Grace and being," in *The Cambridge Companion to Karl Barth,* 107. Trevor Hart also notes that for Barth, while God's grace "penetrates" humanity and gifts it with the capacity to respond to God, humanity is not made divine, but rather human life and act are made to correspond to God. Hart, "Revelation," in *The Cambridge Companion to Karl Barth,* 49. See also Neder, *Participation in Christ,* 73–79.

we have necessarily to draw. . . . And from this being there follows necessarily all that we have to will and to do."[192] Neder says, "Barth is not so much denying that grace inwardly transforms the individual to whom it comes as he is offering that there is nothing more personal or real than the acts in which human beings respond to God's grace. Personal participation in the history of discipleship, the circle of God's action and obedient response, is the most inward and real event possible to human beings."[193]

Colin Gunton has noted Barth's attention to an ontological change in humanity. Attempting to place Barth's ideas in context, Gunton traces a number of views in the Christian tradition regarding salvation and its effects, ranging from an ontological conception in which "the whole being of the person is transformed or completed," through a "moralizing" view in which the person's relationship with God is "reoriented."[194] In assessing Barth's conception of what salvation is and what it achieves for humanity, Gunton argues that Barth's is more than a merely "moral" view because "relation is an ontological category" for him. Because this is so, the effects of salvation also involve the very being of the person.[195] For Barth, "by changing the relationship God reshapes human being" itself through Christ. Human beings receive a new status that creates a new reality out of which they can live.[196]

Barth clearly wants to convey a sense of complete newness, of the regeneration of creaturely life and its freedom for true fellowship with God. He speaks of transformation and participation, and this "ontological declaration" about human being itself through the event

192. Barth, *Church Dogmatics*, 4.2, 276–277.
193. Neder, *Participation in Christ*, 51. See Neder's exposition throughout of the interplay between objective and subjective participation in Christ, and his argument that the objective makes the subjective possible for Barth.
194. Colin Gunton, "Salvation," in *The Cambridge Companion to Karl Barth*, 144.
195. Gunton, "Salvation," 144.
196. Gunton, "Salvation," 148.

and history of Jesus.[197] As John Webster notes, "because it is the history in which the covenant between God and humanity is fulfilled from both sides, Jesus' history is the true essence of created being."[198] In Barth's account, human being itself is changed as the sinful humanity is slain in order to be made alive in Christ. This change in the status of humanity's relationship with God is an objective event, a miracle that definitively reorders human being itself and redirects it toward God.[199] As Neder puts it, "Thus as Jesus Christ encounters those whom he calls, he illuminates and awakens them to their true being—a being in the freedom of his service. In so doing he becomes the ruling principle of their lives, and as such he awakens them to freedom and spontaneity of their own truest selves."[200] Throughout his christological work in Volume 4 of the *Dogmatics*, and in his treatment of special ethics in Volume 3.4, Barth passionately writes of the human moral response that reconciliation with God in Christ makes possible.

Noting this theme in Barth, Stanley Hauerwas argues that, after rejecting the *analogia entis*, Barth reexamined and rediscovered a form of natural theology as he worked with the *enhypostasis* of Christ. In this way, Barth's ongoing concern to preserve the real distinction between God and humans could be preserved, but humans could also be seen to participate analogically in the truth of God through lives of gratitude and witness.[201] In fact, the theme of obedient, grateful responsiveness in witness to this gift from God—and a participation in it—runs through *Church Dogmatics*. Hauerwas argues that, for Barth, if God is properly acknowledged, that knowledge directs human lives in a particular way.[202] It is only through Christ that

197. Barth, *Church Dogmatics*, 4.2, 274–276.
198. John Webster, *Barth's Ethics of Reconciliation*, 85.
199. Barth, *Church Dogmatics*, 4.2, 265, 276–281 for his discussion of the effects of this reordering.
200. Neder, *Participation in Christ*, 77.
201. See Stanley Hauerwas, *With the Grain of the Universe* (Grand Rapids: Brazos Press, 2001).

humans become truly human. To speak of humanity is to speak of humans as sinners in a fallen creation, but it is also to speak of "the unity and wholeness of creation as God's promise" in Christ.[203]

Barth is clear that if the human answer to Jesus is "yes," then this response results in nothing less than the "redirection and conversion" of the entire person.[204] Barth speaks of "transformation," saying there is now a clear division between the old life that has become past in Christ and the new life that is present to us in him—we have been given a new freedom that we must use.[205] In this process "we are claimed as those who are regenerate and converted, as those who are already engaged in that turning to God, and therefore as Christians."[206] Barth speaks in lofty terms of this new freedom given in exaltation and sanctification. "In the determination and limitation given them in their intercourse with God they are men of unconditional and unlimited capacity. They can think rightly and desire rightly, wait rightly and hasten rightly, obey rightly and defy rightly, begin rightly and end rightly, be with and for men rightly and by themselves rightly . . . because in faith they have the freedom of God's partners."[207]

202. Hauerwas, *With the Grain of the Universe*, 39, 142–146, 184–194. Yet, Hauerwas notes that Barth's thought also presents challenges for Christian practices, because his account of the church does not adequately account for the way in which the church is the means through which Christians participate in the new life in Christ. Hauerwas argues that Barth treats the cross as bringing history to a close and short circuits the Spirit's work through the church as that community through which Christians are formed and participate in the divine life through practices. Yet despite these shortcomings, Hauerwas argues that Barth demonstrates that, ultimately, witness is more important than explanation or rationalization.

203. Hauerwas, *With the Grain of the Universe*, 168.

204. Barth, *Church Dogmatics*, 4.2, 157.

205. Barth, *Church Dogmatics*, 4.2, 267.

206. Barth, *Church Dogmatics*, 4.2, 273.

207. Barth, *Church Dogmatics*, 4.2, 242.

The Holy Spirit

How do humans respond to and in this new freedom to live as God's partners that they have received through Christ? Here Barth turns to an exploration of the work of the Holy Spirit. The distance between Jesus' humanity and ours is bridged by the Spirit, who empowers humans for a new life of obedience in faith, hope, and love. Human existence is given a new determination and directed toward God. Within the Trinitarian relations, Barth speaks of the Holy Spirit as the communion or fellowship between Father and Son, as the one who bears witness to the saving significance of Jesus Christ.[208] Hunsinger notes that in this connection, Barth argues the Spirit has no "independent content" but rather a content that is determined "wholly and entirely" by Christ.[209] In addition, the Spirit bears witness to Christ's salvific work in history and also enables humanity to participate in that work here and now.[210] Through the proclamation of the Word, which the Spirit makes possible, Jesus is continually present to humanity and humanity is enabled to belong to Christ.[211] The Holy Spirit makes Christ present in the

---

208. See Barth's discussion in *Church Dogmatics*, 1.1, 448–489. See also George Hunsinger, "Karl Barth's doctrine of the Holy Spirit," in *The Cambridge Companion to Karl Barth*, 180. See footnote 4 in which Hunsinger notes that for Barth, the divine *ousia* is logically prior to the hypostases, even though there is no *ousia* without the hypostases and no hypostases without the *ousia*. "It is therefore in the Holy Spirit, and not directly in the divine *ousia* as such, that the eternal *koinonia* of the three hypostases is to be found." (Hunsinger is here citing *Church Dogmatics,* 1.1, 359, 368, 382.) Does this conception threaten to make relationality in God in some way extrinsic to God's being?

209. Hunsinger, "Karl Barth's doctrine of the Holy Spirit," 181, quoting Barth in *Church Dogmatics,* I.1, 452.

210. Hunsinger, "Karl Barth's doctrine of the Holy Spirit," 181. McCormack argues that for Barth in his doctrine of election, participation in Christ is not something that requires a special action of the Holy Spirit to effect because such participation is already real as Christ carries out the work of election—humans are already elected to participation through the divine election. The Spirit awakens us to this truth. See McCormack, "Justitia aliena: Karl Barth in Conversation with the Evangelical Doctrine of Imputed Righteousness" 190–193, in *Justification in Perspective: Historical Developments and Contemporary Challenges,* ed. Bruce L. McCormack (Grand Rapids: Baker Academic, 2006).

world, guides humanity on the way toward fulfillment of this new reality, and helps human beings to be Christians on the journey.[212] In the time between the present and Christ's return, the Spirit enables humans to take part in the presence and revelation of Christ as they participate in his exaltation.[213] As Barth puts it, humans are now those who are "set in contradiction and opposition to their own sin, who are called and sanctified to true and serious conflict with it and to the fulfillment of the will of God, who constitute His community of service and obedience, who as its members can love in sincerity and truth."[214] It is the power of grace through the Holy Spirit that gives us the assurance that our sins are forgiven and "awakens us to a new life of obedience, the hope of the resurrection of the dead, and everlasting life in which there can be no cessation of His onward movement."[215] Barth writes that this grace of the Holy Spirit "is a new capacity, which in whatever freedom they previously lived or thought they lived, they did not even remotely know."[216] The "Holy Spirit is the subjective reality of revelation," the one who makes possible God's presence to humans.[217] It is only through the Spirit that humans are freed in ways that allow God to work within them so that they can "believe, be a recipient of His revelation, the object of the divine reconciliation."[218] He continues, "The very possibility of

211. Hunsinger, "Karl Barth's doctrine of the Holy Spirit," 181–182, citing Barth, *Church Dogmatics*, 4.2, 654.

212. See Barth, *Church Dogmatics*, 4.3.1, *The Doctrine of Reconciliation*, ed. G. W. Bromiley and T. F. Torrance (Edinburgh: T&T Clark, 1961), 352–353.

213. See Barth, *Church Dogmatics*, 4.3.1, 363. See also *Church Dogmatics*, 4.3.2, *The Doctrine of Reconciliation*, ed. G. W. Bromiley and T. F. Torrance (Edinburgh: T&T Clark, 1962) for an extensive discussion of Christian vocation.

214. Barth, *Church Dogmatics*, 4.2, 266.

215. Barth, *Church Dogmatics*, 4.2, 245.

216. Barth, *Church Dogmatics*, 4.2, 244–245, quote 244.

217. Barth, *Church Dogmatics*, 1.2, *The Doctrine of the Word of God*, ed. G. W. Bromiley and T. F. Torrance (London: T&T Clark, 1956), 242.

218. Barth, *Church Dogmatics*, 1.2, 198.

human nature's being adopted into unity with the Son of God is the Holy Ghost."[219]

Yet, despite his conception of an ontological declaration that changes our very being through the confrontation of Jesus' humanity with the divine made present to us through the Spirit, Barth is less comfortable talking about an indwelling of the Spirit in human beings for many of the same reasons that he is reluctant to speak of "infused" grace. He does have a place for it, but he is reluctant to linger too long on the Spirit's inner work in human beings. Perhaps he fears modern humanity's propensity to stress the subjective character of grace and to think of indwelling grace as a matter of private possession or as an inherent capacity that is simply realized, rather than a divine, supernatural gift from completely outside human being as such.[220] So Barth would surely have qualms about Cyril's conception that, in the incarnation, Jesus' humanity becomes the secure dwelling place for the Holy Spirit, who infuses all of humanity with a graced participation in the life of God.

This hesitancy about a subjective conception of indwelling is also part of Barth's insistence on the objective reality of Jesus Christ and the corresponding truth that humans do not have some independent, subjective reality of their own to which Christ has to be made relevant or to which Christ has to be related. Humans already only truly exist within the objective reality of Christ, and it is precisely this reality that makes them human.[221] For Barth, as Johnson notes, "what humans are *internally* is at every moment in time, a function of the *external* justifying relation of God to them in Jesus Christ."[222]

219. Barth, *Church Dogmatics,* 1.2, 199.
220. See Neder's exposition of the way Barth works from objective to subjective participation and the role of the Holy Spirit in this movement. *Participation in Christ,* 78–84.
221. See Webster, *Barth's Ethics of Reconciliation,* 34–62, 72–73, 87–94. See also Webster's discussion of Barth's ongoing background conversation with Bultmann and the ways in which this affects his conceptions and discussion here. Webster, *Barth's Ethics of Reconciliation,* 91–98.
222. Johnson, *Karl Barth and the Analogia Entis,* 11.

So Barth writes of the Spirit, "He is absolutely other, superior. . . . As our Teacher and Leader He is in us, but not as a power of which we might become lords."[223] Rather, Barth focuses on the Spirit as the ongoing presence and witness of Christ, who instructs, corrects, and guides humans into obedience and the life God intends. Because the Spirit makes the miracle of conversion possible and sustains that conversion, for Barth, the virtues of faith, hope, and love "do not depend upon regenerated capacities, infused virtues, acquired habits, or strengthened dispositions in the soul," Hunsinger notes.[224]

Here, we once again see Barth's conceptions of the relationship between nature and grace come into play as well. In this understanding of the Holy Spirit's work in human life, Hunsinger argues, Barth rejects any sense of emanationism, which he believes stresses divine grace in ways that sacrifice human freedom and response, and he also emphatically rejects any sense of synergism in which human freedom cooperates with divine grace in a way that is considered necessary for salvation. For Barth, Hunsinger argues, "grace is not a matter of repairing this or that human capacity, but of contradicting fallen human nature as a whole, with its capacities and incapacities, so that it actually transcends itself despite its falleness."[225] The relation between nature and grace is miracle—not cooperation or restoration, but resurrection.[226] Through the Spirit, "grace does not perfect and exceed human nature in its sorry plight so much as it contradicts and overrules it."[227] Hunsinger argues that this miraculous conversion of salvation operates within a "Chalcedonian pattern" in

---

223. Barth, *Church Dogmatics*, 1.1, 454. See also Barth's discussion in *Church Dogmatics* 1.1, 450–466.

224. Hunsinger, "Karl Barth's doctrine of the Holy Spirit," 183. See also Neder's discussion of the role of the Holy Spirit as the power by which the objectively true in Christ becomes subjectively true in human beings' lives. *Participation in Christ*, 56.

225. Hunsinger, "Karl Barth's doctrine of the Holy Spirit," 184.

226. Hunsinger, "Karl Barth's doctrine of the Holy Spirit," 184. This of course assumes that restoration, cooperation and regeneration are not miracles as well.

227. Hunsinger, "Karl Barth's doctrine of the Holy Spirit," 185.

which God and humans cooperate without separation, confusion, change, or division of divinity and humanity. Similarly, the Spirit is that which joins the different realities of human and divine together and enables participation by the human in the community of Christ. However, Hunsinger notes that the concept of ongoing regeneration in the believer is underdeveloped in Barth, particularly in relation to resurrection.[228] Further, Johnson notes that the basic contradiction between God and humanity remains—even after justification and reconciliation has occurred.[229]

Alan Torrance has agreed that the work of the Spirit in the ongoing life of the Christian remains underdeveloped in Barth. He argues that Barth's conceptions could have been strengthened by a more complete discussion of the Trinitarian-grounded continuing priesthood of Christ, in which humanity is taken by Christ to participate in his eternal life with the Father, through the Spirit. A stronger development of the Spirit's extension of Christ's ongoing presence and priesthood could have strengthened Barth's theology of the church and his exposition of the sacraments.[230]

Colin Gunton also argues that Barth does not give the Holy Spirit appropriate weight in relation to Jesus' humanity. There is not a sufficient role for the Spirit in mediating the relationship between Father and Son. Rather, Gunton argues, Barth's emphasis is on the relationship of Jesus' humanity to the Father.[231] The result is that the connection between Jesus' humanity and our humanity is weakened.

---

228. Hunsinger, "Karl Barth's doctrine of the Holy Spirit," 187–190, n. 15.
229. Johnson, *Karl Barth and the Analogia Entis,* 115.
230. Alan Torrance, "The Trinity," in *The Cambridge Companion to Karl Barth*, 82–83. "Had Barth's theologies of election and reconciliation, to which Christ's vicarious humanity is central, been more effectively integrated with the theology of worship conceived in terms of Christ's continuing priesthood, a consequence of this would have been a more robust exposition of the intratrinitarian relations as the ground of the existence of the body of Christ." Quote on page 83.
231. Gunton, "Salvation," 152. Stanley Hauerwas also notes difficulties with Barth's account of the Spirit's work in human life. See, *With the Grain of the Universe*, 145.

Barth places more emphasis on the relationship between what happened in the one-time historical event of Jesus and humanity, rather than on the Spirit's continued mediation of the relationship between Jesus' humanity and our humanity in the body of the church.[232] In other words, Barth simply does not have a sufficient account of mediation between the *then* of Jesus' life and the *now* of Jesus' life in the lives of believers.

In addition, Gunton argues that Barth also fails to adequately give an account of the ascension, which, as an account of Jesus' continuing human priesthood, is crucial in making the connection between the then and now of Jesus' humanity. The result, he argues, is a tendency in Barth to "reduce the human life to a series of illuminating episodes" that might be the feature of any human life, rather than attending sufficiently to the unique characteristics of Jesus' human life and its present implications for humanity.[233] The result is that Barth's treatment of Jesus' humanity has an "abstract" quality that insufficiently accounts for the humanity of the risen Jesus and his presence to and effect on humanity now.[234]

However, Douglas Farrow has argued that Barth actually provides an important account of Jesus' ascension, particularly in affirming that the ascended Jesus continues to be fully divine and fully human. Barth's account stresses the humanity of the exalted and glorified Jesus.[235] Yet, Farrow notes that Barth's decision to associate humiliation with divinity and exaltation with humanity creates problems for him. Farrow asks, "can we afford, even occasionally and

---

232. Gunton, "Salvation," 152–153.
233. Gunton, "Salvation," 153. Gunton also argues that Barth makes Jesus too much the one who mediates knowledge of himself rather than providing a more Trinitarian account of that mediation from the Father, through the Son, by the power of the Spirit. These elements also give Barth's account the feature of having more concern with the revelation of the once-for-all act of salvation than for the mediation of a personal relation now.
234. Gunton, "Salvation," 153.
235. Douglas Farrow, *Ascension and Ecclesia: On the Significance of the Doctrine of the Ascension for Ecclesiology and Christian Cosmology* (Grand Rapids: Eerdmans, 1999), 229–254.

as a purely formal device, to use one element in the story of Jesus to speak primarily of divinity and another primarily of humanity? Does that not endanger the story itself, not to mention a sound theology of the incarnation?"[236] While Farrow gives Barth full credit for recovering the significance of Jesus' humanity in the resurrection and exaltation, he nonetheless argues that by actualizing Chalcedon through an argument that Jesus is what he does, and associating each "state" so closely with either humanity or divinity, Barth is then forced, in order to avoid Docetism, "to clamp the two movements" of Jesus' descent and ascent "tightly together" in such a way that they become the same event, which really concludes at the cross.[237] Barth so closely connects soteriology to ontology, Jesus' acts with Jesus' being, that he must "reject any history-related distinction between the humiliated Christ and the exalted Christ."[238] Farrow explains that, as a result, everything seems to be completed at the cross—resurrection and ascension do not actually seem to be new events for Jesus. Jesus' history becomes revelation and humans simply "see and hear and share in what has already been done."[239] The resurrection and ascension function primarily to reveal the climax of history on the cross. There is little room for ongoing human history. Time becomes subsumed in eternity.[240] In addition, the divide between God and humanity is only overcome by death in time and "reconstitution" in eternity.[241]

However, Webster notes that critics of Barth who have argued that creaturely mediation or participation in Christ is conflated into the risen Christ—the criticism that there is really only room for

236. Farrow, *Ascension and Ecclesia*, 243.
237. Farrow, *Ascension and Ecclesia*, 244.
238. Farrow, *Ascension and Ecclesia*, 245.
239. Farrow, *Ascension and Ecclesia*, 245.
240. Farrow, *Ascension and Ecclesia*, 246.
241. Farrow, *Ascension and Ecclesia*, 246.

Jesus and not the world—miss both Barth's purpose in shying away from such mediation, and his way of dealing with the relationship between the objective person and event of Jesus, including the way this life becomes subjectively real in human life.[242] Webster argues that Barth's refusal to attribute such mediation to humanity or the church is actually rooted in a desire to free creatures from responsibility for mediating the divine.[243] Barth wants to ensure that "creaturely agents are not impelled by grace but enabled by grace to be themselves."[244] In addition, such mediation is not necessary because Barth trusts that the Word is living, active, present, and fully able to make himself known. Revelation is presented in a specific form—Jesus. Or as Barth so pithily puts it, "God sets among men a fact which speaks for itself."[245]

Webster argues Barth came to believe that Roman Catholic and Reformed Protestant theology, as well as modern theology, had misunderstood the question of the way in which the "objectivity of Jesus Christ and his salvation becomes subjectively real to the Christian believer" through the mediation of creaturely means—sacraments and church, or morality and experience. For Barth, such misunderstood mediations collapse a necessary distinction and give to creaturely action a significance it does not have. The danger is that such mediations come to be seen as a representation of Christ.[246] Instead, Barth uses the doctrines of Christ and the Holy Spirit to argue that the perfection of Jesus' work is completed and effective. It needs no mediation through creaturely means to be made real in the lives of believers.[247] We are taken into Jesus' history,

---

242. Webster, *Barth's Ethics of Reconciliation*, 93–148, especially 125–146.
243. Webster, *Barth*, 139.
244. Webster, *Barth*, 139.
245. Barth *Church Dogmatics*, 4.3.1, 221.
246. Webster, *Barth's Ethics of Reconciliation*, 126–127.
247. Webster, *Barth's Ethics of Reconciliation*, 87–88.

which is the only true reality, and only here do we truly have our being and action.[248] As Neder notes, "when by the power of the Holy Spirit, faith, love, and hope are offered as responses to the divine verdict, direction, and promise, that which is objectively true becomes subjectively true."[249]

Barth makes the move from the objective event of Jesus to the subjective appropriation of that event in human life through the resurrection and the Holy Spirit in which, Webster argues, the "ongoing, self-realizing character of reconciliation is articulated," but not through any human theories or inherent capacities.[250] In all of this, there is in Barth a strong reserve. "Barth is very unwilling so to emphasize the reality of the human acting subject that it becomes detached from its gracious origin and its sustaining energy in the act of God."[251] Humans are not self-created; rather we live in response to God's grace.

However, true as that is, Barth's conception of the Holy Spirit's work in empowering human life in Christ in the present remained underdeveloped. His continued hesitation about any conception of infusion as necessarily leading to either a diminishment of human integrity or a false elevation of human capacity, coupled with a focus on the change in relationship between God and humanity that stayed primarily at the external level, combine to truncate his conception of the Holy Spirit's ability to empower human life to participate in God's life and to cooperate with God's activity in the world.

---

248. Webster, *Barth's Ethics of Reconciliation*, 90–94.

249. Neder, *Participation in Christ*, 56.

250. Webster, *Barth's Ethics of Reconciliation*, 97. See also Barth, *Church Dogmatics*, 1.2 *The Doctrine of the Word of God*, ed. G. W. Bromiley and T. F. Torrance (London: T&T Clark, 1956), 242–279.

251. Webster, *Barth's Ethics of Reconciliation*, 97. See also Webster, *Barth's Moral Theology: Human Action in Barth's Thought* (London: T&T Clark, 1998) for further discussion of the importance of human response in Barth.

Human Life Between Reconciliation and Redemption

We have seen that in Barth's Christological and soteriological framework, the reconciliation Christ brings humanity is objective, real, and completed. The Holy Spirit makes the living Christ present to humanity, and Christ incorporates them into his exaltation and sets them on a journey of grateful and obedient response to God's gracious acts. However, it is crucial to remember that while reconciliation with God has been achieved fully in Christ, redemption is an eschatological concept for Barth, one that awaits Christ's return. In the present, in the time between the now and the not-yet, human life in Christ retains a provisional quality. As Barth puts it, "We do not exist (yet) in such a way that space and time, nature and history and the human situation are one continuous demonstration of the being of Jesus Christ and our being in Him and therefore of His love."[252] Our new human life in Christ is not yet one of continual obedience and conformance to Christ. "Thus we for our part do not yet exist in a complete and unbroken perception of His being and our being in Him, and therefore in a full and perennial response to His love. . . . we are wanderers who pass from one small and provisional response, from one small and provisional perception and love, to another."[253]

We do not see clearly because the full light of Jesus is concealed and hidden—we cannot see it with our own powers of perception. Our perception is "discontinuous." In order for us to see, Barth argues, there has to be "a penetration and removal of that which hides"—an event. And this will take place only with Jesus' return. Until then, we do not have this kind of direct access to his light. "For we are speaking of the One who is high and lifted up, and of the majesty of

252. Barth, *Church Dogmatics*, 4.2, 286.
253. Barth, *Church Dogmatics*, 4.2, 286.

our being in Him and with Him. And there can be no question of any such accessibility."[254]

And yet, through the Holy Spirit, we have been given the power to see enough—to see the reconciliation with God we have been given in Christ, to turn toward Jesus, and to begin moving toward God. We are truly reconciled, but we are not yet fully redeemed. We are new creatures in Christ, with renewed being and vision, who do not yet have our full sight, who are still in the process of becoming who we truly are. "In Jesus Christ a Christian has already come into being, but in himself and his time he is always in the process of becoming."[255]

While affirming the very real change that has occurred in and for humanity through the exaltation of Jesus, Barth insists on this provisional quality to human life in the here and now. Our exalted life is not something we can securely grasp. It is always a journey, which itself is a gift. In fact, part of Barth's rejection of deification comes from his understanding of deification as implying that grace becomes ours, that grace becomes a secure possession.[256] This means that Christ's mediatorship becomes past and completed—rather than always present. Deification for Barth "claims that we already *have* and no longer need to *receive*, that we already *are* and no longer, precisely at the most important point, need to *become*."[257] In addition, it is important to remember that redemption is a future event for Barth. We are reconciled, but we live in the provisional "not-yet" of a redemption that is an eschatological promise.

254. Barth, *Church Dogmatics,* 4.2, 288.
255. Barth, *Church Dogmatics,* 4.2, 307.
256. See Neder's discussion of Barth's position and his explication of exaltation as Barth's alternative in *Participation in Christ,* 48–49, 65–66. Neder notes that justification/salvation is an objective reality that is true and effective, and not dependent upon human response. Humans do subjectively receive it, but they never possess it and this receiving must be a continually freely offered response of obedience.
257. Karl Barth, *Ethics,* trans. Geoffrey W. Bromiley (New York: Seabury, 1981), 290–291.

Yet, while only in a provisional way, humans are now truly free to live as God's covenant partners, and their actions can be what Barth terms a "formed reference" to Christ's actions. In their exercise of this faithful and obedient action, they are truly new beings. Gunton argues "sanctification is treated ontologically by Barth and represents a move from the transcendent declaration of pardon to a more immanent conception of participation . . . participation in Jesus' holiness."[258] Just as the divine and human natures of Christ are in union through the perfect correspondence of Jesus' human acts with the activity of Father and Son, our lives can be a correspondence of human action to Jesus' pattern of obedience in imitation of this pattern.

Our exaltation calls us to follow the gift of the living Christ, who continually beckons as we are formed and reformed on the journey by those practices of worship, prayer, confession, and service that make us ever more able to follow obediently and joyfully. The Christian story is a story of joyful hope—the story of God who takes on human flesh to dwell among us in Jesus Christ, who lives in joyful obedience to God's way of love even in the face of violence and suffering, who defeats death, and through his resurrection and the gift of the Holy Spirit makes it possible for us to participate in God's own life.

Barth's thought is helpful in affirming the objective, life-changing truth of Jesus' life, death, and resurrection that is revealed and made manifest to humans. But in reading Barth, one comes away with the impression that the human appropriation of this saving event stays primarily at the level of knowledge and will, with insufficient attention to how that human will and knowledge are ontologically

---

258. Gunton, "Salvation," in *The Cambridge Companion to Karl Barth*, 150.

reconstituted by the Spirit in ways that make the living of new life in Christ actually possible.

Somehow the faith, hope, and love made possible by Christ are always provisional gifts of the Spirit that never really take solid root in human being or living. Here again, one senses the struggle in Barth, who still wants to affirm a real change in human life as a result of Christ's life, death, and resurrection. But he wants to do so while also affirming that humans are simultaneously sinners and justified, that there remains a confrontation between God and humans and without resorting to what he understands as a problematic concept of "infusion."[259] But is it truly possible to account for a change in human life without dealing with the inward human being, and is it possible to deal with this change of being without some concept of infusion by the Holy Spirit? In addition, Barth's insistence on continuing to view humans as simultaneously sinners and justified or sanctified makes it difficult to see the possibilities of human participation in Christ. As Neder asks, "Does obedient human action correspond to God's action or not?" [260] If God's grace is really efficacious then the human response it elicits is truly graced good, but Barth's conception of human participation remains provisional. Barth encounters real and persistent problems in extending the effects of the incarnation—the coming together of divine and human in Christ—into a truly changed relationship between God and humanity through Christ, in which human beings are transformed by this event in both inward and outward ways. Here, Cyril provides a more confident and compelling vision of human life as drawn into the

259. See again Neder's argument that Barth does offer a conception of union with Christ as an alternative to what he views as infused grace. Barth's affirmation of Luther's simultaneously sinner and justified, as well as his insistence on a continual confrontation between divine and human, along with his rejection of infusion are connected to Barth's commitment to maintaining that humans never possess grace or righteousness in themselves. *Participation in Christ*, 48–49.

260. Neder, *Participation in Christ*, 85.

truth, goodness, and beauty of the divine life always as a gift, but a gift completely and securely given through the incarnation and the ongoing power of the Holy Spirit, who is at work both inwardly and outwardly in human life to transform human beings into new creatures in Christ.

Summary

Through his emphasis on the covenant of election—in which God chooses to be God in fellowship with humans, acts to save humanity from the consequences of its refusal and disobedience, and exalts human life in Jesus to true fellowship with God as covenant partners—Barth relies on a Christology that emphasizes the one person of Jesus Christ in whom this reconciliation and exaltation takes place. Barth's insistence on the single subject of the incarnation—the second person of the Trinity existing as a fully human being—is intricately tied to his development of the way in which Christ reconciles humanity and exalts them to their intended fellowship with God.

While Barth rejects the term "deification" as a concept that crosses the boundary between divine and human, evacuating humanity and replacing it with the divine, he nonetheless offers a soteriological pattern similar in intent to Cyril. God's intent for humanity is that we live in intimate fellowship and partnership with God. We have broken that relationship through our sin and disobedient refusal to live as God intends. We cannot save ourselves or restore our relationship with God, but God graciously, loving, and wholly takes the initiative to descend into human life to save us so that our relationship with God can be restored and we can be raised to fellowship with God through Christ. All of this salvific pattern happens in Christ himself and is wholly a gracious and free act of the Trinity.

However, in exploring Barth's christological and soteriological conceptions, we have identified areas for analysis and fruitful comparison with Cyril and Balthasar. In his Christology, we have seen a tension in Barth's thought regarding the relationship between divine and human—even in Christ. Does Barth's decision to spend so much of his christological exposition in detailing the two states of Christ and associating each of these states so closely with either the divine or human "nature" cause him problems in expounding the union? While setting his theology within the context of the covenant of election, Barth also is at pains to preserve the "antithesis" and "confrontation" between divine and human, as if only confrontation can preserve difference and freedom. Though he ardently expounds the one person of Christ in whom divine and human subsist, notes of this antithesis are present even in the single subject Jesus. We will have to examine this tension in relation to the conceptions of Cyril and Balthasar, as well as looking at the effects it has on Barth's conception of exaltation and human life in Christ.

We have also seen a tension in the way Barth approaches the humanity of Jesus. He takes all of the necessary steps to affirm, anhypostatically and enhypostatically, that it is the Son of God who fully exists as a human being and that Jesus' humanity cannot be considered apart or abstracted from the incarnational union. And he is emphatic that Jesus' humanity is fully human. However, as we have seen in his development of the theme of exaltation, Barth is quite convinced that any "deification" or "enhancement" of Jesus' humanity with divine grace or power somehow evacuates the humanity, turning it into divinity and thereby destroying Jesus' ability to be mediator because then the humanity he assumes is an enhanced humanness. Yet, he also wants to account for a real ontological change in humans as a result of the change reconciliation brings to their relationship with God, and he certainly wants to create a real acting space for humans to respond joyfully and obediently to God's gracious acts. But as we've seen, given his assumptions and reservations about "infusion" and the work of the Spirit in the subjective as well as the objective realm of human life, Barth struggles to expound this ontological change in human life with the same confidence as Cyril. We will need to examine whether his conceptions reach their intended goal.

No faithful account of Barth's Christology can fail to recognize his vision of God's call to covenant partnership, to genuine fellowship with God, as the telos of human life. Human beings have been changed in that they are free to respond as God's covenant partners through lives of obedience, directed by the Spirit. In our final chapter, we will look closely at the ways in which this account of human transformation in Christ is similar to and different from Cyril's account and what results from such a comparison. Does Barth's account function in the same way as Cyril's? Or are there substantive differences between Cyril's vision of deification and Barth's account of exaltation, differences that have significant impact on a vision of human life in Christ lived with hope and purpose? Barth's enduring proclamation of the Word, who confronts us, saves us, and turns us toward God, making us free to live as God's partners and to witness to this truth, points us forward.

3

―――

Balthasar

The Christological Analogy of Being

God's grace is a participation in his inner divine life. As such, it raises the creature above and beyond any claims or longings it might possess. This participation is neither purely forensic nor purely eschatological; rather it is real, internal and present. It is an event that effects a transformation of the very being of the creature.[1]

—Hans Urs Von Balthasar, *The Theology of Karl Barth*

Hans Urs von Balthasar's theology seeks to place the dramatic event of God's love in Jesus Christ before us. He hopes this allows us to see the role we are invited to play in the Trinitarian life of God, and to actively take our place in this drama of Christ's full redemption and renewal of creation as we are directed and empowered by the Spirit. While adhering to the classical Trinitarian and christological

---

1. Hans Urs Von Balthasar, *The Theology of Karl Barth: Exposition and Interpretation*, trans. Edward T. Oakes (San Francisco: Ignatius, 1992), 377.

understandings expressed in Nicaea and Chalcedon, Balthasar uses this framework to expand our view of the dynamic event of the incarnation, which enacts the ever-greater dynamic love of the Trinity and creates a space for all creation to be redeemed participants in the divine life.

Balthasar's Christology is as intimately tied to his soteriology as is Cyril of Alexandria's. Over and over again, he begins with an insistence that any theological exploration of Jesus' person must be tied to his work in the economy of salvation and the dramatic event of his soteriological work. It is this soteriological event that prompts both inquiry and response to the question of who Jesus is. As Balthasar notes, "the question of his work implies the questions of his person: Who *must* he be, to behave and act in this way?"[2] Then, working from this soteriological event and its relationship to the inner Trinitarian drama of God's life, Balthasar explores the way in which this wondrous exchange frees human life from sin and death and frees it for a rich participation in the life of God. This event transforms human life ontologically and morally in the present and in the life to come.

In Balthasar, we have a theologian who pushes the Cyrillian pattern of single-subject Christology, as well as the wondrous exchange conception of soteriology, to daring edges. Balthasar, responding to both his appreciation of, and concern over, Karl Barth's theology, works with the conviction that Christ—the fully divine Son and a fully human being—takes on the utmost depths of sin and alienation from God on the cross so that humans might be brought into a participation in the divine life. Balthasar further argues that this participation changes humans both ontologically and morally and also actually enriches God's Trinitarian life. While

2. Balthasar, *Theo-Drama: Theological Dramatic Theory Volume III: Dramatis Personae: Persons in Christ,* trans. Graham Harrison (San Francisco: Ignatius, 1992), 149.

Barth exhibits some reservations about the conception of human participation in God's life envisioned by Cyril, Balthasar boldly extends this christological and soteriological conception—some argue beyond traditionally acceptable limits. Does Balthasar take the conception of the wondrous exchange too literally and push its limits too far? Does the Christology he puts forth hold up under the stretching edges of his soteriological vision? In the process, does he disregard or damage the distinction between divine and human or between immanent and economic Trinity in ways that violate the impassibility and immutability of God and thus endanger the giftedness of human participation in God's life that he seeks to lift up? Can his concept of analogy—so critical to his theological conceptions—really hold together the depths he plumbs and the heights he scales? Do Balthasar's understandings of salvation and deification radically exemplify Cyril's christological and soteriological pattern or transgress boundaries Cyril would have insisted on keeping? Does Balthasar's pattern offer a vision of deification that corrects difficulties he sees in Barth, or does it lead to precisely the concerns about the *analogia entis* that Barth expressed?

These are the questions that will occupy us in our exploration of Balthasar. In order to see the form of Balthasar's vision, we must first examine his concepts of the analogy of being and kenotic self-giving, which have a direct bearing on his view of our participation in Christ's mission. In addition, we will need to examine his understanding of the relationship between time and eternity, and his use of the theme of receptivity, if we are to see the vision he lays before us. We then turn to his treatment of themes that are key to concepts of participation or deification: creation and fall, nature and grace. We will then move to a close examination of Balthasar's Christology, with particular attention to his conceptions of the hypostatic union and the two natures, the relationship between divine and human, and the soteriological pattern he establishes within his conception of the wondrous exchange, including his exposition of Christ's descent into hell. Finally, we will look at the ways in which Balthasar's Christology opens before us a vision of human participation in the life of God that, he argues, enriches the Trinitarian life as well. Here, we will highlight issues and questions that will need to be addressed as we look toward a comparison with Cyril and Barth in our final chapter. Our purpose in this chapter is to focus on understanding Balthasar's christological and soteriological pattern of thought in preparation for that fuller analysis and comparison.

The Structure of Balthasar's Conceptions: The *Analogia Entis* and Trinitarian Kenosis

To understand Balthasar's complex christological and Trinitarian positions—and their intricate connection with his soteriology and vision of human life as participation in the divine life—it is necessary first to understand the deeply analogical pattern of his thought and his conception of kenosis as the endless self-giving of the divine persons within the Trinitarian life. To catch the nuances of what he seeks to achieve here, one must also see the relationship he establishes between infinite and finite freedom, between time and eternity, and examine his redefinition of divine perfection to include receptivity. In this section, we will briefly examine these basic structures that are integral to a proper understanding of his christological pattern.

Balthasar's conception of the analogy of being was significantly influenced by Erich Przywara, who argued that the unique Catholic understanding of the analogy of being provides an analogical middle way, which incorporates the duality of existence and essence, of transcendence and immanence, in a unity that does not lose the real distinction between God and creation.[3] A shorthand way of putting it is, as Przywara notes, "God and creation are like one another, and yet even in this resemblance completely unlike." The analogy of being allows us to see that God is at once both "in" and "over" the world.[4] This allows for a true understanding of the incarnation that avoids the extremes of either an immanence in which the divine and human are already so deeply fused that one has no freedom from the other, or a complete transcendence in which God's unity with the bodily, earthly world is only external and removed. Within this understanding, while the human never becomes divine in itself, neither is it erased in its contact with the divine. Creatureliness is preserved and "consecrated."[5]

Balthasar drank deeply from the well of Przywara's insights.[6] His pattern of thought is profoundly analogical, and it is important always to keep this analogical framework in view if we are truly to understand the theological moves he makes in his Christology and in the vision of human participation in God's life he sets forward. Balthasar argues that it is the analogy of being that preserves the real distinction between God and creature, while also creating a genuine space for creaturely response to and participation with God. The analogy of being thus creates the proper space for creatures to respond to God's revelation and to participate in it.[7] Balthasar

3. See P. Erich Przywara, *Polarity: A German Catholic's Interpretation of Religion*, trans. A. C. Bouquet (London: Oxford University Press, 1935). Przywara analyzed the historic philosophical and theological problem of the relationship between essence and existence and the ways in which these two are related in God, in creation, and in the relationship between God and creation.

4. Przywara, *Polarity*, 31–33, quote 31.

5. See also Balthasar, *The Theology of Karl Barth*, 286–287 for his work with this conception.

6. Balthasar argues that Barth's proposal of the analogy of faith, in which "knowledge of God rests on a prior revelation by God," actually is undergirded by an analogy of being, and that it is precisely this concept of the analogy of being that prevents what Barth so greatly feared: the creature's attempt to lay hands on God. See Balthasar, *The Theology of Karl Barth*, 163, 394–396.

7. See Balthasar's discussion throughout *The Theology of Karl Barth*, but especially 282–396, and Balthasar's discussion of Barth's development of the analogy of faith in his chapter "The

takes this concept of the analogy of being he learned from Przywara and gives it a christological structure that animates his theological convictions through and through.

Christology as the Historical Enactment of Trinitarian Kenosis

As he develops his Christology and soteriology, Balthasar insists on a theology that gives proper emphasis to the scriptural account of the full dynamic "event" of the incarnation, which he also insists must be grounded in the unchanging event of the inner Trinitarian life of God.[8] Through a christologically structured analogy, he interweaves his Trinitarian theology and his Christology to meet these soteriological concerns. To accomplish this, Balthasar draws upon a conception of kenotic self-giving that distinguishes the three persons in one, arguing that the Father's generation of the Son is the first divine kenosis, a self-giving of all that he is to the Son.[9] This self-

Centrality of Analogy," in *The Theology of Karl Barth*, 114–167. Balthasar argued that Barth, in his efforts to safeguard God's sovereignty and initiative, in effect unnecessarily constricted the authentic space for creation and its response by narrowing everything to and through the point of Christology and the analogy of faith. See also Stephen D. Wigley, *Karl Barth and Hans Urs von Balthasar: A Critical Engagement* (London and New York: T&T Clark, 2007), xii–xiv for his argument that this conviction of Balthasar's, deeply formed and honed in his response to Barth's theology, became a central conviction throughout the rest of his theology.

8. Balthasar, *Mysterium Paschale,* introduction by Aidan Nichols, (San Francisco: Ignatius, 1990), 23–46. Balthasar argues that Trinitarian language itself is a consequence of allowing the possibility of an "event" in God's self. See also Edward T. Oakes, *Pattern of Redemption: The Theology of Hans Urs von Balthasar* (New York: Continuum, 1994), 282–283 for a helpful discussion of the way in which Balthasar's Trinitarian theology arises from his Christology.

9. Balthasar, *Theo-Drama: Theological Dramatic Theory, Volume IV: The Action,* trans. Graham Harrison (San Francisco: Ignatius, 1994), 323–327. John Webster has responded to Balthasar's conception of kenosis by arguing that kenosis may not be the most helpful concept to describe the inner Trinitarian relations. He notes that "both the relation between the persons of the Trinity and their common relation to creatures are not so much acts of kenosis but *plerosis*. Of that *plerosis* there is indeed a special instance, which is the Word's taking of the form of a servant and his submission to death on the cross. This alone is kenosis; and even here it is the kenosis of the omnipotent Word who can do these things, who can so check his power in the flesh that he may put death to death." See John Webster, "Webster's Response to Alyssa Lyra Pitstick, Light in Darkness" in *Scottish Journal of Theology*, 62, 2 (2009): 207. Webster's words of caution here are well articulated and helpful and he's put his finger on a potentially difficult

giving is received by the Son in complete thanksgiving and is returned. The incarnation is the earthly enactment of this Trinitarian pattern of the self-giving of the divine Son.[10] The Holy Spirit proceeds from this love that is offered and received between Father and Son, bonding the unity within the Trinity and, in the economy, the Spirit empowers the Son's mission. This conception allows Balthasar to develop an account in which "every conceivable moment of Christ's life is always seen . . . as a trinitarian event."[11] It is crucial to see that for Balthasar, kenosis is a self-giving that comes from an inexhaustible fullness. God is absolute love and absolute fullness that is freely self-giving. This full self-giving is the pattern for the Son's mission in the world.[12]

Further, David Schindler argues that, for Balthasar, love is the very "meaning of being" itself and includes all of the "transcendentals in their circumincession . . . to say that love and being co-incide, as it were, is to say that being *is*, not just act, but the simultaneously generous and receptive act that the word 'gift' designates."[13] For Balthasar, he argues, "love is not something being *does* (after being, as it were) in an ordered sequence, but love is that which being truly is in itself, which emphatically includes all that it does and gives."[14] The manifestation of "being—as love" is not the result of either "object

pulse point of Balthasar's theology. However, much revolves around one's concept of kenosis. While Balthasar certainly walks a daring edge here, it is important to note that, for him, kenosis as complete self-giving always moves from a sense of fullness and divine perfection—not from a sense that the Trinity is lacking something that it then comes to possess.

10. Balthasar, *Theo-Drama IV*, 324–333. See also Gerard O'Hanlon, *The Immutability of God in the Theology of Hans Urs von Balthasar* (Cambridge: Cambridge University Press, 1990),37.

11. Mark A. McIntosh, *Christology from Within: Spirituality and the Incarnation in Hans Urs von Balthasar*, Notre Dame: Notre Dame Press, 1996), 73–74. See also Balthasar's arguments throughout *Mysterium Paschale*.

12. Balthasar, *Mysterium Paschale*, 30–37, 80–83, using Barth as an exposition of this kenotic conception.

13. David C. Schindler, "Towards a Non-Possessive Concept of Knowledge: On the Relation between Reason and Love in Aquinas and Balthasar," *Modern Theology* 22:4 (October 2006): 577–607, quote 590.

14. Schindler, "Towards a Non-Possessive Concept of Knowledge," 590.

or subject alone," but instead comes about through their "reciprocal interaction" in mutual encounter.[15] As we will see, this inherently reciprocal character of love is a crucial concept for Balthasar. He will insist that God in God's self *is* this reciprocity of giving and receiving, in which there is not lack, but there is always space for that which is other. This Trinitarian conception is then applied analogically to God's relationship with the world through the one person of Jesus Christ.

Throughout, Balthasar's christological analogy is finely balanced on his understanding that God can be involved in the world and affected by it without this in any way impinging on God's perfection or implying that the world is in some way "necessary" to God. Gerard O'Hanlon explains that, for Balthasar "this drama of the immanent Trinity, revealed in the economic, can be appreciated properly only if one avoids an incorrect notion of the relationship between the immanent and economic Trinity."[16] Balthasar rejects Karl Rahner's conception that "the economic Trinity *is* the immanent Trinity, and vice versa" as too closely identifying the two, thereby overemphasizing the economic Trinity, while rendering the immanent Trinity a merely formal concept. "The laws of the 'economic' Trinity arise from the 'immanent' Trinity, and they do so in astounding variations . . . But the economic Trinity cannot be regarded as simply identical with the immanent."[17] On the other extreme, Balthasar also rejects any Hegelian conception (associated with Jürgen Moltmann) in which the cross becomes the fulfillment of the Trinity and in which temporal change and suffering are

---

15. Schindler, "Towards a Non-Possessive Concept of Knowledge,"593.

16. O'Hanlon, *The Immutability of God*, 37–38. See Balthasar, *Theo-Drama IV*, 319–324 and *Theo-Drama III*, 508.

17. Balthasar, *Theo-Drama III*, 157. Quote from Karl Rahner's *Theological Investigations: Mystery of Salvation 2* (London & Baltimore: Helicon, 1961–1979), 327f, cited in Balthasar, *Theo-Drama III*, 157.

attributed directly into the life of God in God's self. This concept, so popular in process theology, results in a "tragic, mythological God," says Balthasar.[18] Because God is triune, God does not become ensnared in the world process through the incarnation, but rather both unity and difference are possible within the Trinitarian life and economically in the incarnation. Balthasar is clear that the economic Trinity does not constitute the immanent Trinity. For Balthasar, it is crucial to grasp that God is "able to become immanent in the world drama without surrendering his transcendence above and beyond it."[19] Or as he puts it, God "is *above* the play in that he is not trapped in it but *in* it insofar as he is fully involved in it."[20]

However, to understand the way in which Balthasar can insist that the economy can affect God without impinging on God's complete perfection also requires an understanding of his complex conceptions of space, temporality, and eternity.[21] Balthasar argues that the temporal events of the incarnation do "affect God in a non-temporal way."[22] He affirms that God's creation of the world is completely free and non-necessary. Because God loves that which God has created, God is also always present to creation. Balthasar argues that this presence is real. God is involved in creation and this means that God freely makes space for certain creaturely dimensions within the Trinitarian life.[23] These creaturely "modalities," which are expressed

18. See Balthasar, *Theo-Drama IV*, 319–322, quote 322. See also O'Hanlon's discussion in *The Immutability of God*, 37–38.
19. Balthasar, *Theo-Drama III*, 506. See also his discussion of transcendence and immanence, 529.
20. Balthasar, *Theo-Drama III*, 514.
21. In this discussion, O'Hanlon argues that it is important to remember that "eternity and temporality are not in themselves beings, and in particular are not subjects who have a life and personal freedom of their own." See O'Hanlon, *The Immutability of God*, 88.
22. See also O'Hanlon, *The Immutability of God*, 28; see also29, 60. See also Balthasar, *Mysterium Paschale*, 54–65, and *Theo-Drama III*, 197 for his admonition that we must be careful not to conceive the Trinitarian plan of salvation and the decision of Jesus in terms of a temporal "before" and "after."
23. Balthasar, *Theo-Drama: Theological Dramatic Theory, Volume V: The Last Act*, trans. Graham Harrison (San Francisco: Ignatius, 1998), 126–127, 256, 306–307, 389, 399, 412–414, 459,

historically in the event of the incarnation, have always already been incorporated within God.[24] Therefore, the incarnation has its presuppositions in an "event" in God. The incarnation does affect God because God freely and eternally has always already incorporated this real event into the eternal life of God. In this sense, one can—carefully—say that "the incarnation changes God," O'Hanlon notes.[25] Yet, while Balthasar will say that there is a "change" in God in this carefully delineated way, he is adamant that this conception not be seen as univocal with change that occurs in created time or space.[26] O'Hanlon argues that for Balthasar, "God remains eternal and united throughout whatever change is due to the incarnation."[27] The event of the incarnation does not change God because God is always already an eternal event in God's own life. God lacks and needs nothing from creation, but freely makes space for the liveliness and varying modalities of that which is other than God.[28]

513–517, and O'Hanlon, *The Immutability of God*, 19, 60. Balthasar argues that because the Trinity can contain all these modalities, the temporal cross is present eternally in God so that before, during, and after it is an abiding reality in God. Christ is the Slain Lamb in which the temporal is contained within the eternal and thus God remains immutable even in the event. See also O'Hanlon's discussion in *The Immutability of God*, 19–20.

24. See Balthasar *Theo-Drama III*, 48 for his view that God "has always known of human sin and even took account of it in the act of creation" itself. See also *Theo-Drama III*, 516–517 for a discussion of the way in which the mission has always been included in God. See also O'Hanlon's discussion in *The Immutability of God*, 19–20.

25. O'Hanlon, *The Immutability of God*, 24–28, quote 24. Balthasar, *Mysterium Paschale*, 24–25. See also Balthasar, *Theo-Drama IV*, 324–328, 332–333, and *Theo-Drama V*, 387, 412–414, 515–521.

26. See also O'Hanlon's discussion in *The Immutability of God*, 24. O'Hanlon notes that Balthasar affirms the classical understanding that "eternity is thus not measurable by temporal categories." God's perfection is not a "development from potency to act," but is pure act. But Balthasar argues that God's eternity does, in a carefully delineated way, allow for "an event which is characterized not simply by a fixed order of Trinitarian relations but rather by a liveliness of interaction which may, however inadequately, be described as a movement from act to act, from fullness to fullness." O'Hanlon, *The Immutability of God*, 91. For Balthasar's discussion see Balthasar, *Theo-Drama IV*, 26, 57–60, 63, and *Theo-Drama III*, 302–305.

27. See O'Hanlon's discussion in *The Immutability of God*, 24.

28. Balthasar, *Theo-Drama IV*, 60–63, 466–473. See also 470, note 25 for a discussion of change as non-temporal. It is important to note the careful nuances of Balthasar's argument. He does not say that the Father's attitude is changed in a univocal way by secondary, created causes, but

This understanding of the Trinity, and of the relationship between space, time, and eternity within the kenosis of the Trinity, also provides the basis for Balthasar's conception of the ongoing relationship between God and creation.[29] On the one hand, Mark McIntosh notes, the pattern of Trinitarian kenosis, of "mutual self-surrender," this "self-positing as 'other'," creates space and freedom for the otherness of creation, preserving its fullness and integrity. This makes it possible for the created order to participate in the divine life without losing its distinctiveness, without being simply absorbed or overwhelmed by the divine life.[30] On the other hand, this pattern also makes it possible for God to receive the redeemed creation as other, as a non-necessary "enrichment" in God's life.[31] Balthasar argues that in God there is an ability to receive that does not threaten God's being. Thus, this pattern leads to another foundational concept in Balthasar's conceptions: receptivity in God.

Traditional concepts of immutability hold that God is pure act, simple and complete in God's self. This fullness of God's Trinitarian life overflows to creation without being affected or receiving anything from creation. God has no need or lack that makes creation necessary for completion. However, while Balthasar would certainly agree that God has no lack or need of creation, he does argue that

rather that within the openness of the Trinitarian self-giving, these causes can become part of the eternal drama of God's life as God's love reconciles them.

29. Balthasar, *Theo-Drama V*, 67–80, 91–98. 126–127, 181–214, and O'Hanlon, *The Immutability of God*, 55,59–60. O'Hanlon argues that "what is vital to grasp here is that any effect of the world on God does not emanate from a reality external to God; the world on its own is nothing—its power to be, to be distinct and to affect God comes from God." (55) In addition, while created "lives are truly in time, but are present to God all at once, eternally." God can "plan comprehensively and without need to adjust to unforeseen elements."(60) See also Balthasar, *Theo-Drama IV*, 62–63.

30. McIntosh, *Christology from Within*, 74. See also Oakes, *Pattern of Redemption*, 294–295.

31. Balthasar *Theo-Drama III*, 162, and *Theo-Drama V*, 514–515, as well as McIntosh, *Christology from Within*, 74. Balthasar will deny any Hegelian sense that because love must have an other to love, creation is then somehow necessary to God and the economic Trinity is a necessity. For Balthasar this signals a clear violation of Chalcedon's two natures teaching and results in a mythological God who is enmired in worldly becoming.

there is a receptivity in God that does not come from dependency or lack but from the utter completeness and self-giving of who God is.[32] God's self-giving is full and complete, and while for humans this kind of giving is a risk, it is not a risk to God's self because, in the Trinitarian eternal life, the self-gift is always completely received and completely offered back.[33] Being as love, self-giving and reception, a complete reciprocity of giving and receiving—this is what being *is*. Given this understanding, receptivity, which is perhaps better understood as a complete reciprocity of self-giving and receipt of that gift, is a perfection, as are the other transcendentals. As we will see, this move also allows Balthasar to argue that, within the Trinitarian life, creation is an additional gift from God to God, and therefore there is an eternal enrichment of God through creation. Receptivity is thus for Balthasar a divine perfection, not a lack. O'Hanlon notes "to receive is just as divine as to give."[34] This analogical pattern of relationship between God and humanity is lived in human history in the person of Jesus, and through him all of humanity is drawn into relation with God.

Balthasar's redefinition of divine perfection to include receptivity is not without its critics. Steven A. Long has argued that receptivity simply cannot be properly viewed as a divine perfection in the way

32. See Balthasar, *Theo-Drama IV*, 325–326 for the notion of receptivity within the Trinity. This theme of receptivity is a strong note in Balthasar's christological score. While Cyril argues for the importance of receptivity in the humanity of Jesus, Balthasar goes further to argue that, according to the pattern of analogy, receptivity is also part of the very Trinitarian life of God.

33. Balthasar *Theo-Drama V*, 73–74, 82–90, 243–245. O'Hanlon, *The Immutability of God*, 71, 121–122. O'Hanlon argues that while Balthasar will resolutely refuse to say that God is mutable in the sense of being affected by creaturely change, he also rejects the classical notion of immutability in which God's love for creation is completely altruistic and affects creation but not God in God's self. Balthasar's position is a "modified" immutability in which he argues for a concept that is "dynamic enough to describe the divine being, which contains within it the original image of all created temporal becoming and liveliness." Yet the original image within the life of God remains complete and without any need or lack. It remains transcendent and distinct from creation. See 131–133, quote 132.

34. Balthasar, *Theo-Drama IV*, 325–326, and *Theo-Drama V*, 73–87. O'Hanlon, *The Immutability of God*, 121.

that the transcendentals of truth, goodness, and beauty can.[35] But even beyond this philosophical test, Long argues that, when applied christologically, the concept violates the historical affirmation that, in the incarnation, the Word, the divine Son, does not change even though his humanity does change. The Word takes to himself and perfects the humanity. He does not receive it in any way that implies that he is changed by union with it. In addition, because receptivity is not a transcendental perfection, the only way to establish an analogy between creaturely receptivity and divine receptivity is to work "backwards" and to speculate on the inner Trinitarian mystery of the Son's reception of the divine nature from the Father.[36] But "the Son does not 'receive' being as one who 'stands in need of' being or who does not already possess it."[37] Divine receptivity is of a completely different character and Long argues that we have no way of penetrating this divine mystery.[38]

However, while Balthasar does argue that, in the incarnation, the divine Son experiences human life to its utmost extremes, Balthasar would not argue that the divine in any way *needs* to be perfected by the human—precisely the opposite. It is true that Balthasar is speculating on the immanent Trinitarian life, but he is reading it from the economic revelation God has freely offered in the

---

35. Stephen A. Long, "Divine and Creaturely 'Receptivity': The Search for a Middle Term" in *Communio* 21 (Spring, 1994): 156–158. Such transcendentals are more properly predicated of God than humans, and are universal to being itself and involve no potency. Long argues that those working from Balthasar's position move from creation into the Trinitarian life of God, and in a subject, receptivity inherently means a potency, a need to be activated from outside oneself, it is the "taking in of a perfection not already possessed." (154) However, Balthasar would argue that there is no taking in of a "perfection not already possessed," but rather the continuously generous receipt of a continually generous self-giving that denotes the utter fullness and completeness of the inner Trinitarian persons' relations to one another. The receipt of a gift in God's divine life does not imply that God in any way lacks the perfection given—rather the eternal and continuous reciprocity of giving and receiving is what constitutes God's very being as love.

36. Long, "Receptivity," 156–158.

37. Long, "Receptivity," 159.

38. Long, "Receptivity," 160.

incarnation. For Balthasar, it is acceptable to ask who must God be in God's own life for the event of the incarnation to occur? And his answer is absolute self-giving love—a love that is as perfectly received as it is given in God's own life. In addition, O'Hanlon notes, Balthasar insists that if the Trinitarian hypostases exist in a constant exchange of giving and receiving, then "receptivity may be viewed as a perfection." God is primarily pure act, pure being as love in such a way that receptiveness can be incorporated as a positive. [39]

Analogically Structured:
Balthasar's Views of Creation and Fall, Nature and Grace

We've already seen the deeply analogical pattern of relationship Balthasar conceives between God and creation, in which God's intention is for creation to be part of God's own life. In his account of the themes of creation and fall and the relationship between nature and grace, this pattern continues. Balthasar works with Henri de Lubac's insight that we must start with the supernatural order, that which is true and ordered by God, and then see nature and actual history within this light. [40] For Balthasar, creation is originally supernatural and remains so even after the fall. Balthasar denies the existence of "pure" nature, but agrees that nature does provide the necessary ground for the supernatural order of the world and, with it, the freedom and work of grace in the world. [41] In addition, Balthasar notes that for the early church fathers up to and through Thomas, there is only one—supernatural—end for humanity, which is the vision of God. Nature and grace form a unity, in which nature is

---

39. O'Hanlon, *The Immutability of God*, 122–124, quote 122. See Balthasar, *Theo-Drama V*, 73–87.
40. See Henri de Lubac, *The Mystery of the Supernatural*, trans. Rosemary Sheed (New York: Crossroad, 1998). See also Balthasar, *The Theology of Karl Barth*, 296–297.
41. Balthasar, *The Theology of Karl Barth*, 301.

ordered to and for grace. The very nature of humanity is pointed "beyond itself," and it "cannot be fulfilled through its natural possibilities alone."[42] Balthasar sums it up by saying, "We are stuck with the tension that comes from asserting that nature has on its own no access to the world of grace, even though it has finally been created only because of grace and cannot be understood apart from grace."[43]

Using his analogical pattern, Balthasar argues that creation is by definition distinct from God, but it cannot be *completely* dissimilar. In his explorations of the themes of creation, nature, and grace, Balthasar returns to Augustine, Cyril, and the early Fathers to note that they stressed the "unity of creaturely essence and the free gift of grace." However, Balthasar continues, "this is never a necessary unity—it is always a gift."[44] Human nature is ordered toward the beatific vision, but must be assisted by a grace outside itself in order to see or participate in the life of God.[45] By beatific vision Balthasar means "that self-manifestation of the Creator that promises and bestows an intrinsic participation in the divine nature: in God's own life, thought, love, and creation."[46] This is God's intention for creation.

However, humans disobey and misuse the graced freedom they have been given, and this sin and rebellion alienate them from God and distort created life. Yet, while taking sin and its consequences seriously, Balthasar argues that even after the fall, Adam and Eve are not left on their own without the aid of grace. God does not deny or deprive humanity of prevenient grace for even a "single moment."[47] The divine can "irradiate and transfigure creaturely reality only

---

42. Balthasar, *The Theology of Karl Barth*, 261–268, quote 268.
43. Balthasar, *The Theology of Karl Barth*, 301.
44. Balthasar, *The Theology of Karl Barth*, 271.
45. Balthasar, *The Theology of Karl Barth*, 271, 283–285.
46. Balthasar, *The Theology of Karl Barth*, 275, footnote 14.
47. Balthasar, *The Theology of Karl Barth*, 323.

because what is created, as such—which is utterly and absolutely *not* God—is an *image* of God that can never be totally destroyed, even by sin."[48] So with the fall, Balthasar notes, "Adam's loss of the *possession* of grace, does not mean that he has thereby lost the *order* of grace"[49]—order here being humans' "supernatural vocation" directed to God. In addition, "the *nature* of human knowing" remains stable even though the "*act* of knowing" is distorted by sin. The human structure of knowing is not annulled by sin. For Balthasar, "human knowing belongs to its very nature."[50] Balthasar takes up a lengthy discussion of the extent to which the natural knowledge of God remains in humans even after sin. He argues that nature requires some continuing real knowledge of God simply because if humans do not have the capacity to know and relate to God, even in a sinful condition, "then there is neither responsibility in the true sense nor sin nor redemption."[51]

In his discussion of the proper relationship between nature and grace, Balthasar argues that during the Reformation, the Reformers, as well as Catholics like Baius and Jansen, skewed the relationship between nature and grace, leading to either a relationship of opposition, or a positing of a pure nature that developed into a secular humanism with no real place for supernatural grace or a supernatural end.[52] Here, it is important to note again the work of

---

48. Balthasar, *Theo-Drama III*, 525. But if this grace is not accepted, then it is rejected; there is no neutral space or state of indifference.

49. Balthasar, *The Theology of Karl Barth*, 288

50. Balthasar, *The Theology of Karl Barth*, 160, 288.

51. Balthasar, *The Theology of Karl Barth*, 319–322, quote 320. In the more concrete sense, there is a moment of personal "decision of the will" that directs human knowledge. Sin and this negative decision to disobey God darken this, results in a broken relationship with God, and "muddies true knowledge." (319) Yet even the sinner's refusal of knowledge rests on an "original openness" to that knowledge. In both cases, "the sinner refuses what he *de facto* inclusively knows, and what he *could have* known . . . if he had not resisted the knowledge." (322) Thus, "in sin, man cannot know God the way he should know him." (324)

52. Balthasar, *The Theology of Karl Barth*, 270–282 for Balthasar's sketch of this development through Baius and the Reformers.

Long, who argues that while de Lubac and Balthasar correctly sought to affirm the supernatural ordering of humanity to God against an Enlightenment-driven modern understanding of self-autonomous humanism, they both failed to see that Thomas Aquinas *does* develop a concept of pure nature that does not *necessarily* devolve into a nature divorced from God.[53] This concept of pure nature is critical, Long argues, if human nature is not to be evacuated of any real content, if grace is truly to retain its character as gift, and if we are to see the effects of sin and grace on humanity.[54]

Long argues that de Lubac did not attend to Aquinas' distinction between a natural and proximate end and the supernatural end. Balthasar followed de Lubac and expanded this view of a solely supernatural end for humans. The result, Long argues, is that nature in itself is suppressed and robbed of any real context, becoming a "vacuole" or mere placeholder for grace, with the further result that grace is then implicitly reduced to the natural level—precisely what de Lubac and Balthasar were fighting to overcome.[55] Long argues that this has serious christological ramifications because we must properly understand what the human nature that God assumes in

---

53. Steven A. Long, *Natura Pura: On the Recovery of Nature in the Doctrine of Grace* (New York: Fordham University Press, 2010), 79–80.

54. Long's argument proceeds along these lines. God's initial creation is not merely supernatural but both natural and supernatural—there must be a created nature that is ontologically prior if there is to be any nature that can receive grace. Long traces Aquinas' work, noting that 'there is a hierarchy of natural ends . . . that in a different order could have been the *finis ultimus* but is not now." See *Natura Pura*, 77–79.

55. See Long's extensive discussion, *Natura Pura*, 75–100 argues that this supernaturalization of nature causes nature to become "a mere remainder of dialectics" (75) and leads Balthasar to a Hegelian conception in which everything "is inextricably and reciprocally defined by everything else." (80) Balthasar "confuses two related but distinct senses" of pure nature: 1) nature as a "*state* or *condition* lacking divine assistance of supernatural grace" and 2) "nature *simpliciter*," nature as distinct from grace but "affirmed in all the varying states in which it may be found." (82) Further, Long argues that Balthasar's reduction of nature to supernatural grace also provides an explanation for that fact that throughout Balthasar's corpus of work "he never intensively and extensively develops moral theology—precisely that aspect of theology where being and nature are seen to be rich with anthropological and moral content." (83)

the incarnation actually *is*. Long argues that "there is a content of human nature that is neither simply a function of grace nor of sin."[56] If we are to hold that what is not assumed is not redeemed, then we must have an adequate account of the human nature in itself that Christ assumes.[57] Further, Long argues that this misstep causes Balthasar's use of the analogy of being to break down because his understanding of nature and grace is too "reciprocal"—if nature is not given its due and seen in true distinction from the supernatural, then conceptions of the transcendentals and perfection (which cannot include potency) begin to break down, with the result that Balthasar begins to predicate qualities (like receptivity) of God that do not meet the test of perfection in God. Balthasar loses a sense of metaphysical realism required for a true analogy of being and introduces "dialectical distortions into our contemplation of God."[58]

However, Long does not seem to grasp the christological depth of Balthasar's analogical understanding of the relationship between God and creation, in which the participatory relationship between them neither threatens God's sovereignty nor cancels out the integrity of the creature. It is rather only in its relationship with the divine that the creature becomes who it truly is. The very nature of created humanity is to be in this relationship. As Keith Johnson points out, Balthasar argues that "the revelation of Christ to the creature already presupposes that the creature is intrinsically related to God"—our being itself is that we are God's creatures.[59] Further, Long seems to overlook that Balthasar goes to some lengths to assure that the humanity of Jesus is seen in its full dimensions. This is critical for both his single-subject Christology and his soteriology. Balthasar is

---

56. Long, *Natura Pura*, 87.
57. Long, *Natura Pura*, 87.
58. Long, *Natura Pura*, 92–96, quote 95.
59. See Keith L. Johnson, *Karl Barth and the Analogia Entis* (London: T&T Clark, 2010), 196.

insistent that the one person assumes all of what it means to be human in order to redeem and to draw humanity into the life of God. If all of humanity is not completely assumed, then it is not completely redeemed.

In his reading, Long seems to believe that somehow it is only by holding the created nature in a kind of "vacuole" of pure nature that creaturely integrity can be preserved and grace can remain gratuitous. But does this not assume an inherently competitive relationship between divine and human—as if creaturely reality would be evacuated or subsumed by the divine if there is not some protective mechanism in place? Balthasar simply does not have a competitive conception of the relationship between divine and human. His view of the relationship between them is structured by the incarnation.[60]

60. A sense of Balthasar's theological aesthetics may be helpful here as well. Balthasar worked to rediscover a theological aesthetics that seeks the "unrepresentable mystery" of the divine not by abstracting *from* the creaturely form, but rather *in* and *through* those very creaturely mediums seen through a Christic lens. Drawing on Balthasar, Frederick Bauerschmidt argues that the divine glory shines through the cross, through the earthly elements of creatureliness, and gathers them to reintegrate them in the promise of a restored future through the divine life. In this incarnational form of beauty, humans are drawn to the good and the true. As Balthasar puts it, "The form as it appears to us is beautiful only because the delight that it arouses in us is founded upon the fact that, in it, the truth and goodness of the depths of reality itself are manifested and bestowed, and this manifestation and bestowal reveal themselves to us as being something infinitely and inexhaustibly valuable and fascinating. The appearance of the form, as revelation of the depths, is an indissoluble union of two things. It is the real presence *of* the depths, of the whole of reality, *and* it is a real pointing beyond itself *to* these depths." Hans Urs von Balthasar, *The Glory of the Lord, Vol. 1: Seeing the Form*, trans. Erasmo Leiva-Merikakis (San Francisco: Ignatius, 1982), 118. Bauerschmidt argues, Christ's death and resurrection are signs that "present us with the reality of God as triune love, and not simply a representation of that reality . . . the human nature of Christ is 'assumed' by the reality (Word of God) to a personal union in which there is difference without division or separation." See Frederick Bauerschmidt, "Aesthetics: The theological sublime" in *Radical Orthodoxy*, eds. John Milbank, Catherine Pickstock, and Graham Ward (London: Routledge, 1999), 209. Bauerschmidt argues that far from evacuating the fullness or integrity of creaturely form and reality, Balthasar's theological conceptions are built around this form of a mediatory realism that insists that creaturely forms have a real integrity through which the divine goodness, truth and beauty are truly revealed and show forth in and through that creaturely reality, without erasing it or canceling it out.

Balthasar argues that to posit "pure nature," even if only hypothetically, inevitably leads to a divorce between nature and grace, rather than seeing them as distinct but inseparably united by God's purpose of a supernatural end for the humanity God has created.[61] To hold a concept of a hypothetical "pure nature" is to lose sight of the Christology affirmed at Chalcedon. It is revelation—God's own self-disclosure in the incarnation—that truly allows us to see the distinction between God and created nature. Nature can be really and truly seen only in the light of revealed grace.[62] We will visit the charge that Balthasar does not give a sufficient account of Jesus' humanity during the discussion of his Christology. Here, it is important to see that Balthasar's argument is that nature simply cannot be truly or adequately understood, or even seen, without the irradiation of grace precisely because this graced participation in God's life is what God intended for creation from its inception. To posit "pure nature" as separate, rather than simply distinct, from supernatural grace is to rob it of the only true light that can bring its real form into view. The incarnation, in which the divine graces and irradiates the human, is this real form and shows us what nature truly is. Within the christological analogy of being, Christ shows us what humanity truly is and becomes the foundation and model for the unity of the natural and supernatural, the divine and the human.[63]

61. Balthasar, *The Theology of Karl Barth*, 282–292.
62. Balthasar, *The Theology of Karl Barth*, 251–325.
63. Balthasar, *The Theology of Karl Barth*, 287, 353, 364–366.

Hypostatic Union:
Identity through Mission

Thus far, we've seen the way in which Balthasar develops his conception of the christological analogy of being, which is based on the self-giving of the Trinitarian kenosis, and we've explored the way in which this analogical pattern of thought forms his concept of the relationship between space, time, and eternity and leads him to posit receptivity as a divine perfection. We've also examined the way Balthasar uses this sense of analogy to describe the relationship between God and creation in a christologically-centered pattern. Within this tightly interwoven interplay, Balthasar's thought is driven by an effort to give full weight to the historical enactment of the divine life in Jesus Christ as fully human and fully divine, and the saving ways this makes it possible for humans to participate in God's life. As with Cyril and Barth, Balthasar's understanding of the one person of the incarnation as the divine Son in his mode of existence as a fully human being is both impelled by and crucial to his soteriological pattern of thought. McIntosh points out that Balthasar focuses on two key insights from Chalcedon. First, Jesus' unchanging personal identity is the eternal Son of God.[64] Second, Jesus has two natures, one fully divine, the other fully human. Jesus is the eternal person of the Word who, in the incarnation, has entered a completely human existence and lives a completely human life. Further, like Cyril, Balthasar argues that humanity is perfected in the eternal Son. So from Chalcedon, McIntosh notes, Balthasar understands that "Christ is the divine Word existing humanly" in history.[65]

---

64. See McIntosh, *Christology from Within*, 4–5. See also Balthasar, *Theo-Drama III*, 208–225 for a discussion of the development of Christology's affirmation of the one person, as well as 237–240 on the importance of the fact that it is only as the divine Son that he can enter into humanity and transform it.

65. McIntosh, *Christology from Within*, 4–5. See Balthasar, *Theo-Drama IV*, 475–476.

Balthasar then uses a dramatic structure to develop what McIntosh terms a "Christology from within," weaving together scripture, the Christian tradition, and the insights of Christian mysticism in a dynamic conception that seeks to overcome what Balthasar sees as problems with historical Christologies from "above" and "below." McIntosh argues that Balthasar uses the basic pattern of Chalcedon, but also uses the insights of Maximus the Confessor and the spiritual exercises of Ignatius of Loyola combined with the imagery of a dramatic production to add depth and dimensions that more fully describe this dynamic, divine event enacted in history.[66]

Within the traditional understanding of Chalcedon, Balthasar sees a difficulty in fully articulating the completely human life of Jesus with its dynamic, dramatic moments of tension and suffering. He attributes this difficulty to deficient understandings of both Antiochene and Alexandrian conceptions. Balthasar sees Nestorius' problem as what he terms "the inability to distinguish individuality from person."[67] Balthasar also sees Cyril's tradition as defective in two ways. He argues that the *Logos-sarx* Christology Cyril received from Athanasius had been "falsified in a heretical direction" by Apollinarius, which results in historical tendencies to "put the divine Person in the place of Christ's human soul" (even though Balthasar is careful to acknowledge that Cyril affirms the existence of Christ's

---

66. McIntosh, *Christology from Within*, 4–5. Edward Oakes argues that this conception of Theo-Drama is Balthasar's way of altering the perspective within which divine freedom/omnipotence and human freedom can be reconciled. A successful theatrical production always depends on the harmonious cooperation of three freedoms, which are *not* however equal: for the director must serve the script and the actor must serve both. Yet the actor simply cannot afford to be an automaton if the production is to be successful: some unnamed element (which we approximate by calling "talent," and which entails the actor's free cooperation) must be engaged if the play is to emerge before the audience as playwright and director intended it. See Oakes, *Pattern of Redemption*, 217–218. For Balthasar, the incarnation is the ground for the possibility other dramas in history. See Balthasar, *Theo-Drama III*, 21, 38, 41.

67. Balthasar, *Theo-Drama III*, 213. However, recent studies of Nestorius, as we have seen in previous chapters, suggest that the problem was that he could not adequately distinguish between nature and person.

human soul). He accuses the Greeks of seeing the incarnation not "as 'becoming man,' but as 'becoming corporeal.' "[68] Balthasar concedes that "doubtless in his formula of the one *physis-hypostasis*, Cyril meant the personal unity of the incarnate Son, but he had no conceptual tool whereby he could distinguish this from the 'nature.' "[69] Continuing his historical reading, Balthasar argues that after Chalcedon, the driving issue was how a distinction could be shown "between the divinity of the person and the humanity of his conscious nature."[70] The search continued for an adequate means to express the "fundamental mystery of Christology, namely, that a perfect man, endowed with reason and even possessing a free will . . . can be God."[71]

Balthasar argues that it is Maximus who provides the resolution to this dilemma and he uses Maximus's thought to develop a Christology that affirms that Jesus is the divine Son in his mode of existence as a fully human being who lives all the tensions of human finitude—including suffering, death, and separation from God. Balthasar clearly grasps the critical affirmation of a single-subject Christology for soteriology, noting that "it is only possible to apply qualities and attributes of the one nature to the other because both are united in the one person of the Logos—not by way of nature, but by way of person."[72] Yet, in affirming this single subjectivity, Balthasar wants to ensure that the human consciousness and will of Jesus are given their proper due, arguing that the theory (which he associates with Aquinas) that only a single being (*esse*)—that of Jesus'

---

68. Balthasar, *Theo-Drama III*, 214.

69. Balthasar, *Theo-Drama III*, 213–214, quote 214. Again, it's important to note for our understanding of Cyril that recent studies suggest that Cyril understood quite well the distinction between nature and person—the problem between he and Nestorius was precisely Nestorius' inability to see the distinction.

70. Balthasar, *Theo-Drama III*, 214.

71. Balthasar, *Theo-Drama III*, 215.

72. Balthasar, *Theo-Drama III*, 222.

divine nature—activates his creaturely existence comes unwittingly close to Monophysitism, "like many of the Father's statements about Christ's humanity being 'divinized' but not transformed into divinity (Gregory of Nyssa, Cyril, Hilary)."[73] The view (which Balthasar sees as common to Irenaeus, Athanasius, and Cyril) that Christ established a relationship to all humanity at the level of nature results in formulations (what Balthasar terms the *Logos-sarx* model of Christology) that lead in difficult directions. Here the material "flesh" is what mediates between Jesus and humanity. But taken to extremes, this view ends up denying Christ's human soul in favor of the divine Son merely occupying human flesh or results in a conception in which Jesus seemed to adopt human nature as a universal "nature," which then lost sight of the fullness and historical particularity of Jesus' humanity. [74] However, Balthasar argues that theology must hold on to the fullness of Jesus' humanity in all of its historical particularity.

Given his analysis of the historical strands of Christology leading up to and through Chalcedon and its aftermath, Balthasar uses the traditional understandings of Nicaea and Chalcedon, but expands them to deal with what he sees as three historically problematic conceptual difficulties: the union of the two natures and the related issue of Christ's self-understanding, the full reality of Jesus' humanity in the hypostatic union, and the relationship between the incarnate Word and humanity in the incarnation.

73. Balthasar, *Theo-Drama III*, 229, footnote.
74. Balthasar, *Theo-Drama III*, 234–237.

The Two Natures in the One Person:
Union through Mission

In his efforts to affirm the one person of Jesus Christ, while doing full justice to the full soteriological scope of Christ's saving event, Balthasar uses his studies in mystical theology and the thought of Maximus the Confessor to re-envision the categories for expressing the unity of Christ, while also attending to the fullness of both the divine and human. His Christology is an effort to move away from a concept that tries to bring together divine and human at the level of "nature," to one that brings about the union through the enactment of obedience and mission in Jesus' life, death, and resurrection.[75] He makes this move by using what he learned from Maximus: "the eternal Son possesses the divine essence according to his particular mode of existence as the Son," as McIntosh puts it.[76] For Maximus, the "mode of existence" is distinct from essence or nature. McIntosh notes that Balthasar uses this insight to argue that "the unity is not at the level of nature. . . . instead, both natures are preserved in their integrity and fullness, and the union is at the level of existence" of the one person.[77] Balthasar argues that the traditional conception of the *communicatio idiomatum* does not resolve the issue of the relationship between the divine and human as long as the discussion remains at the level of nature. In relating the human and divine natures, it is not possible to abolish the complete difference between created and uncreated natures, and because there is such a complete difference, it becomes difficult to truly posit a union. Balthasar argues that a proper conception of union cannot be developed at the level of *nature*, only

---

75. See Balthasar *Theo-Drama III*, 224–226. See also McIntosh, *Christology from Within*, 4–5. See also Balthasar, *Cosmic Liturgy: The Universe According to Maximus the Confessor*, trans. Brian E. Daley (San Francisco: Ignatius, 2003), 212–214.

76. McIntosh, *Christology from Within*, 5.

77. McIntosh, *Christology from Within*, 5, 39–40, quote 40. See Balthasar, *Cosmic Liturgy*, 232, 247–249 and Balthasar, *Theo-Drama III*, 221–222 for a fuller exposition of his thought.

at the level of *person*.[78] So the union can only be properly conceived as one in which Jesus is the divine Son in his mode of existence as a fully human being. The union of the natures is in this one person, and that union is realized through the identity of missional enactment.

In other words, Jesus is the eternal Son who is perfectly and completely human, and Christ's human life is lived fully in accordance with the mode of existence of the eternal Son's life within the Trinity.[79] As Balthasar puts it, that which "distinguishes the Logos from the Father (the Son's mode of existence) is, in the state of union, no longer itself distinguishable from that which distinguishes the incarnate Logos from other human beings" (Jesus' pattern of life.)[80] With this insight, Balthasar develops a conception that can affirm that Jesus is the divine Son, while also giving a full and active account of his humanity.[81]

Balthasar's movement from a focus on natures to one of activity or personal mode of existence is an attempt to alleviate what he sees as the historical metaphysical difficulties associated with positing a union at the level of nature, as well as an attempt to do justice to the event and drama of Jesus' historical existence. Additionally, he does not want to allow Christology to become separated from the Trinity. As a result of this transposition, McIntosh argues, Balthasar conceives the incarnation as a divine pattern of activity—an "activity of perfect Sonship" . . . "which takes place in analogical human terms in Christ."[82] This pattern of Trinitarian activity is seen as the divine

---

78. Balthasar, *Theo-Drama III*, 221–222. See also Balthasar, *Cosmic Liturgy*, 207–209. While Balthasar learns this from Maximus, who completed the Cyrillian insight by providing the concept that in the incarnation, it was the divine Son in his mode of existence as a completely human being, nonetheless as we've seen, this conception that the union occurs at the level of person and not nature is consistent with Cyril's insight and was the key issue in his debate with Nestorius.
79. See Balthasar, *Cosmic Liturgy*, 214–215, and McIntosh, *Christology from Within*, 40–41.
80. Balthasar, *Cosmic Liturgy*, 247.
81. McIntosh, *Christology from Within*, 41–42. See also Balthasar, *Cosmic Liturgy*, 256–271.

Father's complete self-giving to the Son and the Son's complete self-giving, obedient response to the Father in the unity of the Spirit. Balthasar emphasizes the defining role of divine mission in Jesus' life and his complete abandonment to this mission. His mission *is* his identity.[83] Balthasar argues that "Jesus understands that his purpose is to give expression to the Father with every aspect of his humanity and that humanity reaches true fulfillment as he lives in obedience to that mission."[84] So McIntosh explains that for Balthasar, "mission fulfills, and even in a sense creates, identity."[85] McIntosh also notes that the key in this concept is Maximus's sense that *"the humanity of Christ reveals the divine precisely by being so human.* Every human feature of Jesus' existence is translated into a divine mode; the least human gesture enacts the most characteristic traits of the eternal Son's existence."[86]

Balthasar then uses these insights to deal with the conceptual difficulties he identifies in historical christological understandings. In dealing with the first conceptual difficulty—the issue of Christ's self-understanding in the union of fully divine and fully human—Balthasar uses this concept of missional identity to argue that

82. McIntosh, *Christology from Within,* 5–6. See also Ben Quash, "The theo-drama," in *The Cambridge Companion to Hans Ur von Balthasar,* ed. Edward T. Oakes and David Moss (Cambridge: Cambridge University Press, 2004) 150–152.

83. Balthasar, *Theo-Drama III,* 509. See also McIntosh, *Christology from Within,* 6.

84. Balthasar, *Theo-Drama III,* 172.

85. McIntosh, *Christology from Within,* 43–44. See Balthasar, *Theo-Drama III,* 172. See also Oakes, *Pattern of Redemption,* 222–223 for an exposition of role and mission in Balthasar.

86. McIntosh, *Christology from Within,* 40–41. Wigley also notes that Balthasar's Christology is one that attends both to "being" and "consciousness." Wigley, *Barth and von Balthasar,* 96. In addition, for Balthasar only the concept of mission can adequately account for the simultaneity and paradox of Jesus' sublimity and lowliness and the historic affirmations of both his full divinity and his full humanity. Balthasar argues that it is critical to note that Jesus knows "he is identical with his mission from the very beginning. . . . in view of God's foreknowledge of what is to become of it, the world cannot be created without account being taken of this sending of the 'beloved Son'; this means, in turn, that he-who-is-sent cannot be given this mission subsequently, a posteriori, without having been consulted when the original decision was made." The Son, sharing the divinity of the Father, thus freely accepts this reconciling mission. Balthasar, *Theo-Drama III,* 515–516, quote 515.

Jesus experiences this consciousness in terms of his mission, which unifies his humanity and divinity without collapsing the distinction between them. In terms of Christ's consciousness, Balthasar sees in Jesus' self-understanding an openness to the kingdom and the Father. Jesus' self-consciousness is "I am the one who must accomplish this task. I am the one through whom the kingdom of God must and will come."[87] Balthasar is here trying to find what McIntosh terms "a middle way" between a conception in which Jesus has "super-historical self-awareness" of everything and a conception of a "two-story consciousness" that splits human and divine knowing in Christ. Rather, God and human consciousness "coincide, but only within the limits of his mission." Jesus knows he is the one who is sent and he must enact this mission.[88]

As Balthasar notes, "The task given him by the Father, that is, that of expressing God's Fatherhood through his entire being, through his life and death in and for the world, totally occupies his self-consciousness and fills it to the very brim. He sees himself so totally as 'coming from the Father' to man, as 'making known' the Father, as the 'Word from the Father,' that there is neither room nor time for any detached reflection of the 'Who am I' kind."[89] As Balthasar develops the concept of identity as mission, he argues that the Son's divine pattern of self-giving is lived out in Jesus' obedient self-surrender to this mission. Again, it must be remembered that Balthasar's conception of self-surrender is one of free and joyful response to God's love, a wholehearted desire to be obedient to God. So in the incarnation, Jesus' complete surrender to the divine mission does not evacuate the humanity, but it is rather through that very surrender that the humanity achieves its fullest being and

---

87. Balthasar, *Theo-Drama III*, 166.
88. McIntosh, *Christology from Within*, 48. See also Balthasar, *Theo-Drama III*, 172.
89. Balthasar, *Theo-Drama III*, 122.

expression. As McIntosh notes, "The process of self-abandon is an act of personal love or communion, echoing the Trinitarian perichoresis (and instantiating it in the case of Christ) in which one person comes to ever greater consummation in giving self over to the other, only to receive an ever greater return of love."[90]

Further, Balthasar argues that Jesus does not have to completely understand himself to be the eternal person of the Son. He does have to surrender all that he is and does in obedience to being the Word in history.[91] So while Balthasar affirms that the hypostatic union is complete from the moment of inception, Balthasar paints Jesus' enactment of mission as unfolding each moment in obedient surrender to the coming "hour" in which God's salvation will unfold.[92] With this concept, Balthasar argues that it is possible to say Jesus progressively grows in knowledge and understanding as he practices obedience in the progression of his mission. Through this deepening practice of living his mission, Jesus develops an increasing awareness of the depth and breadth of the abyss between God and humans and that his mission calls him is to move toward this abyss, by approaching his "hour."[93]

---

90. See McIntosh, *Christology from Within*, 61.

91. Balthasar, *Theo-Drama III*, 153, 172–173. See also McIntosh, *Christology from Within*, 48–49 for his discussion of Jesus' human consciousness.

92. McIntosh, *Christology from Within*, 68–81, 140. See Balthasar, *Theo-Drama III*, 157–183. Balthasar says, "Since the Subject in whom person and mission are identical can only be divine, it follows that 'God's being' really 'undergoes development'; it follows that he who is born the Son of God has a nature that exhibits development." Thus, Jesus' historical existence affects God—though in a completely non-necessary way.

93. Balthasar, *Theo-Drama III*, 110, 169–182. See also McIntosh, *Christology from Within*, 81–82. Jesus' awareness is that he must entirely "abolish the world's estrangement from God." (Balthasar, *Theo-Drama III*, 110) In terms of a distinction between Jesus and the "Son of Man," Balthasar argues that there is not any division in Jesus, but rather is a manifestation of Jesus' awareness of the gulf between sinful humanity and God. This is an abyss he must move toward but in which his "own future state remains unknown to him" because he is willing to leave that future completely to God. McIntosh, *Christology from Within*, 34. McIntosh also explains that the Spirit's guidance does not diminish Jesus' freedom "because the Spirit remains within him" and "his predisposition to receive and send the Spirit." At times, Jesus experiences the Spirit

The second conceptual difficulty of traditional Christology that Balthasar seeks to address is ensuring the full reality of Jesus' humanity in the person of the Word. Balthasar describes how he sees the historical conundrum. "Here we have someone who is entirely human, an unabridged human being, who 'became like us in all things but sin'; how then, when he uses the word 'I' can he be speaking not as a human person but as divine? Or, if he also speaks with a human 'I' how can there be two persons in him, be they ever so intimately united?"[94] Balthasar argues that the major question in light of Chalcedon is how to understand that the identity of the human *is* the eternal Word. Again, missional identity is brought into play as Balthasar traces back the concept of "person" and then reinterprets the conception of person as "mission." It is the mission that constitutes the person because humans come to know who they are only through interaction with God.[95] Once again, this is an enactment of the Trinitarian pattern of relationship: the Father gives the Son his identity, and the Son's mode of existence in the Trinitarian relations is to receive all that the Father is and to return self-giving to the Father.[96] Balthasar's way of dealing with the christological conundrum he has identified is to argue that the incarnation is the human enactment of this divine mode of existence, "Sonship." In Jesus, "mission and person coincide perfectly," McIntosh argues. Jesus' "mission is to *be* the Son."[97]

both as a free consent and as a "rule" that requires complete obedience. McIntosh, *Christology from Within*, 49.

94. Balthasar, *Theo-Drama III*, 202.

95. Balthasar, *Theo-Drama III*, 207.

96. See Balthasar, *Theo-Drama IV*, 323–327. See McIntosh, *Christology from Within*, 52, citing Balthasar in *A Theology of History* (New York: Sheed and Ward, 1963) 26. See also Balthasar, *Theo-Drama III*, 207.

97. McIntosh, *Christology from Within*, 52. See also Balthasar, *Theo-Drama III*, 157 and *Theo-Drama IV*, 323–328 for Balthasar's discussion of the way in which Jesus' identity is only possible on a Trinitarian basis: the eternal Son's procession is the pattern for Christ's mission.

The third problem of Christology that Balthasar seeks to address is the question of how the humanly incarnate Word can wholly adopt human nature itself without compromising the concrete human existence of Jesus. Balthasar here argues that issues of ontology cannot be separated from soteriology. Who Jesus is and what Jesus does are inseparable.[98] As Balthasar deals with the long-standing controversies regarding the distinction of the two natures, it becomes clear that, for him, the real "ontological difference" between God and creatures is the deep chasm created by humanity's sinful rejection of God's intentions. Jesus' humanity and consciousness must take account of the depth of this alienation and his mission is accomplished within a full awareness of this human sin.[99] In the face of this sin and the abyss it has created, Jesus' self-giving requires real sacrifice as he enters into that divide between God and humans.[100]

As he lives out his mission, Jesus freely offers obedient and self-giving love to the Father precisely in all of the places where humans have refused God's love in disobedience.[101] In this journey into the depths of human alienation, in his free offering of himself, Jesus is also led beyond himself towards God. McIntosh argues that for Balthasar this means that, in Jesus, the divine will and human will are no longer competitive because Jesus' human will is already part of the Trinitarian life. Jesus' human obedience gives him the fullest freedom possible because "his every desire, every act, every word becomes the direct expression of God—with all the power and authority of God."[102]

---

98. Balthasar, *Theo-Drama III*, 149–150.
99. Balthasar, *Theo-Drama III*, 110, 168–172, 239–240, and McIntosh, *Christology from Within*, 44–45, 54.
100. See McIntosh, *Christology from Within*, 61, 67, 75–84.
101. See Balthasar, *Theo-Drama III*, 168–169 and McIntosh, *Christology from Within*, 69.
102. McIntosh, *Christology from Within*, 84–85. Balthasar argues that Jesus' obedience is possible because it is the direct expression of the divine Son's love for the Father. It is the historical "translation" of the Son's eternal response to the Father. Balthasar, *Mysterium Paschale*, 90–91.

Jesus thus moves toward his "hour" on behalf of humans. He knows that he is the only one who can accomplish this mission. But he also knows that he can only make the painful journey through this hour by offering himself and trusting himself completely to God.[103] The divine Son, in his mode of existence as a particular, fully human being, enters into every place that humans have been disobedient and offers complete obedient self-surrender in their place.

Also crucial to Balthasar's thought here is the role of the Spirit. He develops the concept of the "Trinitarian inversion" to explicate the Trinitarian pattern of the incarnation more fully.[104] While in the life of the immanent Trinity the Spirit is the bond of love between Father and Son, in the economic pattern of Jesus' life, the Spirit takes on an active role, forming the bond between immanent and economic, and empowering and impelling Jesus' earthly mission.[105] The Spirit in Jesus is totally concentrated on attending to the Spirit above

McIntosh also notes that for Balthasar, obedience is "always an active response of love," and it is made possible by "a divine gift of interior freedom and energy." *Christology from Within*, 76. This obedience is always a free response to the costly and prior self-giving of the Father. Further, obedience is only true obedience when undertaken in freedom and joyful response to divine love. Yet, while Balthasar sees obedience as a free response to love, this does not mean that the will of God does not take the form of a command. See McIntosh's discussion in *Christology from Within*, 59–87.

103. Balthasar, *Theo-Drama V,* 246; *Theo-Drams IV,* 232–234; and *Theo-Drama III,* 166–170. See also Oakes, *Pattern of Redemption,* 236–237. See also Ben Quash's account Jesus' passivity as the " 'superaction' of his obedience" in this surrender. Ben Quash, "The theo-drama," 151.

104. Balthasar, *Theo-Drama III,* 183–202. While in the eternal Trinitarian life the Spirit proceeds from the Father through the Son and then the exalted Christ sends the Spirit with the Father, Balthasar inverts this understanding during the early ministry of Jesus, making the Spirit the bond of freedom and love between Father and son. It is the Spirit who sends the Son into the world and continues to send and direct him in his earthly enactment of the eternal Son's mission. See Quash, "The Theo-Drama," 150–151 for an account of the way Balthasar extends the kenosis of the second Person in the economy and "extends it to apply to all three Persons of the Trinity." (151) See also Balthasar, *Theo-Drama IV,* 318–328.

105. Balthasar, *Theo-Drama III,* 183–191, 522–523, 533. Within this analogical understanding, the incarnation does not require any "mythical change" in God, but rather is a change in relationship to the form of the hypostatic union "This prevents the Son's Incarnation from implying a 'mythical' change in God. It is not that God, in himself, changes but that the unchangeable God enters into a relationship with creaturely reality; and this relationship imparts a new look to his internal relations. This is not something purely external, as if this relationship ad extra did not really affect him: rather, the new relationship to worldly nature,

him. Further, through the Spirit's indwelling and direction, the Son experiences his economic mission in both subjective and objective ways and this varies according to the needs of the mission.[106]

We have seen how Balthasar's conceptions affirm the single subjectivity of Jesus as the basis of his soteriological use of the wondrous exchange. So it is critical to affirm that Jesus is both fully divine and fully human united in the one person of Jesus Christ. While the Son is doing the Father's work, it is also genuinely his work, which he freely does and offers. "If his works were not divine as well as being his, they would not be his at all. How could he give his life for his sheep if it were a mere human life or even if the Father were merely to ascribe divine value to this purely human work?" Balthasar asks. He continues, "the Fathers rightly asserted, against the Gnostics, that if Christ were not a real man with flesh and blood, we men would not be saved; they were just as right to stress, in opposition to the Arians, that we would not be saved either if Christ were not God just as truly as the Father is. The fact that the Father generates the Son is the soteriological presupposition of our salvation."[107]

This emphasis on the one person, in which the divine and human are united in soteriological mission, is key because it is intertwined so intricately with Balthasar's affirmation of the "wondrous exchange." The universal mission of Jesus can only be carried out through this exchange and, as we shall see, Balthasar radicalizes this exchange, which sounds the major chord in his soteriology.

which is hypostatically united to the Son, highlights one of the infinite possibilities that lie in God's eternal life." Balthasar, *Theo-Drama III*, 522.

106. Balthasar, *Theo-Drama III*, 521–522.
107. Balthasar, *Theo-Drama III*, 519.

The Wondrous Exchange:
Assuming Sin Itself

We're now in a position to see the ways in which Balthasar has developed his argument to express his soteriological convictions, which are grounded in his taking seriously "the wondrous exchange" first expressed by Paul in 2 Corinthians 5:21, "For our sake, he made him to be sin who knew no sin, so that in him we might become the righteousness of God." This concept, as we have seen in earlier chapters, was developed through the early church, expressed by Gregory of Nazianzus's "what is not assumed, is not redeemed," in concert with the conviction that, as Cyril put it, "he took what was ours to be his very own so that we might have all that was his."[108] As we've seen, Cyril was adamant in his insistence that only a single-subject Christology could account for this wondrous exchange, which he was convinced was the central soteriological conviction of the Christian faith.

Balthasar's soteriological thought takes these ideas utterly seriously and he refuses to back away from exploring their utmost depths and heights. The full import and drama of God's saving action—both for God and for creation—must be seen in the events of Jesus' life, death, and resurrection. Here, Balthasar takes the concept of the wondrous exchange and extends it. He wants to account for the fact that in this exchange something really happens between God and humanity and, for him, this can only happen if God in his divinity enters into the situation of humanity to literally change places with us—suffering sin and death on our behalf and lifting us up into the divine life. Further, Balthasar argues that this exchange in some way affects not only Jesus' human nature but is truly experienced by his

---

108. Cyril, *On the Unity of Christ*, trans. John McGuckin in John McGuckin, *Saint Cyril and the Chistological Controversy: Its History, Theology, and Texts* (Crestwood, N.Y.: St. Vladimir's Seminary Press, 2004), 59.

divine person as one of the Trinity. "For it is only by virtue of his divine person that he can enter into the desperate situation of a free human being vis-à-vis God, in order to transform it from a dead-end to a situation full of hope."[109] For Balthasar, *pro nobis* means more than on our behalf or for our benefit—it means in our place. Additionally, throughout his tracing of the historical understandings and development of soteriology, Balthasar insists that soteriology must account for five motifs: "the Son gives himself, through God the Father for the world's salvation; the Sinless One 'changes places' with sinners . . . man is thus set free (ransomed, redeemed, released) . . . he is initiated into the life of the Trinity . . . the whole process is shown to be the result of an initiative on the part of divine love."[110]

However, while Balthasar pushes against the historically perceived limits of the wondrous exchange, he also guards against some of its more penal understandings as a punishment inflicted by the Father on the Son. Rather, Balthasar stresses over and over that this exchange is one willingly and freely entered into by the Son in agreement with the Trinitarian persons. "One thing we must never forget: the atonement wrought by Christ must not be interpreted as a penance imposed on the Son by the divine Father; rather, as we have often repeated, it goes back to that salvific decision made by the Trinity.

---

109. Balthasar, *Theo-Drama III*, 240. In his historical tracings, Balthasar notes that for the Greek Fathers, even in this wondrous exchange, God could not suffer in his divinity, yet the incarnate Son must be able to experience human emotion and circumstances without being overtaken by them—he is in control. But Balthasar thinks it is only with the western tradition of Augustine and Anselm that the full soteriological implications of this are drawn out. "It is on the Cross that the sinner changes place with the only Son." *Theo-Drama III*, 239. Thus, it cannot be just any man who suffers on the cross. It must be one of the Trinity "both in his human nature and in his divine person." Balthasar, *Theo-Drama III*, 239–241, quote 240. He notes, "we can also see that Christ's mission on our behalf is more than a work and a suffering on his part to spare others the punishment they have justly deserved (as is emphasized by the Protestant version of the doctrine); it involves his coworking and cosuffering with those who are estranged from God." 241.
110. Balthasar, *Theo-Drama IV*, 317.

Jesus Christ sees himself as coming forth from that decision in perfect freedom."[111]

It is precisely this wondrous exchange that points to the single subject of the incarnation as the divine Son who enters history as a fully human person. In this exchange, God the Father hands over the entire responsibility for the salvation of the world into the hands of the Son. In doing this, he is "not imposing on a finite subject a task that can only be carried out by the infinite God; the bearer of such responsibility in this subject can be none other than a divine Person."[112] Balthasar notes that "the Fathers reached this conclusion primarily for soteriological reasons: no mere man, even were he to have the most awesome mission laid upon him, can 'take away the sin of the world.'"[113]

Suffering, Death, and Hell

We have seen Balthasar's extension of the height and depth of the wondrous exchange through his conceptions of kenotic self-surrender and complete obedience, based on the Trinitarian pattern of God's life enacted in human history in the one person of Jesus Christ. These convictions lead Balthasar to develop some of his most controversial soteriological patterns of thought—on suffering, death and hell. Balthasar explores the concept of self-surrender and obedience in the events of the cross, death, and descent to hell, where Jesus experiences the utmost depths of human alienation.[114] Jesus willingly, out of love, assumes all of humanity's alienation from God within himself, and this all must "be handed over to God's

---

111. Balthasar, *Theo-Drama III*, 242.
112. Balthasar, *Theo-Drama III*, 509–510.
113. Balthasar, *Theo-Drama III*, 509–510, quote 510.
114. Balthasar, *Mysterium Paschale*, 12–14.

saving justice, which must reject it—this accounts for the experience of abandonment" on the cross, O'Hanlon explains.[115] When Jesus' relationship with the Father seems broken on the cross, Balthasar argues that Jesus experiences real desolation. Jesus' suffering comes from a deep love for God and humans that is profoundly painful when the full depths of the broken relationship between them, and the consequences of that sin, are experienced. Jesus completely takes on and experiences human sin and death, and in this process Jesus' humanity completely hands over everything to God in utter surrender and obedience. In this way all of human alienation, to its deepest dregs, can be dealt with and humanity can then be renewed and drawn into the Trinitarian life.[116]

It is crucial to note that Balthasar affirms the Chalcedonian conception that Christ in the divine nature is immutable and impassible, while in his human nature he can change and suffer. He is also firm in upholding the real distinction between God and creation and between the divine and human natures in Christ. However, while Balthasar emphatically affirms the single subjectivity of Christ as the divine Logos, he also refuses to bracket off Jesus' suffering and humanity to his humanity alone.[117] The cross reveals both the immanent and economic Trinity. The complete self-giving of the persons of the Trinity is what makes creation and redemption

---

115. O'Hanlon, *The Immutability of God*, 32. See also Balthasar, *Theo-Drama IV*, 334–338, 349, and *Mysterium Paschale*, 72, 90–92, 101–104, 112, 120–122, 137–140.

116. See McIntosh, *Christology from Within*, 105, 109. See also Balthasar *Theo-Drama IV*, 132, 189–191, 493–500.

117. See Balthasar, *Mysterium Paschale*, 24–25. See also *Theo-Drama V*, 387, 412 for a discussion of the real distinction and the way in which the incarnation unites this distinction. See also O'Hanlon, *The Immutability of God*, 43. For Balthasar's discussion of the necessity of the Son of God's suffering see *Theo-Drama IV*, 191–195. See *Theo-Drama IV*, 131–134 for a discussion of the importance of Christ experiencing the depths of human pathos, and *Theo-Drama V*, 218–223 for a discussion of the patristic view of impassibility/immutability. Balthasar's concept of soteriology is primarily one of substitution (not necessarily penal substitution but one that requires a strong sense of representation) that "must be on the ontological, and not merely social or psychological level." See O'Hanlon, *The Immutability of God*, 32.

possible. Thus Balthasar argues, quoting Bulgakov, "the cross is inscribed in the creation of the world."[118] Within this framework, the union of divine and human in the one person is the "condition of possibility for a real assumption of humanity's universal guilt," as Christ gives himself as the one in whom all that is counter to God can be judged and overcome.[119] In the incarnation, Balthasar argues—this time echoing Barth—God becomes both "subject and object of judgment and justification and places himself on the side of man so to defend, on their behalf, the cause of God."[120] God no longer judges from "outside" but from within, as God becomes the full measure of humanity. Through this not only is the world saved, but God also reveals most fully and authentically God's glory.[121] In dealing with Jesus' passion, death, and presence in hell, Balthasar argues that it is precisely in these moments when humanity would seem to be most threatened that Jesus is at once "most completely human and the Word most fully incarnate."[122] It is in the events of the cross, death, and a descent to hell that Jesus enters most completely into the depths of human alienation from God in order to redeem it.[123]

---

118. Balthasar, *Mysterium Paschale*, 35, quoting Sergius Bulgakov, *Du Verbe incarne: Agnus Dei* (Paris, 1943), cited in Balthasar, *Mysterium Paschale*, 35. See Quash's discussion in "The Theo-Drama," 153 of the descent into hell as upholding and showing the unity of God. There is nothing "outside" or "beyond" God, even the farthest points of sin's alienation. See also Balthasar, *Theo-Drama IV*, 319–331, 476, 500–501.

119. Balthasar, *Mysterium Paschale*, 101, 111–112, quote 101. The atonement is not a penance imposed by the Father, but rather a salvific decision made by the whole Trinity—the Son is sent in perfect freedom and Christ suffers voluntarily. See Balthasar, *Theo-Drama III*, 242, and *Theo-Drama IV*, 258 for a discussion of Anselm. For a discussion of the relationship between freedom and necessity using Aquinas, see *Theo-Drama IV*, 264: "Only if we keep in mind his free decision to save the world can we speak of a (consequent) 'necessity.' "

120. Balthasar, *Mysterium Paschale*, 121.

121. Balthasar, *Mysterium Paschale*, 122–124.

122. McIntosh, *Christology from Within*, 90.

123. See McIntosh, *Christology from Within*, 90. See Balthasar, *Mysterium Paschale*, 164–168. This leads Balthasar to emphasize Christ's total passivity in hell—unlike the tradition's emphasis on his activity. Balthasar's logic is that if Christ is truly to assume our full humanity, then he

Balthasar's conviction that the saving power of Christ reaches to the furthest points of the past and stretches forward to the eschaton is, according to Edward T. Oaks, a key impetus in his thought. The one Person of Christ—in his life, death, descent into hell, resurrection, and ascension, as the historical enactment of the Trinitarian self-giving love—must outweigh and deal with the very depths of creaturely alienation from God, evil, and all its effects.[124] Throughout his work, Oakes argues, Balthasar seeks to explain

> how Jesus can be the savior of all, for if he is to lift up humanity (indeed the whole cosmos) back to the Father, he must be able to sink to the bottom with such a reverberating "thud" that not only will he lift up the world into heaven but also that he will land at the bottom so heavily that he will continue to radiate outward in both directions in such a way that his ripple effect will never fade. And this requires that the entire process, from incarnation and earthly ministry all the way to his death, descent into hell, and resurrection, *be a trinitarian event*.[125]

Or as Balthasar himself put it, "The central issue in theo-drama is that God has made his own the tragic situation of human existence, right down to its ultimate abysses; thus, without drawing its teeth or imposing an extrinsic solution on it, he overcame it."[126] Oakes argues that "dark as this view of God might seem at first glance, it also provides the perspective that allows Balthasar to entertain the

---

experiences death in a total human passivity and alienation from God, though the Spirit keeps the bond of Father and Son from breaking. Balthasar, *Mysterium Paschale*, 148–149.

124. Oakes, "The Internal Logic of Holy Saturday in the Theology of Hans Urs von Balthasar," *International Journal of Systematic Theology* 9, no. 2 (April 2007): 191–193. Oakes argues that for Balthasar this can "only happen if somehow the claim is already true of the pre-existence of the *Logos* and the reality of the incarnation, so that Christ's descent into hell is an event within the Godhead, by which the entirety of the evil of the world has been fully plumbed" and will continue to be dealt with until the end of the age. (191).

125. Oakes, "Hans Urs von Balthasar: The Wave and the Sea," *Theology Today* 62, no. 3 (October 2005): 364–374, here 372.

126. Balthasar, *Theo-Drama: Theological Dramatic Theory Volume II: Dramatis Personae: Man in God*, trans. Graham Harrison (San Francisco: Ignatius, 1990), 54.

possibility of universal redemption. This is because any place that Christ touches is, by definition, a locus of salvation."[127]

Balthasar argues, "If Jesus has suffered on the Cross the sin of the world to the very last truth of this sin (to be forsaken by God), then he must experience, in the solidarity with the sinners who have gone to the underworld, their (ultimately hopeless) separation from God, otherwise he would not have known all the phases and conditions of what it means for man to be unredeemed yet awaiting redemption."[128]

Balthasar thus argues that Christ's humanity, through its union with the divine Son in this universal mission, actually is brought to a new and fuller state of existence. McIntosh argues that death is not Jesus' loss of humanity but rather its fulfillment and liberation. As Jesus' humanity completely surrenders to God, God uses it to redeem all of humankind.[129] Stephen Wigley notes that for Balthasar, God saves humanity in a way that does not simply erase the dimensions of creaturely finitude but rather gives them "new value and meaning."[130]

However, it is crucial to recognize that for all the emphasis that Balthasar gives to Holy Saturday, there is no mistake that salvation through the incarnation is only fully accomplished in the resurrection, through which Jesus' self-giving love to humanity becomes an ongoing presence. It is the resurrection—not the cross or even hell—that is the full extent of Christ's abandonment and

---

127. Oakes, "The Wave and the Sea," 373.

128. Balthasar, "Descent into Hell," in *Explorations in Theology, Vol. IV: Spirit and Institution*, trans. Edward T. Oakes, S.J. (San Francisco: Ignatius, 1995), 395. Balthasar makes this move through a "radicalization of the meaning of the hypostatic union" as the place where, through the Son, the Trinity itself is involved in this descent. Oakes, "The Internal Logic of Holy Saturday," 196. Oakes, like McIntosh, argues that it is Balthasar's reading of Maximus, which he believes guards against the tendencies of both Nestorianism and Monophysitism, that is critical to his understanding of the hypostatic union and this soteriological pattern.

129. See McIntosh, *Christology from Within*, 107–108. See also Balthasar, *Theo-Drama III*, 157–160, 530, *Theo-Drama IV*, 189–191, 200–201.

130. Wigley, *Barth and von Balthasar*, 100.

self-giving because it is here that Christ is eternally given to the world through the Spirit in the church and sacraments.[131] Jesus thus becomes the dramatic acting space for redeemed human participation and fulfillment. Creation, via the hypostatic union, is repositioned in the Trinitarian life.[132]

Suffering and Descent into Hell:
The Depths of Love

These aspects of Balthasar's work as they relate to Christ's suffering and his entrance into hell have been the focus of recent sharp criticism from Alyssa Pitstick.[133] Although she is not the first to be made uneasy by Balthasar's conceptions, she is pointed in her complete rejection of his thought and her assertion that not only does his thinking push against the boundaries of traditional Christian thought, it transgresses it. While Pitstick's arguments with Balthasar are plentiful and complex, the elements of her criticism that are pertinent here are her objections to Balthasar's theology of suffering and hell, which she argues have a deleterious impact on his Christology and Trinitarian theology.[134] Because she is so expansive in her criticism of Balthasar's thought, we will spend some time looking at her objections because

---

131. See Balthasar *Theo-Drama IV*, 134–135, 362–367, 390–393. See also McIntosh, *Christology from Within*, 128, citing Balthasar, *The Glory of the Lord, Vol. VII: The New Covenant* (T&T Clark, 1990),148.

132. McIntosh, *Christology from Within*, 132–133. See also *Theo-Drama III*, 231, 527–528.

133. See Alyssa Lyra Pitstick, *Light in Darkness: Hans Urs von Balthasar and the Catholic Doctrine of Christ's Descent into Hell* (Grand Rapids: Eerdmans, 2007). Pitstick's chief concern seems to be the depth and extension of Christ's suffering in Balthasar's treatment (particularly his treatment of the wondrous exchange, which he reads as calling for Jesus to be made sin by taking on all of the sins of the world in himself). In addition, she rejects any notion that Christ entered the hell of the damned itself.

134. Unfortunately, the sheer polemical tone and uncharitable style of Pitstick's work threaten to overwhelm the more substantive points deserving of serious reflection. A significant part of the problem is that Pitstick simply misreads Balthasar's theology in serious and comprehensive ways. See also Tracey Rowland's review of Pitstick's book in *International Journal of Systematic Theology*, 10, no. 4 (October 2008): 479–482, and Mark McIntosh's review in *Modern Theology*

they highlight the areas of Balthasar's christological and soteriological thought that have drawn questions and critical appraisal by a number of scholars.

In essence, Pitstick argues that Balthasar inappropriately prolongs the redemptive work of Christ and the concept of ransom beyond the cross—it is not at the cross that redemption happens but rather in Christ's suffering in hell. This, she argues, violates a number of traditional understandings, beginning with the belief that Jesus completely accomplishes salvation at the cross on Good Friday and that on Holy Saturday he freed the just who died before him.[135] Working from her unrelenting critique of his theology of the descent, she argues that Balthasar's conceptions evacuate Jesus' divine knowledge in the incarnation, collapse the immanent Son's life into the incarnation, rob Jesus' humanity of its saving significance, fail to distinguish between "nature" and "person," and impinge on the immutability and impassibility of the Trinity.[136]

24, no. 1 (January 2008): 137–139 for their critique of Pitstick's reading of Balthasar. Pitstick's approach is an unfortunate mismatch for Balthasar's whole style of thought and presentation.

135. See Pitstick, *Light in Darkness*, 98–114, for her view of Balthasar's improper use of substitutionary atonement and the relationship of cross and descent. See also page 449, note 4 for a list of authors Pitstick cites as questioning the conformity of Balthasar's thought to traditional Catholic doctrine. Additionally, see Paul Griffiths "Is There a Doctrine of the Descent into Hell?" *Pro Ecclesia*, Vol. XVII, no. 3, 257–268, where Griffiths concisely sums up Pitstick's exposition of what the Catholic tradition has affirmed: "Christ's descent was only to the limbo of the Fathers; the descent made Christ's power and authority known throughout hell . . . the descent accomplishes two purposes—liberating the just from limbo . . . and proclaiming Christ's power even in the realms of the dead . . . the descent was glorious, which she takes to imply that it involved no suffering on Christ's part." Griffiths, 261. However, Griffiths notes that both scripture and tradition have characterized the suffering and death of Christ on the cross as glorious. This is how God has chosen to reveal God's glory in the world—and "if in the world, why not all the more in hell?" Griffiths, 264–265, quote 264.

136. John Webster in his response to Pitstick provides a concise summary of the errors Pitstick accuses Balthasar of making. Pitstick argues that Balthasar's conception collapses the immanent being of the Son into the economy, robs Jesus' humanity of redemptive significance because the work of salvation is accomplished by the Trinity, admits "voluntarism" into the Trinity by positing an "antecedent consent" of the Son to the Father, has damaging effects on divine mutability and possibility, and improperly glorifies the cross. Underlying all of this is what Pitstick characterizes as a misunderstanding of the relations between divine persons and divine essence. Pitstick argues that Balthasar proposes that "the divine essence exists *in* these self-

Pitstick repeatedly asserts that in Balthasar's Christology, the divine Son "deposits" his divinity and its attributes (including the beatific vision) with the Father during his incarnation.[137] This particularly irritates her regarding Balthasar's conceptions of Jesus' human knowledge of his mission. She argues that here Balthasar divides the Son's divine essence from his divine attributes by saying the Son "lays up" the form of his divinity with the Father during the incarnation. While Balthasar does say this, in the overall context of his thought, what he means is that the Son trusts the Father with the totality of who he is as he is sent into the world as a fully human person to carry out the salvific mission. Balthasar is adamant that the single subject of the incarnation is the divine Son. John Webster also helpfully corrects Pitstick's view that Balthasar's conception involves the Son's surrender of deity in the incarnation. Webster reminds us that Balthasar does not view God's self-surrender as a giving up of divinity but rather sees this surrender as the "consistent expression of the mutual self-giving or primal kenosis of the triune persons."[138]

This is one of many places where Pitstick, as Tracey Rowland has noted, "has a tendency to take statements from von Balthasar which are theologically rich and complex, and then force them through

subsisting relations" (Pitstick, 282) and here, Webster notes, we "see the perils of expanding the notion of kenosis to the immanent Trinity." See John Webster, "Webster's Response to Alyssa Lyra Pitstick, Light in Darkness" in *Scottish Journal of Theology*, 62, 2 (2009): 206–207. See Pitstick, *Light in Darkness*, 115–140 for her analysis of Balthasar's Trinitarian theology. See also 281–313 and 337–340 for her critique of Balthasar's conception of the relationship between nature and person.

137. Pitstick, *Light in Darkness*, 148–160.
138. Webster, *Response to Alyssa Pitstick*, 209. But Webster adds that Reformed theology avoids this by saying that the unity of Christ occurs in his personal hypostasis. This avoids the trouble that arises with the "excessive employment of the communication of attributes." The Word does become flesh, but the Word does not give up divinity. Rather, remaining fully divine, the Word assumes full humanity. However, Balthasar would scarcely argue with that conception. The key point here is what constitutes divinity. For Balthasar, this complete self-giving is what it means to be divine. The incarnation is the historical enactment of that divinity in a fully human person. See also *Theo-Drama III* for Balthasar's extensive discussion of the way in which Jesus' identity is only possible on a Trinitarian basis. See also Mark McIntosh, *Christology from Within*, 50–57.

a scholastic sieve, squeezing them into a tight definition which is subsequently subjected to ridicule."[139] Pitstick's assertion that Balthasar has denied the divine Son his own immanent life are somewhat reminiscent of Bruce McCormack's charge that Barth denied the *Logos asarkos* and are just as overstated. Balthasar has a robust Trinitarian theology and never denies the divine Son his own immanent life. However, much like Barth, he does want to avoid the "abstractions" that he believed plagued scholastic theology and so he focuses on the dramatic event of revelation through the incarnation. He argues this is the way God has revealed God's self in the flesh and in human history, and this is the focal point of theological consideration. If one loses sight of the whole of Balthasar's corpus, it might be possible—as with Barth—to look at specific elements and believe that the immanent has been collapsed into the economic. However, within the whole context of his thought, Balthasar understands the crucial need for the distinction and maintains it.

Second, Pitstick accuses Balthasar of evacuating the Incarnate Christ of humanity by arguing that in his conception of the descent, the humanity is actually emptied of content and only the divine Son is left to suffer and be responsible for redemption.[140] Thus, she argues, "the redemption is accomplished as an expression of the Trinitarian processing and the Son's human nature has relatively little, if any, essential role to play."[141] Pitstick's charge that Balthasar fails to give Jesus' humanity its redemptive significance is odd considering that one of Balthasar's chief concerns in developing his Christology is to give appropriate weight and significance to the humanity of Jesus and his human consciousness. As we've seen, he gives lengthy treatment to the issue, and his development of the concept of missional identity

---

139. See Tracey Rowland's review of Pitstick's book in *International Journal of Systematic Theology* 10, no. 4 (Oct. 2008): 479–482, quote 480.
140. Pitstick, *Light in Darkness*, 196–216.
141. Pitstick, *Light in Darkness*, 125. See also 305–312.

between divine and human is an effort to see the salvific work of the incarnation as precisely residing in the one person who is both fully divine and fully human. Balthasar's soteriology revolves around the wondrous exchange. It is, in fact, precisely his insistence that the Incarnate One has assumed full humanity—including utter passivity in death and in hell—that seems to have so aroused Pitstick's ire.

Third, she argues that this failing is a result of Balthasar's inability to see the distinction between person and nature and that a "person suffers in a nature."[142] This seems to be at the heart of her argument against Balthasar. However, her charge that Balthasar does not recognize that a person suffers in a nature simply fails to register that, as we have seen, Balthasar has consistently affirmed both natures of Christ but has moved the weight of his christological conceptions to the concept of the mode of existence of the one person. He argues that *all* predicates can be said of this one person. The predication of suffering is made to the one person, in order to move away from what Balthasar sees as historic problems with making predications at the level of each nature. While one may take him to task for transposing "nature" into a radicalized form of Maximus's "mode of existence" as a way of allowing suffering to be predicated of the entirety of the one person—both divine and human—that move is more the case of a radical reading of the one person than a failure to recognize that "a person suffers in a nature."[143] Balthasar might well respond

---

142. Pitstick, *Light in Darkness*, 133. She argues that this also results in Trinitarian problems for him as he misconceives the relationship between the divine persons (who are made too much independent persons with their own personal properties) and the divine essence—resulting in tri-theism. Balthasar is not a tri-theist and the attention he gives to the relations between the divine persons is impelled by a concern that we see the entire Trinity acting in the economy of salvation.

143. Of those who are critical of Balthasar on this point, Thomas Weinandy approaches his critique by arguing that Balthasar and Barth both fail to properly appreciate the Cyrillian insight of the one Person and thus attribute an improper sense of mutability and possibility into the life of the Trinity. See Thomas Weinandy, *Does God Suffer?* (Notre Dame: University of Notre Dame Press, 2000).

that to so precisely and rigidly confine actions and properties to a specific nature of Christ carries a whiff of the so careful distinctions of Nestorius that aroused Cyril's suspicions.

The crux of the issue that Pitstick's argument highlights is whether the concept of the one person in the hypostatic union properly allows suffering to be predicated of both Jesus' humanity and his divinity in its *economic* mode of existence—which is precisely the move Cyril argued was necessary in the fifth century. And the second issue is whether predicating suffering of the one person of the incarnation properly allows one then to postulate that this suffering is somehow present in the inner Trinitarian life in a non-necessary way that implies no lack of perfection or completion in God's inner life.

This Trinitarian dimension leads to Pitstick's additional objection that this perceived Balthasarian failure to distinguish nature and person also results in his introduction of mutability and passibility into the immanent Trinity.[144] She argues that because Balthasar fails to see this distinction, he essentially collapses the entire being of the Son into the incarnation—the Son's divinity is not held immutable and impassible in the immanent Trinity while only Jesus' humanity undergoes suffering. As a result of Balthasar's insistence that the divinity of Christ is present in the redemptive act of suffering, change and suffering are admitted into the inner Trinitarian life.[145]

---

144. Pitstick, *Light in Darkness*, 131–133, 189.

145. Her concerns about Balthasar's extension of the events of the economic Trinity back into the Trinitarian life are well noted and have been the subject of a number of fine studies, which space here does not permit us to explore in any depth. Balthasar does not collapse the distinction between immanent and economic, but his distinction is perhaps less rigid than some would comfortably allow. However, much as we have seen with Barth, there is a whole complex structure of thought behind Balthasar's argument for a certain internal mutability in God. This structure relies on God's freedom to embrace what is other without being in any way necessarily changed or affected by it, as well as the complex relationship between time and eternity Balthasar envisions. He is certainly open to critique here, but for a more informed and nuanced presentation of his thought see O'Hanlon and for a more finely drawn critique, see Thomas Weinandy.

Finally, Pitstick argues that Balthasar actually does violence to the wondrous exchange formula by incorrectly reading it as "what is not endured" is not healed or redeemed, rather than "what is not assumed" is not healed. [146] Here Pitstick is really concerned that Balthasar's thought leads him to take seriously the conception that Jesus takes on sin-in-itself in his person (though she misreads him as positing that this is taken on in the divine nature). Pitstick reacts strongly to this conception of substitutionary atonement or any sense that Jesus would take on reprobation in himself. Rather, she argues that the truly proper theory is that of meritorious satisfaction.

I would argue that what runs throughout all of Pitstick's objections to Balthasar is her conception of a rigid distinction and separation between person and nature, which she then has difficulty bringing into a real union.[147] This creates problems for her reading of Balthasar. She seems to either miss or disregard Balthasar's insistence on and radicalization of the one person, of whom—as the divine Son in his mode of existence as a fully human being—all predicates can be properly attributed. While Pitstick attributes her formula "a person suffers in a nature" to Maximus, she seems to have not attended to Maximus's distinction between essence and mode of existence, which

---

146. See Pitstick, *Light in Darkness*, 98, 110–114, 176–177, 181.

147. In her fervor to uphold the distinction between the two natures, Pitstick makes some moves that are reminiscent of Nestorius' insistence on precisions of terminology that so aroused Cyril's suspicions. In a section discussing person and natures, she argues for great linguistic precision between the use of "Son" and "Jesus," arguing that "Son" must be used to connote the divine nature and "Jesus" to denote the human nature, and that when speaking of suffering and dying, these must always be qualified with reference to Jesus' human nature. See Pitstick, *Light in Darkness*, 296–298. Now, this is not to argue that the distinction between divine and human must not be maintained, but perhaps Pitstick is so concerned about protecting the divine immutability through the sharp distinction between the two natures that she loses sight of the one person as the central affirmation of Christology. With this in mind, she should perhaps be more wary of quoting Cyril (page 295) as a backup for her insistence that "the Word suffered *in the flesh*," because, as we have seen, Cyril's stress in that sentence would more than likely fall on "the *Word* suffered in the flesh" than Pitstick seems to realize. One can almost hear Cyril's words that the issue that caused Nestorius and the Antiochenes such trouble was their "exaggerated fear of passibility."

is precisely the distinction that Balthasar picks up and uses to develop a Christology that can argue it is the divine Son, the second person of the Trinity, in his *mode of existence* as a fully human being who we see in Jesus Christ. The living of his mission in the economy, even to suffering and dying, is predicated of this *one person*—the divine Son in his *economic mode of existence.*

This is in no way to uphold an attribution of suffering to the immanent Trinity. Balthasar's theology certainly is not immune to scrutiny in this area, but overall Pitstick simply misreads the basic thrust of Balthasar's theology partly because she insists on reading it through her sharp distinctions and separation of person and nature rather than through Balthasar's one person and mode of existence categories. So she reacts quite viscerally to Balthasar's soteriology, particularly his insistence on substitutionary atonement as an embodiment of the wondrous exchange—Jesus, the one person, the divine Son in his mode of existence as a fully human being, takes on the very depths of sin and death in his person.[148] For Balthasar, if the full depths of human experience are not fully assumed by and

---

148. See also Thomas J. White, who has responded to Pitstick's concerns about Balthasar's view of substitutionary atonement and treatment of Holy Saturday by noting that Balthasar is actually working with and altering Barth's reinterpretation of election—that all are elected in Christ and that Christ accepts reprobation for all others. See Thomas Joseph White, O.P., "On the Possibility of Universal Salvation," *Pro Ecclesia* Vol. XVII, no. 3 (Summer 2008): 269–280. However, White argues that a focus on the concept of penal substitution that is then developed into a sense that Christ suffers the hell of damnation for us does not take into consideration that the tradition has portrayed damnation not as "outward 'punishment' or inward desolation," but as "a creation of the human will: it is the voluntary refusal to love." Thus, hell is "essentially a 'place' in which God cannot be present because it is the one place from which God's love and agency have been banished." (280) Christ cannot become sin in this sense. White thus argues that Christ, as the embodiment of God's love, simply "could not experience the 'hell of damnation' in this way." (280) However, here White also seems to miss a key feature of Balthasar's proposal: there is no "place"—even hell, even the refusal of love—that is outside the sphere of God's love. Within the inner Trinitarian life there is a space for every modality of love, even its refusal by creatures. In the incarnation, Jesus takes on that very refusal and overcomes it. God deliberately enters every "place" of human sin and refusal and redeems it. Humans may still refuse God's grace, but that refusal never puts them beyond the reach of God's love in Christ.

predicated of the one person, then humanity is not fully redeemed and healed.

Balthasar's thought is complex and highly nuanced, built in intricately linked layers that do not fit neatly into tidy, labeled boxes. Any exploration of Balthasar's christological and soteriological conceptions firmly needs to keep in sight that his primary concern is to capture the dramatic height and depth of the Trinitarian love for humanity. This is a love that extends even to sending the eternal Son to live a fully human life that assumes the full measure of what it means to be human—including the depth of humanity's separation and alienation from God—in order to redeem and draw humanity into the very life of God. Wigley reminds us that for Balthasar, the "sufferings of Christ on the cross can be comprehended fully only in light of the Incarnation, something which is crucial to the teachings of the Fathers. What is important about God in Christ coming to take on human flesh is that it also involves God in Christ coming to share our common humanity and point the way by which human beings can come to share in the life of God."[149] In other words, Balthasar believes that God in Christ plumbs the depths of human life and all that can separate us from God *so that* humans can be freed and drawn into the very intimacy of the divine life. He seeks to take utterly seriously the wondrous exchange—regarding both the depths that Christ assumes and the heights of divine life in which humans then share—because he believes this is God's intention for created life.

149. Wigley, *Barth and von Balthasar*, 146.

The Christological Analogy of Being:
The Way of Human Participation in God's Life

Pulling together the threads of Balthasar's theology thus far, we have seen that his Christology and soteriology are intimately linked within a pattern of redemption that moves creation toward its intended supernatural end of life with God through the incarnation, in which God assumes and overcomes the depths of humanity's sin, disobedience, and alienation from God. Balthasar has radicalized Cyril's single subject Christology and the concept of the wondrous exchange, arguing that by assuming human sin and death to its deepest dregs and farthest reaches—even to the depths of hell—the second person of the Trinity in his incarnate mode of existence as fully human and fully divine takes upon and into himself everything that could separate humans from God and truly overcomes it. Because Christ has fully assumed everything of what it means to be human and has overcome the distance between God and creatures, all of creation can once again be properly positioned in the life of God—both now and eternally.

As we have explored, the story of this pattern of redemption that Balthasar tells in dramatic form goes like this: Because created life is patterned on the relationship of the Son to the Father in the power of the Spirit, there is room in God's plan for humans to be truly free and to have space within which to act. This is possible because God's Trinitarian self-giving love makes space for multiple modalities of love within the relationship of the Trinity itself.[150] However, creatures have used the space of this freedom in disobedience, and it either has collapsed into idolatrous self-assertion or become distorted in fear and alienation.[151] By entering, through the incarnation, into

---

150. Balthasar *Theo-Drama V*, 91–102, and O'Hanlon, *The Immutability of God,* 60.

151. Balthasar, *Theo-Drama IV* 162–188. It is an analogical understanding that provides the framework for the real distinction between God and creation. The creature is like God,

every place where humans have disobeyed and are alienated from God, Christ assumes and removes the very depths of sin, death, and all that alienates creatures from God, and he does so in order to "re-situate human being within its true acting space" in the divine life.[152]

We have seen that the christological analogy of being provides the framework for the proper relationship between creature and God. Because in Christ humanity and divinity are united in the one person without losing their distinction, the pattern of relationship between God and creatures reflects this structure and participates in it. Within this christological analogy of being, Balthasar argues that Christ is the "measure of human existence," "the foundation and model of the unity of the natural and supernatural," of God and human.[153] Christ then becomes the space in which humans are repositioned in the Trinitarian life.

Balthasar argues that as Jesus opens up the space for humans to participate in his mission, he also opens the way for them to participate in the life of the Trinity.[154] Wigley notes that Balthasar establishes a "trinitarian origin for his ontology." The entire worldly order's being originates through the Trinitarian personal relations and so, in order for creation to find its true end, it must participate

possessing both essence and existence, but in God, essence is identical with existence, while in the creature essence and existence are distinct and in tension with one another. Balthasar explored this theme in depth through the relationship between infinite and finite freedom. Stephen Wigley notes that Balthasar works with two understandings of freedom from his work with the Fathers—"freedom as 'autonomous motion,' as actively willing to pursue a chosen course, and freedom as 'consent,' as joyfully and obediently agreeing to that which is in our best interests." Real freedom is discovered only "when the two freedoms conform—when we actively choose to consent to that which is best for us"—exactly what we see in the incarnation. Wigley, *Barth and von Balthasar*, 94.

152. Balthasar, *Theo-Drama IV* 361–362. See also McIntosh, "Christology," in *The Cambridge Companion to Hans Urs von Balthasar,* 35.

153. Balthasar, *The Theology of Karl Barth*, 332.

154. Kevin Mongrain has argued that Balthasar's vision is greatly influenced through Irenaeus's view, read through de Lubac, of the mutual glorification of God and humanity in Christ. See Kevin Mongrain, *The Systematic Thought of Hans Urs von Balthasar: An Irenaean Retrieval* (New York: Herder & Herder, 2002).

in that divine life.[155] In addition, Balthasar argues that within the Trinitarian life, "creation is an additional gift from God to God." Therefore there must be an "eternal enrichment of God through creation," O'Hanlon notes.[156] Balthasar is clear that creation is nonnecessary to God, yet he argues that the world and each person do enrich the life of God because, in God's eternal liveliness and self-giving, God freely makes space for and welcomes that which is other.[157] As we have seen, for Balthasar there is in God a mysterious "capacity to receive" that allows for the "not yet" of eschatological hope and makes space to receive that which is "other" as a gift.[158]

This repositioning within God's life as the true, supernatural end that God intends for creatures is envisioned by Balthasar as an ongoing participation in the life of God, beginning in history as humans participate in Christ's mission. As humans receive their own vocation within that mission, they discover their real identity and become true "theological" persons within God's community of the church. Further, as they analogically participate in Christ, humans experience not only an interior, spiritual transformation, but a true ontological transformation into a likeness of Christ in which they live out their share in Christ's mission and identity.[159] Balthasar shares Cyril's conviction that redemption through Christ brings about both a change in human *being* and a change in human *doing*. Like the

---

155. Wigley, *Barth and von Balthasar*, 105. See also Balthasar, *Theo-Drama V*, 394–401. In arguing for this space for genuine human action, O'Hanlon notes that Balthasar argues that secondary, created causes can become part of God's life as God's love reconciles them; "God is not "changed in any univocal sense," but through God's choice to be affected. O'Hanlon, *The Immutability of God*, 34. O'Hanlon explains that created lives are "taken up into this relationship between Father and Son in the Trinity" and "from within this relationship itself, 'introduce' different modalities into the divine life." See O'Hanlon, *The Immutability of God,* 60 and Balthasar, *Theo-Drama V,* 387–399, 412, 502–521.

156. O'Hanlon, *The Immutability of God*, 75.

157. Balthasar, *Theo-Drama V,* 387–399, 412, 506–521. See also O'Hanlon, *The Immutability of God*, 76.

158. See O'Hanlon, *The Immutability of God*, 75.

159. Balthasar, *Theo-Drama III*, 527–528.

church Fathers, he wants to keep a distinction between divine and human, but also to account for the real inner and outer transformation of humanity through Christ.

Yet, Balthasar notes, Vatican I reiterates that in the supernatural order, exaltation and transformation do not obliterate human nature or turn it into divinity.[160] It is rather precisely a proper understanding of the analogy of being that provides the framework for a faithful understanding of deification and human participation in God's life. Nature and grace "operate in harmony or analogy," and through Christ, "a way from nature to grace has been opened up."[161] Yet the distinction between nature and grace remains.[162] Balthasar argues that when "grace is flowing out" from God and "nature is receiving" that grace, then nature is already a "transformed, exalted nature."[163] All things that grace touches retain their natural qualities, yet they are transformed and irradiated by grace. Grace truly enables a participation in the divine life. It allows the creature in some way to truly know the "ever-greater and thus the ever-more unknown God."[164] However, this participation comes not through any natural or inherent ascent of the creature, but through God's descent in the incarnation—the taking on of a sinful humanity utterly dissimilar to God.[165]

In addition, this grace brings about an ongoing personal relationship with ontological aspects, not just a forensic change in status before God. God has revealed and given God's self in Christ,

---

160. Balthasar, *The Theology of Karl Barth*, 307.
161. Balthasar, *The Theology of Karl Barth*, 311.
162. Balthasar, *The Theology of Karl Barth*, 307–314.
163. Balthasar, *The Theology of Karl Barth*, 281.
164. Balthasar, *The Theology of Karl Barth*, 286.
165. Balthasar, *The Theology of Karl Barth*, 281–287. Nature is never "the measure of grace." But it is never simply an inactive appendage either. "Grace, like the vine, is the exclusive principle of fruitfulness, but nature, like the branches, can bring forth much fruit when united to the vine." See the discussion on 387–389, quote 387.

and through this grace God shares God's life with the world and allows humans to participate in it. That sharing is both "conscious and ontically real." It "involves both an event aspect as well as an ontological aspect."[166] Balthasar argues that if God has truly entered human history, then there is a "real encounter" between God and humans. Something ontological occurs. "If it is to be a real history made up of real events, then we cannot avoid the real ontological elements in the exchange: there is a real participation and a lasting ontic effect."[167] Because we are dealing with God's active and free self-revelation, then "we must grant an unconditioned priority to the ontological over the cognitive."[168]

Here, Balthasar is working to account for the ontological transformation of the human creature's being—an account he thought was lacking in Barth's theology.[169] At least some of the divergence between Balthasar and Barth in this area may be due to differences between Roman Catholic and Protestant understandings about justification and its relationship to sanctification. For Roman Catholics, operating with a sense of infused grace, both justification and sanctification take place through Baptism as God infuses the grace of the Spirit, making the baptized righteous with God and enabling them to live out that righteousness through life in the church, participation in the sacraments and moral living.[170] Many Protestant reformers, looking to stress the objective reality of God's saving action, have insisted on a more forensic understanding of

166. Balthasar, *The Theology of Karl Barth*, 364.
167. Balthasar, *The Theology of Karl Barth*, 365–367, quote 366.
168. Balthasar, *The Theology of Karl Barth*, 366.
169. See Wigley, who argues that Balthasar develops his conceptions in response to his worry that Barth's focus on the "event" of salvation did not adequately account for a change in the actual *being* of the creature as a result of the incarnation and Christ's salvific work. Wigley, *Barth and von Balthasar*, 12–13, 36–37.
170. See the essay by Anthony Lane, "Two-fold Righteousness: A Key to the Doctrine of Justification?" in *Justification: What's at Stake in the Current Debates*, ed. Mark Husbands and Daniel J. Treier (Downers Grove, Ill.: Intervarsity, 2004) for a helpful discussion here.

justification. It is the imputation of Christ's alien righteousness that saves—there is nothing inherent in the human being, there is no "infusion" of grace, we never cease to be sinners even while at the same time being justified.[171] For these Protestant theologians, there is no basis outside of Christ's alien righteousness that makes us right with God. It is something completely outside of human being, and confers a remission of sins and a change in our status before God. But it does not "make" us inwardly righteous, and any hint of such inward righteousness anchors human justification in something (infused grace) beyond Christ's life, death, and resurrection. Justification makes us right with God, and sanctification is the result of that change in status before God.[172]

At the risk of oversimplifying a complex and highly nuanced debate, the dispute really turns around how humans are made righteous and sanctified through Christ. For many in the Protestant tradition, particularly in the Reformed tradition, it is Christ's righteousness that is imputed to us in a forensic way—that is, it changes our status before God from those who are guilty to those who are acquitted. Justification does not come about because of an inward renewal through an infusion of grace in Baptism. But for Catholics, we are accepted by grace on the basis of the righteousness of Christ that God infuses into us, and the process by which we live out that justification is our sanctification. McCormack has argued that Barth evidences the Reformed theological trajectory by arguing that justification is not based on any inherent capacity of humans to receive grace or by any infused, inward righteousness.[173] Barth

---

171. See also the essays of Bruce McCormack, Simon Gathercole, Henri A. Blocher and Carl Trueman in *Justification in Perspective: Historical Developments and Contemporary Challenges*, ed. Bruce L. McCormack(Grand Rapids: Baker Academic, 2006) for a helpful analysis of these issues.
172. See helpful essays in *Justification in Perspective*, ed. McCormack, as well as in *Justification: What's at Stake in the Current Debates*, ed. Mark Husbands and Daniel J. Treier for thorough expositions of Protestant thought regarding justification.

retains the forensic framework of the Reformers but, as we have seen, argues that Christ is both subject and object of election in which, through this wondrous exchange, Christ takes on our sin and guilt and sanctifies humans, who then participate in his election and exaltation. However, McCormack argues that it is critical to see that in Barth's and the Reformers' view of forensic, imputed justification, God's righteousness does actually "create the reality it declares"—it is transformative and ontological, but not through infusion.[174] The transformation is at the level of will, obedience, and action because for Barth, we are what we do.[175] The Holy Spirit does not perform "divine surgery" on the human will, but rather enlightens it in ways that enable us to see and to obey.[176]

But the Catholic view continues to be one of infused grace, whereby we are justified because we are *made* righteous by God in Baptism. Grace perfects nature. God can and does do this. It is a different understanding of the way nature and grace are related in the act of justification. God truly does remove sin, transforming nature and ordering it to its supernatural end through the church and sacraments and through participation in the moral order, and this act in no way compromises the integrity of nature or the gratuity of grace. Perhaps the real source of disagreement is whether there can be real ontological change without some form of infused grace. The Catholic tradition, as well as a number of Protestant and Orthodox traditions, would argue that such change, to truly encompass a real change of being—including a transformation of will and knowledge to obedience—requires the gift of an infused grace through the Spirit

---

173. Bruce L. McCormack, "Justitia aliena: Karl Barth in Conversation with the Evangelical Doctrine of Imputed Righteousness," in *Justification in Perspective*, 167–196.

174. See Bruce L. McCormack, "What's at Stake in Current Debates over Justification? The Crisis of Protestantism in the West" in *Justification: What's at Stake in the Current Debates*, 107.

175. McCormack, "What's at Stake in Current Debates over Justification?" 112–115.

176. McCormack, "What's at Stake in Current Debates over Justification?" 116. Perhaps the real issue is whether there can be ontological change without some sort of infused grace.

that is never an inherent capacity of human being, but is rather always a gracious gift of God.

Balthasar, working within this Catholic understanding, argues that knowledge of God and grace does not reside purely at the cognitive level, but rather there is "a genuine ontological transformation, a genuine imparting of divine Being and a genuine sharing of the creature in God's Being that affects the creature's own being as well as the creature's awareness of the world of divine Being."[177] Otherwise, we are dealing with a merely "eschatological transformation, with a justification that is merely forensic and imputed"—in short one that stays at the cognitive level but leaves the being of the creature essentially unchanged.[178] If humans are not truly incorporated into God's life through Christ, then "the event of revelation does not truly touch them."[179] It is critical that we can trust God's action in the incarnation through which humanity can participate in God without the evacuation or collapse of human being itself. The analogy of being allows us to give full due to both the divinity and the humanity of Christ and all creatures, and to attend to more than a merely eschatological, future transformation or a merely cognitive one. As Wigley notes, Balthasar was convinced that "the biblical witness was not just concerned with God's revelation in Jesus but with the transformation of believers in Christ."[180]

Balthasar argues that a completely postponed transformation that remains at the cognitive level (which he believed is where Barth's conceptions led) is simply inconsistent with the transformational grace of the incarnation.[181]

177. Balthasar, *The Theology of Karl Barth*, 364–365.
178. Balthasar, *The Theology of Karl Barth*, 365.
179. Balthasar, *The Theology of Karl Barth*, 365.
180. Wigley, *Barth and von Balthasar*, 152.
181. Balthasar honed this conception of human participation in God's life with both an ontological and moral aspect in his concern over Barth's conceptions. Balthasar thought Barth's theology was beautiful and he incorporated many themes of Barth's work, particularly his christocentric

And why can something that is going to happen to the creature in the age to come also not take place, in some hidden way, here and now? If we invoke analogy to understand how the creature will not be destroyed in the future upon entering the divine world, why cannot the creature gain access to God in the present too? And if this access is real, why should the real and ontic sanctification of the creature through grace be postponed for the future aeon alone and only be treated as merely a forensic sanctity here and now in the face of all the statements of revelation?[182]

For Balthasar, there is a real "par-taking" in the divine life. It is not simply passive reception. Rather, humans can and must actively allow God to act in and through them. "God's grace is a participation in his inner divine life. As such, it raises the creature above and beyond any claims or longings it might possess. This participation is neither purely forensic nor purely eschatological. Rather it is real, internal, and present. It is an event that effects a transformation of the very being of the creature."[183]

Here we see the crucial role Balthasar's understanding of analogy plays in his conceptions of human participation in the divine life. The analogy of being provides a framework of similarity within an already always greater dissimilarity that provides the space for this rich participation of humans in God's life, without dissolving the differences between divine and human or impinging on God's wholly otherness. Analogy creates space for real transformation and thus it functions, as Oakes notes, not simply as a concept but as "a whole way of life."[184] Through the christological analogy of being,

---

focus, into his own work. However, Balthasar also took Barth to task for using a christocentric lens to such an extent that he robbed creation of any real breathing space or room for true response. Balthasar, *The Theology of Karl Barth*, 393.

182. Balthasar, *The Theology of Karl Barth*, 366. Here again, we see that in contrast to Long, Balthasar argues that creaturely integrity and fullness is actually brought to its fullness and perfection precisely through its analogical participation in the divine life through an infusion of grace that is always a gift. See also 376–378.

183. Balthasar, *The Theology of Karl Barth*, 377.

Jesus' life provides the pattern for redeemed human life and Jesus becomes the dramatic space for human participation.[185] As humans carry out their role in Jesus' mission within the family of God, their identity is formed and they begin, here and now, to participate in the divine life.[186]

Perhaps in light of Balthasar's conception of Jesus as the enactment of the Trinitarian relationships that creates space for creation—a conception given concrete form in the hypostatic union—the moral life can best be pictured as a dramatic performance in which each participant truly becomes part of God's "play." Each person acts out the unique missional role he or she has been given as a sharing in Christ's drama, made possible through the re-situation of creation within the Trinity.[187] As participants move through the play, they not only perform their own roles, but those roles are inescapably linked to all the other players on the stage with whom they interact. They give to and receive from one another as they work together with Christ to bring forth the beauty of the drama, by persisting in prayer, suffering on behalf of one another, and opening themselves to the ever-flowing direction from the author through the powerful direction of the Spirit.[188]

184. See Oakes, *Pattern of Redemption*, 36–37 for a discussion of what Balthasar learned from Przywara. Quote 37.
185. See Balthasar *Theo-Drama II*, 67–69, 86 and *Theo-Drama III*, 231, 258–259. For a more lengthy discussion of this issue, see McIntosh, *Christology from Within*, 133–134. Balthasar argues, "Christ can be called the only concrete analogy of being, since he constitutes in himself, in the union of his divine and human natures, the measure of every distance between God and man." See Balthasar, *Theo-Drama II*, 267.
186. See Mark McIntosh, "Christology" in *The Cambridge Companion to Hans Urs von Balthasar*, 34–36.
187. McIntosh, "Christology," 35.
188. Given these frameworks, Balthasar's exposition of the moral life is visible primarily as he deals with the tensions of finite freedom lived within the missional acting space created by infinite freedom. The tensions of human life cannot be truly resolved outside of this Trinitarian and christological drama. Jesus forms the pattern for creaturely participation in God's life and forms the space for humans to accept or reject this offer of participation. Further, as Ben Quash notes, infinite and finite freedom are not in a competitive relationship. Finite freedom is not destroyed by infinite freedom, but participates in it, and is respected and improved by that

While Balthasar is often criticized for his failure to tackle specific moral and ethical issues in extended ways, this may be because his assumption that Christ is the analogical pattern for human life, lived out through the gift of the church and the sacraments in the power of the Holy Spirit, is so deeply embedded in his thought. In addition, there is a strong contemplative strand in Balthasar. Humans know what is good and are empowered to do that good only as they contemplate the life, death, and resurrection of Jesus. For each person, that contemplation will reveal a part for them to play in the mission of Christ and that mission will provide their unique personal identity and mission. Each person finds his or her freedom for good human action only within a participation in Christ's self-giving mission, and this space cannot be prescribed without violating the acting room God has given us.[189]

In Christ, the finite and earthly constraints of human life are taken up and then transformed by the divine through the event of the incarnation, in which the life, death, and resurrection of Jesus are a Trinitarian act. Wigley argues that for Balthasar, "it is this 'irruption' which takes place in the presence of Christ that brings a new understanding of time and space, in which the patterns of creaturely existence are transformed by the divine and it becomes possible to see

proper relationship. See Quash, "The Theo-Drama," in *The Cambridge Companion to Hans Urs von Balthasar* 149. However, Quash has noted that Balthasar is in danger of a tendency, which he criticized in Hegel, of supplying a comprehensive framework that too quickly and totally resolves the tensions in the drama and, in effect, reduces the real freedom of the characters on the stage. See Quash, *Theology and the Drama of History* (Cambridge: Cambridge University Press, 2005). See also Wigley's discussion, *Barth and von Balthasar*, 114–123. This participation is empowered by the Holy Spirit, who liberates human freedom authentically to embrace its finite freedom. Balthasar, *Theo-Drama II*, 230–231, 258–259. Human freedom is both an autonomous motion and yet something that cannot be possessed or properly exercised without relationship to that which is other—infinite freedom. See Balthasar, *Theo-Drama II*, 258–259.

189. See Balthasar's discussion in *Theo-Drama II*, 158–169 of the various views of Christ's life and work that seek to account for the interplay between divine action and human response and Balthasar's stress on the free, dramatic space for human response.

how heaven, far from being a state to be hoped for at some time in the future, can by the grace of Christ be present in the world today."[190]

Balthasar's insistence on the soteriological pattern of the wondrous exchange, made possible through the one person of Jesus Christ with the purpose of transforming humanity both ontologically and morally and drawing human life into the divine life, is remarkably compatible with Cyril's vision. However, Balthasar stretches the depths and heights of the descent and ascent and vividly portrays the dramatic tensions of this saving event. In our next chapter, we will explore whether Balthasar's conceptions result in a crossing of boundaries that ultimately undermine the goals he seeks to achieve, or if his work is a faithful extension of Cyril's pattern.

Summary

Throughout this chapter we have explored Balthasar's presentation of the drama of God's love for creation. It is a drama in which the Trinitarian persons make space for the "otherness" of humanity and the Trinity acts to save human beings from the consequences of their refusal of God's love—even to the extent of the divine Son entering the full depths of human alienation from God in order to lift humanity once again into the divine life of God. Balthasar's soteriology is inextricably tied to a single-subject Christology in which this enactment of the wondrous exchange takes place in the one person of Jesus Christ. Balthasar refuses to back away from the depths and heights of this exchange as he explores the reality of what it means to affirm that the second person of the Trinity, in his mode of existence as a fully human being, embodies the utter extent of God's self-giving to humanity in order that the depths of humanity's

190. Wigley, *Barth and von Balthasar*, 104.

alienation from God can be overcome and human life can be raised up into God's life.

Balthasar's conceptions offer a christological basis and a soteriological pattern that are remarkably similar to what we have seen in Cyril. God creates humanity as a pure gift of self-giving love. When humans refuse that love and turn away in disobedience, alienating themselves from God in ways that they cannot undo, God freely and graciously descends into human life as the divine Son in his mode of existence as a fully human being. Balthasar pushes single-subject Christology and the soteriological pattern of the wondrous exchange to its depths and heights in arguing that the Incarnate Son assumes and experiences the full extent of human alienation from God—through suffering, death on the cross, and a descent into hell as the furthest reaches of human separation from God—in order to overcome that alienation from within and to open the way for humans to be drawn into and repositioned in the life of the Trinity. Balthasar's theology is animated by his conviction that the telos of human life God intends is a supernaturally graced ontological and moral transformation enabling humans to participate in the life of God. In the encounter of God and humans in the space of Jesus' death and resurrection, a real transformation occurs for humans that then enables and empowers human response and obedience.

However, in exploring Balthasar's theology, we have also identified areas for further analysis and comparison with Cyril and Barth. In particular, Balthasar's stress on reciprocity as a vital feature of analogy, and his distinctive view of receptivity as active, rather than merely passive, enrich his conception of participation. But these convictions do lead Balthasar to some highly speculative thought regarding the immanent Trinitarian life, and he certainly pushes against some of the boundaries of traditional Christian thought regarding God's immutability and impassibility. Balthasar extends the economy of the incarnation both into the world and into God, arguing that the entirety of the incarnation is a Trinitarian event that affects both creation and God, without endangering God's distinctiveness from creation or threatening God's wholly-otherness. Does this then imply that Balthasar has crossed a line that Cyril was adamant in drawing—the line of impassibility? Does Balthasar make this mistake by arguing that not only is humanity affected by the incarnational events of Jesus' life, death, and resurrection, but God chooses to be affected as well? Can Balthasar's modified view of God's immutability and impassibility retain the necessary distinction between divine and human while securing human participation in God's life as God's free and non-necessary gift? What is the effect of Balthasar's understanding of human life as an enrichment in the Trinity on the traditional understanding of deification?

Additionally, does Balthasar simply push the edges of a single-subject Christology that takes seriously the logic of the wondrous exchange—pushing at the extreme depths of Christ's suffering in hell and the extreme heights of human life as an enrichment in God's life—or does he stretch the concept beyond its acceptable boundaries? While in Barth we see the ongoing tension of conflict and antithesis between divine and human even in the incarnation, does Balthasar's vision of a complete identity of mission between divine and human in the incarnation threaten to collapse the distinction between them and endanger the soteriological and teleological pattern he seeks to uphold?

As we proceed to our section of comparison and analysis, which conceptual framework—that of Barth or of Balthasar—provides a fuller account of deification and a more compelling vision of human life as a participation in God's life, while remaining faithful to the Christology of Cyril and the Chalcedonian definition?

While Balthasar's conceptions are certainly daring and make a number of scholars uneasy on any number of fronts, it is important to keep in mind that it is precisely his profound conviction that the most beautiful and enraptured form of God's love for creation is revealed on the cross where we see the Father's willingness to send, the Son's willingness to be sent, and the Holy Spirit's power to keep the unity of that love in the face of all human rejection and alienation, overcoming that alienation forever. He reminds us that God's vision for human life is even now being fulfilled through Christ. Human life—now and eternally—has changed, and we have been given a share in the divine life that empowers our present with hope and moves us toward the future through graced participation in the Trinitarian life. Balthasar's vision draws us forward to richly imagine the beauty, goodness and truth of life with God.

4

———

Realizing the Promise

Barth's and Balthasar's Conceptions of Participation
in the Life of God

It is the property of human nature not to possess any trace of the heavenly graces of its own will, or, as it were, by its own nature . . . Rather, it was enriched from outside and by acquisition, that is, from God, with that which transcends its own nature."[1]

—Cyril of Alexandria, *Commentary on Isaiah*

The search for transformation, the drive for something more, the poignant yearning to become fully human continues. We continue to oscillate between a cynical despair that any such transformation is possible and a false hope that, given enough time, humanity will find its own way through the development of its inherent capacities—that we will become the gods of our own world. In such a landscape, it is

1. Cyril, *Commentary on Isaiah*, trans. Norman Russell in Norman Russell, *Cyril of Alexandria* (New York: Routledge, 2000), 83.

critical for Christians to understand and to confidently proclaim and embody a proper understanding of participation in the life of God as a pure gift of grace that truly does transform human life—never as an inherent capacity we can develop or achieve on our own but only as God's grace in the life, death, and resurrection of Jesus Christ transforms our created nature. Within the proper limits of that understanding we can, in a humble confidence, proclaim and live in that new reality because we trust the power and grace of God, the God who became human that we might become humans who participate in the divine life.

As we have seen, that soteriological conviction was the animating force for Cyril of Alexandria's Christology. In chapter 1, we explored the concept of deification in some detail and then examined Cyril's concept within the tradition's understanding. We then turned to an examination of the Christology and soteriology of Karl Barth and Hans Urs von Balthasar, who both assert a strong Cyrillian emphasis on the single subjectivity of Christ and a strong reliance on the ancient exchange formula in their soteriology. But despite significant similarities in their thought, both with Cyril and with each other, Barth and Balthasar end up in quite different places when it comes to the effect that the life, death, and resurrection of Jesus have on humankind. This chapter brings together the work of the previous four by analyzing the conceptions of Barth and Balthasar in the light of Cyril's understanding of deification.

Using Cyril's insights provides a helpful lens through which to examine the work of Barth and Balthasar and the similarities and differences between their visions of human life as a participation in God's life. Their similarities have been noted by any number of scholars. Both Barth and Balthasar seek to work within a Chalcedonian structure, upholding the one person of Jesus Christ, fully human and fully divine. Both see a need to move away from what they perceive as the "static" conceptions of Christology bequeathed by scholasticism and both respond by developing conceptions that actualize and attend to the dramatic action of the Christ event. Both clearly want to attend to the transformative effects of Jesus' life, death, and resurrection, and both offer a Christic lens through which all of creation—past, present, and future—is viewed. Both offer a compelling, if controversial, critique of modernity and its effects, and hold up the Christian life as a radical alternative.

However, as we have seen, despite their similarities, their christological and soteriological frameworks result in different conceptions of the role and acting space for human beings, different perspectives on how and to what extent humans participate in the divine life, and different understandings of the effects of that participation. In this chapter, we examine to what extent each of them captures Cyril's insights into the redemptive and transformative union of humanity and divinity in Jesus Christ, who draws humanity into the life of God.

As we begin, it is crucial to review the conception of deification with which we are working. Deification as a participation in Christ that leads to a new creation emerged as a central theme early in the church's life as a way of giving expression to the salvific work and purpose of the Trinity on behalf of the creation. Norman Russell, Donald Fairbairn and A. N. Williams have argued that deification became what Williams calls the "dominant model of the concept of salvation."[2] The predominant soteriological pattern was a belief that God created humanity in the image of God to live in relationship with God; that through the fall, this gift of relationship is broken and humanity became subject to sin and death; that through the

---

2. A. N. Williams, *The Ground of Union:Deification in Aquinas and Palamas* (Oxford: Oxford University Press, 1999), 27. See also Donald Fairbairn, *Grace and Christology in the Early Church* (Oxford: Oxford University Press, 2003) and Norman Russell, *The Doctrine of Deification in the Greek Patristic Tradition* (Oxford: Oxford University Press, 2004) for similar arguments.

incarnation, and the life, death, and resurrection of Jesus Christ, humanity is transformed and restored to a life with God; and that humans are given a real participation in the life of God as a pure gift of grace.

Further, it is important to note the boundaries established for the conception of deification and the exchange formula so closely associated with it. The exchange is one of properties, not an exchange of essence or nature, and the properties are predicated of the one person of Christ, not of the natures themselves. There is no mixture or confusion of divinity and humanity and neither is evacuated or overruled.[3] Inheriting this basic structure, Cyril uses three guiding premises that provide an analogical framework for his conception. These are designed to uphold the distinction between divine and human while also providing for a real participation of humanity in the divine life, resulting in transformation and moral response. Those premises are: 1) as human beings who participate, we are distinct in kind from the divine in which we participate; 2) we receive the qualities in which we participate only partially and in an external way, while that in which we participate possesses those qualities in an intrinsic and fully complete way; and 3) as those who participate, we can lose that which we have by participation, while that in which we participate possesses those qualities by nature and can never lose them.[4] Deification is thus never an innate quality of humanity. It does not come about through any realization or development of some innate self. It is *always* a supernatural gift from God, realized through Christ in faithfulness and obedience.

Finally, in our examination of Cyril, we saw that the reason for his passionate insistence on the single subject of Christ is his conviction

3. See again Russell, *The Doctrine of Deification,* 108, and Williams, *The Ground of Union,* 28.
4. See Cyril, *Commentary on John,* 1.9, trans. Russell in *Cyril of Alexandria,* 100–101. See also Daniel A. Keating, *The Appropriation of Divine Life in Cyril of Alexandria* (Oxford: Oxford University Press, 2004), 162.

that it is only through the unity of humanity and divinity in Christ that a transformed life is made possible for all creation. It is *in* this one person, fully divine and fully human—through his life, death, and resurrection—that humanity is transformed, that we are freed from sin and death, and actually given a share in the life of God. We have seen that, for Cyril, Jesus Christ is both agent and recipient of this transformation. In the Word's hypostatic union with his own humanity, he infuses his life into all of humanity through participation, resulting in an ontological re-creation of our being that truly *overcomes* the power of sin and death and makes possible an obedient moral response by humanity. This inward, ontological transformation is always coupled with an outward transformation of moral response that cooperates with the divine initiative. Further, this transformation is not merely an eschatological hope, but makes possible a change in our being and moral pattern of life here and now.

We turn now to an analysis of Barth and Balthasar, examining their christological and soteriological patterns in comparison with Cyril's strong conception of God's intention for human life realized through Jesus Christ.

Barth

We turn first to Barth. Despite his strong insistence on the single subjectivity of Christ, his central use of the exchange pattern in his soteriology, and his discussion of the analogous relationship between God and humans as covenant partners, he flatly refuses any talk of deification, preferring instead to speak of the exaltation of humanity. While he seems to uphold Cyril's insistence on the one person, and relies on an exchange-based, "what is not assumed is not redeemed" view of atonement, he categorically refuses the very conviction that drives Cyril's Christology. Throughout his life, Barth developed a deeper appreciation of analogy and for the response of humanity—as we have seen in his reworking of the covenant of election, as well as in his rich and finely drawn discussion of ethics—but he continued to refuse any conception of deification.[5] This rejection, coupled with his refusal to consider the sacraments of Baptism and the Eucharist as any real participation in Christ, seems at best deeply puzzling in light of his strong concept of the covenant partnership between God and humanity established in Christ. What accounts for this difference? In trying to hold to a single-subject Christology that is still preoccupied with keeping the divine and human in confrontation—and that refuses to follow through on Cyril's insistence that in the union of divine and human in Jesus, God infuses the humanity with power and grace, accomplishing the regeneration of human being itself—does Barth offer an account that is cohesive and that provides a telos of human life that is at least as confident and hopeful as Cyril's?

As we have seen in our examination of Barth's christological and soteriological pattern of thought, his conceptions have much to offer that is positive and helpful. Certainly foremost among his positive achievements is his transformation of the doctrine of election in favor of an exuberantly gracious God who so determines to be a God in fellowship with humankind that God, in the person of Jesus Christ, becomes both the subject and object of election, both judge and judged, in order to save humanity and make that fellowship possible. In addition, Barth works to develop a lively account of Jesus' life, death, and resurrection that captures the heights and depths of God's love and action on humanity's behalf. In terms of his Christology proper, we have seen Barth emphatically affirm the single subjectivity of Christ, which is crucial to his concept of election. In addition,

5. Neder argues that Barth does affirm an analogy of being, but it never resides in created nature itself. Rather it is one of action—active participation in Christ in response to God's initiative. Adam Neder, *Participation in Christ: An Entry into Karl Barth's Church Dogmatics* (Louisville: Westminster John Knox, 2009), 76.

Barth has worked to uphold the real distinction between God and humanity that often has become blurred in modernity. In his work with the relationship between divine and human in Christ, we have seen him develop a framework that attempts to uphold both the fully divine and fully human agential complexity, to use Jones's term, with both the divine and human wills of Jesus working in complete harmony to initiate and enact God's saving activity in the world.[6] Finally, we have Barth's attention to the moral implications for human life in Christ. Clearly, humanity's response to God's saving initiative, which has freed humans to truly stand on their feet and walk as God's obedient covenant partners, is a major focus of Barth's work. Barth's work sings as he speaks of human obedience in response to God's commands as humans share in the exaltation of Christ's humanity through witness to God's gracious love in the world.

Throughout, Barth shares many of Cyril's most emphatic convictions and most compelling insights. He shares with Cyril a definitive emphasis on a single-subject Christology in which the divine Son is the primary acting agent. He shares with Cyril a view that Jesus is both the subject and object of salvation, both the giver and the recipient in his one person. He shares with Cyril an emphasis on the wondrous exchange as a primary soteriological pattern.

But the outcome of that exchange is different for the two theologians. For Cyril, God became human so that, in the union of divine and human in Christ, humanity might be refashioned and empowered for a truly new being and life through participation in Christ—not as a result of any inherent capacity or work of human being as such, but solely as a gift of God who, in and through Christ,

---

6. As Neder points out, for Barth the hypostatic union is really a continual event in which Jesus enacts the divine initiative and perfect human obedience to it. The union is not an issue of being or essence but of act and decision, because for Barth, act and decision constitute being. Neder, *Participation in Christ*, 9–19.

transforms human being and doing. While there are similarities in Barth's pattern of humiliation and exaltation that, at first glance, look almost identical to Cyril's, on closer examination there is nonetheless a significant difference in what takes place in and for humanity, both in the person of Christ and through him to the rest of humanity. For Cyril, the wondrous exchange through the one person makes possible an ontological transformation, in which an infusion of grace perfects humanity and makes it truly and fully human, empowering humans for an ongoing dynamic growth in Christian living within the pattern of Christ, a pattern that truly is present and effective in the lives of the faithful here and now. Salvation is clearly the divine initiative, but Cyril also argues that this divine initiative enables a human response that cooperates with God. Barth argues that humanity is exalted to its true status as God's covenant partner in Christ; insists that, in Christ, divine and human come into harmonious and non-dialectical relationship; and asserts that Christ's humanity is definitive for all humans in that they are elected in him, and this election is their primary determination, even in their sinful state. Neder argues that this concept of participation in Christ is a key theme in Barth's theology, but this participation is not an inward transformation or healing. Rather, it is a correspondence of action between divine initiative and human response.[7] Yet Barth has trouble extending the effects of the incarnation to the rest of humanity itself, continuing to insist that God and humans remain in confrontation, even in the reconciliation brought about by Christ.[8] This insistence on confrontation lends a reserve to his conception of human transformation and exaltation in Christ.

---

7. Neder, Participation in Christ, 19–20.

8. See Neder, *Participation in Christ*, 69–79, who offers a positive construction of Barth's insistence on confrontation. However, the question is why does discipleship and the freedom of humans require confrontation? Why not a gifted grace of cooperation? Is there underneath this need for confrontation the sense of a competitive relationship between divine and human?

What might account for this disjunction? Several interrelated reasons have become evident throughout this study. First, Barth's Christology, while focused on the single subject of Christ, nonetheless has some troubling nuances that emanate from his view of the antithesis between divine and human, and his deep concern to preserve this confrontation. Part of the difficulty stems from a related issue—Barth's rejection of the ancient church's conception that grace perfects and elevates nature. This rejection means that he simply cannot make room for the transformation of created nature itself by grace because he views such a concept as erasing the distinction between God and humanity.[9] This concept would lead humanity to see itself as "divine" and to indulge further its propensity to think too highly of itself, to couch its self-centered conceits, ambition, and quest for power—the inevitable and lasting effect of its sinful corruption—as a participation in God's plan. This outcome is exactly what Barth observed in the two World Wars and what he feared would happen again.

In addition, Barth sees the concept of grace perfecting nature as evacuating human nature. This nature would no longer be human. It would be divine. Here we see Barth's basic understanding of the relationship between human and divine as irrevocably in confrontation with one another. Despite his affirmations that in Christ the relationship is direct and undialectical, one senses that he is not always comfortable with the concept because he continues to place hedges around it, both in his treatment of the two natures and particularly in his view of the relationship between divine and human after Christ. Neder points out that, positively, this confrontation creates "distance" in which humans have freedom to respond without

9. Neder, *Participation in Christ*, 11, 19–38 argues that for Barth, union in Christ is not transformation or healing but death and resurrection in which humans are empowered to decide and act in ways that correspond to Jesus' pattern of response to God. "Human nature is as Jesus Christ does it, not as he does something to it." *Participation in Christ*, 22.

being overwhelmed by God.[10] But, if he is truly comfortable with the harmonious and non-competitive union of divine and human in Christ, and if he views this as an event that truly changes the world and the relationship between God and humanity, then why does he remain so uncomfortable with the concept that, through the union of divine and human in this one person, God graciously transforms and perfects humanity itself as a participation in Christ? Why would God's grace and action necessarily overwhelm humanity? Why does the event of interaction between God and humans after Christ necessarily involve confrontation?

An additional reason for the disjunction between Cyril and Barth results from Barth's rejection of metaphysical, substantialist views of ontology, which he reads through scholastic Protestantism and perceives to be static, dry, and unable to give full due to the dramatic event of Jesus Christ and the sheer eruption of God into human history. Barth moves to actualize his theological account and, christologically speaking, this means that his conception of what happens between divine and human in and then through Jesus Christ is focused on the level of willed activity and obedience. While act constitutes being for Barth, and any number of scholars are adamant that Barth does have an ontology of act and relationship, it nonetheless is an ontology based on an extrinsic relationship (given Barth's insistence on imputation).[11] Barth's rejection of infused grace and inherent righteousness, and his adherence to the Reformed Protestant conception of justification by grace through faith based solely in Christ's alien righteousness—which is imputed to us and changes our status before God but does not transform human nature

---

10. Neder, *Participation in Christ*, 79,

11. See Keith L. Johnson, *Karl Barth and the Analogia Entis* (London: T&T Clark, 2010), 182–190 for his discussion of the importance of this concept for Barth.

itself—makes it difficult for him to speak of an inward or intrinsic transformation of humanity in Christ.

Finally, Barth never really becomes comfortable with the language of "being" or with an analogical understanding of the way in which creaturely being's participation in God's being is possible without erasing the distinction between them. This discomfort with the analogy of being, of the language of being, leads Barth, like many modern theologians and philosophers, to assume that epistemology can somehow be separated from ontology. This false divide between human being and knowing leads to a pattern in Barth's thought in which simply the act of knowing, of enlightened cognition, is completely determinative and transformative of being. This assumption may in part contribute to Barth's primarily cognitive conception of human transformation in Christ. But right knowledge—even knowledge as action—is not always transformative. There are countless examples in human history, and our own lives, where right knowledge has not produced a transformation of being and doing. That is not to discount knowledge, but rather to say that questions of knowing and being and doing are inextricably intertwined and that the Holy Spirit works not simply in one of these arenas, but in all of them. What we know certainly informs who we are and what we do. But who we are influences what and how we know, just as what we do becomes part of our knowing. Barth's reliance on a primarily epistemological account of transformation causes him difficulties in conveying the full depth and breadth of human transformation in Christ through the power of the Spirit.

Christology

We turn first to Christology because Barth's theological conceptions turn so completely on his Christology within the covenant of election. While in his discussions he is thoroughly adamant about the single subjectivity of Christ, who is the divine Son living a completely human life, as he moves to discussions of exaltation versus deification, there are places beneath the surface where one wonders if he has truly grasped the complete significance of Cyril's insistence on the one person. For Cyril, while the two natures must be complete, unmixed, and unconfused, once the incarnation has created a union of the two in the one person of Christ, there is no need to keep talking about them separately, as if they are in competition with one another, or as if one is threatened to be impinged on or evacuated by the other. The divine and human are held in a mysteriously perfect union in distinction in which worries about safeguarding one or the other can be set at ease in the confidence of God's action in the incarnation. In this confidence, every divine and human word and action of Jesus Christ is predicated of the one person and it is that one person who becomes the focus of all christological conversation.

However, Barth focuses in on an extensive discussion of the two natures that in places leaves one in doubt that he has escaped a somewhat competitive conception of the two natures after all. This may be in part because he follows the Reformed tradition in its emphasis on keeping in sight the two natures' distinction from one another, and also in large measure because he follows his own Kantian-based insistence on keeping divine and human utterly separate. Some would no doubt disagree here, arguing that Barth's conception of the humanity and divinity of Jesus is that of a harmonious relationship, which is true in his sections on Christology proper.[12] However, his way of bringing the human and divine into relationship in Christ also leads to some difficulties. Because Barth

12. See for example Kenneth Oakes' discussion, "The Question of Nature and Grace in Karl Barth: Humanity as Creature and as Covenant-Partner," *Modern Theology*, 24: 4 (October 2007): 608–609.

reacts so strongly to the concept of "being" as static, and instead focuses on the total actualization and event of Jesus' life, he is in danger of creating a false divide between being and act, and between being and knowing that focuses on extrinsic knowledge and relatedness while neglecting intrinsic dimensions. God's act and being are one, and while Barth would certainly affirm that on one level, he nonetheless tries to create an ontology of relationship based on will and act and, if Jones is correct in his assessment, this is the way Barth ultimately relates the divine and human in Jesus.

As both subject and object of election, Jesus as the divine Son chooses himself for election, and Jesus as the fully human one accepts that election and then actively enacts it. Of course, there's nothing intrinsically problematic about affirming Jesus' human active agency—that is certainly to be applauded. And such a concept is certainly not foreign to Cyrillian Christology. Cyril also viewed Jesus as both giver and active recipient of salvation. However, in making the necessary affirmation of two wills and both divine and human agential activity in Jesus, if one is not careful to keep the single subjectivity of Christ in view and in the foreground, and to attend to both the extrinsic and intrinsic dimensions of the union, one walks a knife edge toward Nestorianism. And given Barth's insistence on keeping divine and human separate for fear that one or the other will impinge on or evacuate the other, the danger is heightened. While Paul Jones's reading that Jesus' humanity in some way "constitutes" God may be an overstatement of Barth's position, certainly the nuance is there in Barth's expositions of the Son's humanity choosing election.[13] In other words, does the concept

---

13. Jones actually sees this move of Barth's as expressing a radicalizing of Cyril's conceptions in that "the union of the Son with the man Jesus is pressed back into the divine life" and Jones argues that this actually strengthens Barth's description of human agency in Christ. (129) Jones also argues that for Barth, Cyril, and Nestorius provide complementary views of the incarnation—one attending to Christ's personal simplicity and the other attending to the moral

of "choice" imply a separate, second subject—the Son of Man, Jesus' humanity—who actively chooses to accept the election chosen by the divine Son of God? Jones's reading certainly heightens this tendency beyond what Barth intends, but nonetheless the nuance is troubling. Not only is the concept of choice within God problematic, but in setting up his incarnational thought in such a fashion, Barth then must work to keep divine and human separate—even in the union—in order for the humanity to effect this choice to be elected. So Barth continually strives to protect the humanity in Jesus from becoming infused or enhanced with any divine grace in order to preserve this as a purely human choice. Because Barth seems unable to conceive of a divine grace that would enhance but not evacuate or overrule humanity, he struggles with the need to keep human and divine separate even in the one person—despite his sincere conviction in the single subject of the incarnation.

Barth certainly does *not* have a purely Nestorian Christology, but he does struggle with the same hesitancy about allowing divine and human into close contact with one another, the same propensity toward an extrinsic pattern of relation between divine and human at the level of will and action.[14] This is both because his doctrine of election calls for Jesus to be both subject and object of election, in which his actions as both subject and object must be kept separate,

union in which divine and human act "conjunctively." See Paul Dafydd Jones, *The Humanity of Christ: Christology in Karl Barth's Church Dogmatics* (London: T&T Clark, 2008), 143–147, especially 144. Of course, as we've explored in chapter 2, Cyril and Nestorius do not provide complimentary patterns of Christology. There are paradigmatically different and one does not arrive at a single-subject Christology following Nestorius' pattern of thought.

14. Neder disagrees here, arguing that Barth is really avoiding Pelagian tendencies to believe that humans cooperate in their own salvation. "The question is not so much a comparison of whether Barth's Christology is more like that of Cyril or of Nestorius. It is rather a referendum on the theology of Pelagius and its variants." *Participation in Christ,* 72. I think Barth is certainly resistant to Pelagian conceptions regarding any inherent human goodness or action, but Barth also exhibits a consistent thought pattern in which there is a hesitancy to bring human and divine too closely together for fear that one will overwhelm or evacuate the other. While *not* Nestorian, Barth does share a similar reserve to the one that motivated Nestorius.

and also because, overall, Barth's primary way of envisioning the relationship between divine and human—outside the specific instance of the incarnation—is one of antithesis. These patterns, particularly within a dialectical structure of thought, inhibit his ability to fully explicate the outcome of a single-subject Christology for all of humanity.

While Barth may have developed a stronger analogical understanding throughout his career, he also never abandoned dialectics as a way of enforcing his consistent theme of the absolute antithesis between God and humanity. This insistence on such a strong antithesis makes it difficult for him to truly move through the implications of Christ's total union of divine and human. This does not occur in his formal discussions of the hypostatic union per se, but rather seems to lurk beneath the surface when he moves to conceptions about the effect of the incarnation on the rest of creation. While some argue that Barth moved in a more analogical direction in his thinking, others maintain that he remained a dialectical theologian all his life. The issue is complicated by the reality that in both analogy and dialectic there is a treatment of the dissimilar and the similar. In analogical patterns, the stress is on seeing the similarity within an always-greater dissimilarity. In dialectics, the stress is on seeing each of the points of comparison in opposition to one another. In Barth, they sometimes seem to operate within a hair's distance of one another. So untangling his use of analogy and dialectics in something as complex as the hypostatic union is no easy task. However, it seems clear that dialectic is not just a stylistic device for Barth—it expresses his abiding goal of keeping divinity and humanity not just distinct but in confrontation. Barth's conceptual framework of a dialectical confrontation between divine and human at times threatens to become a larger category than his conception of the hypostatic union. The suggestion that we truly see only the veil of Jesus' humanity, and that the humanity—or vehicle of revelation—while hypostatically united to the divine, is not itself God, seems dangerously close to maintaining the kind of distinction the church found so problematic in Nestorius. Despite his strong development of the single subjectivity of Christ, beneath the surface seems to run his strong dialectical, antithetical understanding of the relationship between God and creation, and a framework of competitive relationship, in which either humanity or divinity might dominate or evacuate the other if the antithesis or contradiction is not constantly enforced.

Related to this issue, Barth's efforts to focus on extrinsic action as that which constitutes being creates nuances in his Christology that are troubling. We've seen Barth's strong reliance on the exchange in which God comes to humans so that humans might come to God. And we've seen his insistence on seeing this event as taking place in the one person of Christ, which necessitates a strong single-subject Christology. However, Barth undermines this focus by spending so much time talking about the divine and human essences and activities of Christ—particularly the lengths he goes to in order to preserve Christ's human agency, as if it is in danger within the incarnational union. Despite Barth's intentions to strongly affirm only one active subject, if we are to speak of the relationship between Christ's humanity and divinity primarily, or only, at the level of will and obedient action, and if we are to preserve his human agency as something that works cooperatively and in complete harmony with the divine agency—while at the same time denying any enhancement of that humanity that would enable such cooperation—then it becomes more and more difficult to avoid undercurrents of two subjects. In addition, it is interesting that in his christological framework Barth relies on a strongly synergistic conception of the way in which divine and human agency operate in Christ, but then completely rejects any hint of synergism between God and humanity in and after Christ in the power of the Spirit. Barth consistently struggles to extend what happens in and through Christ to the rest of humanity in the present moment.

While Barth strongly argues that in Christ, and only in Christ, there is no dialectic or antithesis, somehow he cannot seem to extend the effects of the reconciliation—in which the division between humanity and God is overcome—to any kind of substantial change for human nature itself. One can see this in Barth's rejection of any "enhancement" of Jesus' humanity. Because Barth refuses to admit any infused power and grace for Jesus' humanity, believing this would rob it of its complete humanness and either transmute it or evacuate it, he has trouble accounting for the way in which Jesus is both the same and yet different from us. He turns to a conception of the union of the divine and human in Jesus at the level of will and obedience, but it is not completely clear how Jesus is able to act completely and obediently with God's will. If his humanity is in no way different than ours, then that would imply that we too are able to be so obedient. But would that not then imply an inherent capacity in human beings to be in harmony with God's will and intention? In which case, Jesus is only different in degree in that he realizes this capacity more fully than we do. Is this not exactly what Barth seeks to avoid?

Barth rejects an affirmation of Cyril's concept that Jesus' humanity is completely and fully like ours and yet also different because, in the incarnational union of divine and human, his humanity is infused with a unique grace and power that render his humanity true and complete in a way that ours is inherently not. But it is precisely this Cyrillian insight that preserves Jesus' uniqueness as the one person who is both fully divine and fully human and, *in his person*, takes on all that separates humanity from God and overcomes it, thereby re-creating humanity itself. How does Cyril's affirmation of the unique enhancement of Christ's humanity, in which divine grace perfects and elevates human nature in his one person and makes possible the extension of this gift to all of humanity, undermine the integrity and fullness of human nature? This is of particular importance since Barth affirms the sinfulness of human nature that keeps us sinners, even in the midst of our reconciliation with God. Why is there so much concern to preserve that human nature and to leave it untouched by the incarnational union of divine and human? Barth seems to believe that otherwise humanity would be somehow evacuated by divinity, rather than seeing the possibility that human nature could be made different or better, while still remaining *human* nature. While his strong dialectic between humanity and divinity helps him preserve the real distinction between God and creature, it does seem to make it difficult for him to conceive of the human as being able to participate in the divine without one or the other being compromised.

Here Cyril's confidence and caution are helpful. While humanity is certainly full and active in Jesus, we must keep our sights fully on the one person who is the divine Son in his mode of existence as a fully human being: the one who both gives and receives salvation that draws us into his life, death, and resurrection. God is not threatened by this act—nor is humanity. God is capable of, and indeed has achieved, the bringing together of divine and human in Christ without impinging upon or evacuating either. God is capable of bringing together, surely and completely, that which cannot be united any other way. And when God does this in the incarnation, it changes everything.

Grace and Nature

We also see throughout this discussion the way in which Barth's conception of the relationship between nature and grace continues to come into play. Cyril and Barth simply have different views of the relationship between nature and grace and the effect of sin upon that relationship. For Cyril, sin perverts and distorts God's intention for humanity and results in death and broken relationship with God, but it does not completely destroy humans' ability to receive God's grace. In the incarnation, the power and grace of God unite with humanity in the one person of Christ, healing and transforming humanity from the inside out. Grace heals, perfects, and elevates a nature that was, from the beginning, a gift of grace from God. Barth's view of sin lends a more complicated dynamic to his thought. On the one hand, sin so destroys and perverts humanity that there is no inherent capacity to see and know God that remains. The *analogia fidei* asserts that any ability to know God or to receive God's grace is completely a gift of grace from outside human being. Humans have become "radically and totally evil, without qualification" for Barth.[15] Yet God does not allow sin to be the primary determining factor of humanity—election is, and through that election, Jesus' humanity is what defines human being. So on the one hand, Barth asserts that humanity is now defined by election in Christ and that through the cross and resurrection, grace has not perfected created nature—it has killed and overruled it. The relationship between humanity and God is one of miracle and resurrection. Nonetheless, sin still exerts a pull

---

15. See Barth's discussions throughout the *Church Dogmatics*, especially in *Church Dogmatics, Vol. 3.2, The Doctrine of Creation*, ed. G. W. Bromiley and T. F. Torrance, trans. J. W. Edwards, O. Bussey, and Harold Knight (Edinburgh: T&T Clark, 1960); however, this theme remains even in his mature work in *Church Dogmatics, Vol. 4.1: The Doctrine of Reconciliation*, ed. G. W. Bromiley and T. F. Torrance, trans. G. W. Bromiley (Edinburgh: T&T Clark, 1956); see his discussion of the "Fall of Man" in 478–513, this quote 500.

on humanity in the here and now, as humans remain simultaneously sinners and those justified by Christ.

Given Barth's strong conception of the overruling of sin through the miracle of resurrection, one might expect a highly transformational account of human life as a response to this miracle. One might expect this strong affirmation of a complete killing of sin and overruling of sinful human nature to result in an even stronger sense of rebirth for humanity and a stronger confidence in human response. And there are places where Barth's theology of human response shines brightly. As Stanley Hauerwas notes, despite the confusion and apparent nothingness brought about by sin, Barth assures us that there are still evidences of the goodness of God to be seen in creation through things as simple as the laughter of children, the beauty of nature, and the work of poets and musicians. Christian lives bear witness to God's promises and gift in Christ. Against a notion that humans live in a universe governed by fate, Barth insists that, as Hauerwas puts it, "Christian hope is not 'just a virtue' but a metaphysical draft of the universe that denies we are creatures subject to a closed causal system."[16] It is the language of faith, with which theology begins, that instructs and helps develop the moral and intellectual virtues necessary for a proper understanding of God, and those skills are necessary if we are to become faithful witnesses to God amid the violence and moral fragmentation of the current culture.[17]

Yet Barth's affirmation of this human response always has a provisional quality to it. On the one hand, he is adamant that

---

16. Stanley Hauerwas, *With the Grain of the Universe: The Church's Witness and Natural Theology* (Grand Rapids: Brazos, 2001), 187, footnote 30.

17. Hauerwas, *With the Grain of the Universe*, 174–176. For Barth, metaphysics is not epistemology but a mode of speech in which we become part of that about which we speak—Jesus. (189, citing Robert Jensen, footnote 34.) Yet for Hauerwas, Barth's theology of the church and the Holy Spirit's agency is open for further development because, he argues, Barth does not adequately account for "how the church is necessary for our knowledge of the world" (192) and for training Christians to live lives of faithful witness. See 192–193.

reconciliation has occurred as an objective fact in Jesus Christ's death and resurrection. Given his assertion of the sheer miracle that God has performed to actually kill and overcome sin and death in Christ's own person and his certainty that knowing this produces an ontologically new reality, one might expect Barth's account of human life in Christ to reflect such a miraculous transformation. But, here Barth draws back and instead places hedges around the ability of humans to truly manifest that miracle of Christ in their lives here and now. We have explored the ways in which Barth's conception of the Holy Spirit plays a role in this hedging, and also the ways in which his reaction to the events of the World Wars so deeply influenced his need to keep humanity and divinity separate from one another. In addition, several scholars, Johnson among them, have argued that Barth was deeply influenced by Martin Luther's assertion that humans are always simultaneously sinners and justified, that they cannot escape their sinfulness or propensities to sin this side of the *eschaton*. Barth clearly wants to prevent humanity from suffering under the misapprehension that their activities become "divine," and he is constantly on the alert for any theological conception he thinks provides warrant for that belief or activity. This leads him to reject any hint of an analogy of participation in God's being and life that posit a real human capacity to see or respond—even this response is miracle.

But here is the crux of the issue—if it is miracle and it truly has occurred solely because of God's gracious activity in Jesus Christ, does that not call for an even stronger sense of participation in God's life precisely *because* God has intervened so powerfully and miraculously. Is this not the power of the resurrection? Surely, God fully and completely achieves what God intends in this miraculous event. Why can Barth not allow the possibility of that miracle being more fully and completely lived out in human life, here and now?

Despite protestations to the contrary, does Barth really believe the power of sin has more hold over current human life than does the miraculous event of the incarnation or the resurrection?[18] Here we see that redemption is an eschatological concept for Barth that is promised but yet to come. Human life in the here and now remains always and only a provisional response, as humans remain sinners even in the midst of their real change of status and relationship with God in Christ's atonement and resurrection. The power of that event really is delayed until the *eschaton*, with only a shaft of light penetrating the yet prevailing shadows of a world still caught in the power of sin. Ultimately, in Barth that vision only shimmers on the horizon of a future *eschaton*. Humanity in the present tense lives in the paradox of still being caught up in a sin that has already been defeated.

Given that understanding, Barth offers us a vision of human life and fellowship with God that operates primarily at the level of cognition, will, and obedience, and while he talks of conversion by the Holy Spirit, he is much more reticent to talk about any transformation of inward being. However, his approach raises the question about how human being, human knowing and human action are related. For Barth, we are what we know and do. But are we only what we know and do?[19] Further, if Barth is insistent

18. Neder notes that Barth extends Luther's "simultaneously justified and sinner" to "simultaneously holy and sinner." Humans remain sinful in themselves and holy only in Christ. Yet Neder also argues that "This is an extreme and unnecessary assertion, one that ultimately cuts against Barth's affirmation of de facto [subjective] participation in Christ." If Barth is genuinely concerned to offer a real participation in Christ, then Neder says, this "should have led Barth to conclude that as this event takes place, there is nothing left to say about such people than that they are holy." *Participation in Christ*, 85. Clearly, I agree.

19. Keith Johnson argues that for Barth, being is constituted as the free decision to act in correspondence to Jesus' actions in faith and obedience. Human "nature" as such does not exist because the only "true human nature" is Jesus' humanity. We only exist in relationship to our election in him and this existence is at the level of act through obedience as our actions correspond to his. See Johnson, *Karl Barth and the Analogia Entis*, 209–211. Again, we see Barth's insistence on defining being as correspondence of act, and again we see the difficulties

on defining humanity in terms of action, in affirming our fallen and sinful nature, and then refusing any transformation or elevation of it, how does that nature then *act* in different ways after Christ's death and resurrection? In other words, Barth does a masterful job of describing the external effects of Christ's salvific event, but he is distinctly uncomfortable about discussing any inward change that goes hand in hand with an ability to actually be, know, and act in new and different ways—including the ways in which the power of the sacraments and the practices of the church enable those new practices. If we remain the same at the level of being, what changes us and enables us truly to act in new ways? What would account for that changed ability to be obedient? Certainly, we have the model of Christ and the witness of the Holy Spirit that gives us new knowledge, but where is the power of transformation that can overcome the power of sin in both our being and our doing?

Barth draws up short of the radical affirmation that his own soteriology demands. If Christ is both subject and object, both giver and recipient of election and salvation, if divine and human come into completely harmonious relationship in this one person, then surely something radical happens here. Why can that not be extended to humanity without either evacuating humanity or impinging on God's divine sovereignty? God is surely capable of extending such a miraculous participation. If sin and death are truly killed and overcome in the miracle of the cross and resurrection, then why shy

---

this raises for his conception of the intrinsic dimensions of the union. Johnson argues that Barth develops an analogy of relationship rather than an analogy of being, but the relationship between divine and human is defined solely by extrinsic action. (214–218). However humans are not solely and completely what they *do*. Johnson's exposition also raises another interesting question: if there is no human nature *qua* nature and everything is defined solely by Jesus' human nature, then why would it matter to Barth if that human nature might be "enhanced?" If everything is defined by Jesus' humanity, then there is no human nature in itself to protect or to worry about evacuating by the divine, which is Barth's argument against deification. Barth's worries about deification seem to be based on arguments of "essence" or intrinsic being, which he elsewhere denies have validity for defining being. See Johnson, 209–218.

away from the conviction that humanity is recreated as part of being given a new identity and a new future in which we are set on our feet and freed to live as God's covenant partners? Is overruling and killing sinful human nature not also an evacuation of it? How is that any less an abrogation of created nature than its elevation and perfection?

Because we are always both sinners and justified, for Barth we can never trust our own response. The event of Christ's life, death, and resurrection has changed our status before God but has left us fundamentally unchanged this side of the *eschaton*. At its root, is there not a danger here of ascribing more power to sin than to God's grace actually working in human being? If one can trust the God revealed in Jesus Christ, who Barth assures us goes to unimaginable lengths to save us and restore us to fellowship, why can we not trust that same God to be at work in us to heal and restore human nature and empower us to live in new ways? Certainly, humans have had, and continue to have, the ability and freedom to rebel against or misuse that freedom. Humanity can and does believe and act as if all that is necessary already lies within us as an inherent capacity of our nature with no thanks to God and no humility in our use of God's gifts. One can sympathize with Barth's caution. But does seeing ourselves as simultaneously sinners and justified—with the power of sin still holding sway over us and with limited and provisional capacities to respond to God's grace—move us any further in the desired direction? Can not false humility or a cynicism with regard to our ability to actually live new lives do just as much damage as arrogance and a falsely inflated sense of our own capacities? Can we live into a new life in Christ if underneath it all we do not believe it is actually possible?

Here is the real difference between Cyril's and Barth's view of the union of divine and human and the participation in God's life that results from the incarnational union between divine and human.

For Cyril, the humanity is infused with divine power and becomes, not divine, but more fully and truly human as sin is healed, death is destroyed, and humans undergo an ontological transformation as they participate in Christ's life-giving person. They are then empowered to live in morally transformed ways, continually undergirded by the sacraments and the practices of the church. For Cyril, there is no competitive relationship between divine and human, or between ontological transformation and moral obedience. The humanity of Jesus is never diminished or evacuated by its infusion of power from the divine but is rather brought to perfection and completion. There is no moral obedience without transformation at the level of being and there is no ontological transformation without holiness of life. However, for Barth, outside the incarnation divine and human are always in confrontation and the harmony of divine and human in the incarnation is not extended to all of humanity. It's interesting that Barth develops an incredibly strong covenant of election in which he affirms that God determines to be God in fellowship with humans and that humans are created to be this partner—even to the extent of making this decision potentially constitutive of God's being—and yet he refuses any hint of change for human being itself. God's being is affected by the decision of election and the incarnation, but human being remains ever as it is.[20]

Barth does posit an ontological change in human being as a result of the change in the status of relationship with God through the reconciliation achieved in Christ. But his insistence on defining "being" almost solely in terms of act, manifest in knowledge, will, and obedience, raises interesting questions about how this change is actually brought about. Barth insistently denies any place to

20. Again Neder notes, "Among other things, Barth's otherwise successful counter to the Roman Catholic charge that justification is a legal fiction is undermined to the extent that he casts doubt on the reality of the transformation of the believer that takes place in de facto [subjective] participation." *Participation in Christ*, 86.

regenerated capacities or infused grace or habits. As we've seen, this rejection has its impetus in Barth's fear of a "high-pitched anthropology" and a justified horror that humans can come to believe they can "lay hands on God." Barth steadfastly denies that the grace of Christ and the empowerment of the Holy Spirit are ever anything other than a pure, supernatural gift that is completely extrinsic to human being. This view, coupled with his collapse of Roman Catholic understandings of infused grace into the trajectory of "pure nature"—which is not a uniformly held conception in that tradition—leads Barth to reject the concept of infused grace's long and legitimate history in Christian thought up to and through the Reformation. The indwelling of the Holy Spirit, the infusion of divine power and grace, and the inward transformation of human being through grace are not human "possessions," they are not a product of human progress or a capacity inherent in a humanity that is abstracted from its original giftedness by the supernatural grace of God. Yet Barth's fear of the misappropriation of infused grace, and all attempts that might try to lay hands on God, make him too hesitant to grasp the gift that is offered.

Because of Barth's fear that somehow humanity will be conceived as "divine" and that the distinction between human and divine will either be blurred or collapsed, he maintains a strong antithesis and confrontational quality to the relationship between humanity and divinity. But this fails to adequately attend to a fully developed soteriology that accounts for more than simply a change in human cognition and status before God and instead moves toward a realization of the power of Christ to truly transform humanity in the process of restoring relationship with God. Barth loses the fullest sense of the two-fold, dynamic participation one sees in Cyril, a participation that envisions an ontological change in humanity, while still retaining the full distinction between divine and human, and progress in moral life and Christian living through which that change is developed and evidenced.

On the positive side, Barth has grasped and articulated well Cyril of Alexandria's crucial insight about the single subjectivity of Christ: the Word, the second person of the Trinity, becomes human and all that Christ does as a human is done by the Word. Yet, while Barth's Christology is often characterized, and sometimes criticized, for being highly Alexandrian, he fails to follow through on Cyril's soteriological insights. In some ways, Barth is more reminiscent of the Antiochenes with their zealous concern to keep divine and human from impinging on each other. If Barth were to completely follow through on his work with Cyril's single subjectivity, he would also have to confront the reasons for Cyril's passionate insistence on this concept—and one of those key reasons was his insistence on the transformation of humanity. Both divinity and humanity are united in the incarnation without either being diminished, but the Logos infuses the humanity with the glory and power of his own divinity.[21] While Barth speaks eloquently of Jesus' exalted humanity, his refusal of all concepts of an "infused grace" also seem to make it difficult for him to grasp Cyril's concept that, in his one person, Jesus truly transforms human being itself and extends that transformation to all humanity. For Cyril, Jesus restores the divine image and likeness in humanity, not simply by remaking nature or destroying authentic humanness, but rather by reappropriating the divine life through the indwelling of the Holy Spirit. Jesus provides a stable grounding for the Holy Spirit in humanity that cannot be lost as it could be and was with Adam. It is this indwelling that makes possible an ongoing

---

21. Cyril argues: ". . . he made his own the flesh which is capable of death so that by means of this which is accustomed to suffer he could assume sufferings for us and because of us, and so liberate us from death and corruption by making his own body alive as God." *Explanations of the Twelve Chapters*, in John McGuckin, *Saint Cyril and the Christological Controversy: It's History, Theology, and Texts* (Crestwood, N.Y.: St. Vladimir's Seminary Press, 2004), 292–293.

transformation of humanity. The one person of Christ becomes *the* place for all human participation in God.

Cyril's conception sees participation both as God's initiative—as pure gift—and as our response to and cooperation with that divine grace. Nature and grace, divine and human are truly united but remain distinct from one another. Cyril has something to offer to Barth regarding the ways in which the fullness of salvation is lived out in creation. As a result of the union of divine and human in Christ, humanity can now truly transcend its original condition and become a new creation. It is the logic of the incarnation.

Balthasar

In Balthasar, we have seen themes that resonate strongly with Cyril's christological and soteriological convictions. Indeed, Balthasar's theology explores the radical dimensions of single-subject Christology and the wondrous exchange through this one person who redeems humankind and draws humanity into the life of God. Balthasar's analogical framework, his christological analogy of being, strongly shapes his understanding of human participation in the divine life. He appropriates well the christological understandings of Cyril regarding the one person of Christ, and he extends the thought of Maximus the Confessor regarding the two wills of Christ into an understanding of the identity of Jesus' person and mission. Through the transforming event of Jesus' death, resurrection, and ascension, a way is opened for humans to participate in Jesus' mission within the Trinitarian life. Jesus becomes the space for humans to respond to and participate in the divine life. Further, echoing Cyril, this participation must be both an ontological participation and a cognitive and moral participation. In the encounter of God and humans in this one person, and through Jesus' life, death, and resurrection, a real transformation occurs for humans that then enables and empowers human response and obedience.

Yet, we have also identified areas of potential difficulty and concern arising from Balthasar's stretching of his deeply analogical understanding of single-subject Christology and the wondrous exchange. Balthasar extends Cyril's conceptions, testing their heights and depths, but in doing so does he go too far? We have seen questions raised about whether his understanding of grace and nature evacuates human nature of any real content. We have seen questions raised about whether Balthasar's predication of suffering to the divine Son takes place in his economic mode of existence, or whether Balthasar steps over a traditional boundary and predicates suffering of the divine Son in his immanent Trinitarian life. Further, Balthasar's affirmation of receptivity as a perfection of God, a perfection that allows God to receive redeemed creatures into the Trinitarian life as an actual, though non-necessary, enrichment in God's own life causes a good deal of uneasiness and threatens to blur the necessary distinction between divine and human that Barth was so careful to preserve. Because Balthasar's christologically centered analogy of being dominates his theology, we will begin our evaluation by briefly revisiting the strength of that conception before turning to its more potentially problematic uses.

Christological Analogy

Balthasar's analogical framework for the relationship between nature and grace, between divine and human, is given its impetus from the incarnation. Because God has joined humanity and divinity in the union of the one person of Christ, clearly God can do this, and this act tells us something about the created structure of the world. God truly does reveal God's self in and through creaturely reality—foremost in the incarnation, but through the incarnation God also reveals something about the way God relates to all creaturely reality. There is not a competitive relationship between God and humanity. Certainly there is a real divide and sin has serious consequences, but God and creatures can be in relationship without competing for "space" because God, as harmonious Trinitarian relationship within God's own life, has already graciously created space for what is completely other than God, without evacuating it of content or blurring the distinction between Creator and created.

Because God freely makes space for that which is other than God, creation or nature is always already in a participatory relationship with God, and supernatural grace irradiates and transforms creation without in any way impinging on its creaturely status—it remains created nature. Through this analogical and non-competitive structure of thought, Balthasar argues that the hypostatic union does not either supersede or suspend the differences between divine and human. Rather, the union renders these differences perfect in their respective natures. As Nicholas Healy and David Schindler have noted, for Balthasar "on the one hand, the two natures are genuinely unified in a single hypostasis, such that they can no longer be rightly conceived as merely external, or juxtaposed, to one another. On the other hand, the two natures remain genuinely distinct, but only from within their intrinsic relation—union—with one another."[22]

It is precisely because Balthasar has such a strong analogical conception of this union and the single subject of Christ that he develops a treatment of the wondrous exchange that strikes some as too extreme. First, we have seen that Balthasar takes utterly seriously the ancient maxim that what is not assumed is not redeemed. For

22. Nicholas Healy and David Schindler, "For the life of the world: Hans Urs von Balthasar on the Church as Eucharist," in *The Cambridge Companion to Hans Urs von Balthasar*, ed. Edward T. Oakes and David Moss (Cambridge: Cambridge University Press, 2004), 61.

him, that means that Christ must take on all of what it means to be human, which means he must not only experience sin and its most dire consequences, but actually take them into himself. Christ assumes the very deepest dregs of all that alienates humanity from God, with all the alienation and suffering that entails—even to the depths of hell. Here, Balthasar tells us, in the one person of Christ, *all* that separates humanity from the love of God is taken into the person of Jesus Christ and overcome. We have seen Alyssa Pitstick, among others, take Balthasar to task for these conceptions, arguing that he transgresses acceptable boundaries and predicates suffering of the divine Son himself in his immanent life by failing to explicitly limit suffering to only the human nature of Christ.

But how one reads Balthasar here is influenced in large measure by which lens—the single person in the union or the distinction between the two natures—is the primary focal point for looking at the pattern of salvation and redemption. In many ways, the issue is reminiscent of the debate between Cyril and Nestorius, in which Nestorius was simply horrified that Cyril spoke of Christ as suffering and dying on the cross—of saying that the Impassible suffers—without constantly clarifying that it is only the humanity to which he refers. Cyril, while acknowledging the distinction and affirming God's divine impassibility, nonetheless argues that once the union has occurred in the incarnation, to continue dividing up what Jesus does between divine and human undermines the very union God has freely entered into and thus undermines the salvific work Christ has undertaken. Balthasar's theology moves from a similar conviction.

However, the question remains: does Balthasar predicate suffering of the divine Son in his immanent life? Here Balthasar is often mistaken for edging over the abyss into process theology with its positing of creation as necessary to God's own fulfillment. Some are troubled about his Trinitarian and christological conceptions in that they allow for creation to in some way "affect" God or to be received by God into God's inner life. Do we here see Barth's worries about the *analogia entis* given full flower? Does Balthasar push the possible danger of the analogy of being to its daring edge and in doing so transgress the boundaries Barth was so adamant in maintaining?

Balthasar's extension of receptivity into God's immanent life makes not a few scholars uneasy. Does this then imply that Balthasar has crossed a line that Cyril was adamant in drawing—the line of impassibility? Certainly, some scholars argue that this is the case. Such conceptions make uneasy those who want to confine any notion of passibility exclusively to the human nature of Christ in the incarnation. Perhaps Thomas Weinandy's concerns about Balthasar are a good illustration of these misgivings. Weinandy worries that Balthasar's allowance of a kind of internal mutability within God violates the immutability of God, thus undermining the saving power of Christ's salvific work and capitulating to a modern failure to distinguish between love and suffering. Suffering becomes a *necessary* aspect of love rather than merely a *possibility* because of the consequences of sin, thus the idea of any kind of suffering in the life of God is problematic.[23] Rather, Weinandy argues, if one understands the traditional conception of impassibility, the "benefits" of a passible God simply disappear. As Weinandy notes, *in the incarnation*, "the person of the Son of God is truly born, grieves, suffers, and dies, not as God, but as man for that is now the new manner in which the Son of God actually exists."[24] To posit suffering in God's self is a failure to acknowledge that it is the divine Son of God, in his existence as a human being, who truly experiences authentic, genuine human suffering.[25]

---

23. Thomas Weinandy, *Does God Suffer?* (Notre Dame: University of Notre Dame Press, 2000). See 152–168, especially 160.
24. Weinandy, *Does God Suffer?* 200.

Does Balthasar cross the line Weinandy highlights and thereby threaten God's impassibility? The answer is not a simple yes or no. Balthasar does argue that the event of the incarnation, and all that has been assumed by the Son in his incarnate union with humanity, does become part of the divine life. This event that God has freely entered into does "affect" God. But this effect is never necessary. It never completes anything lacking in God and it does not "change" God in the sense that God now becomes other than who God has always been. Rather, Balthasar argues, God has always, out of the complete fullness of God's inner Trinitarian relations, made room for that which is different and other. This is who God is as the being who loves. That which the Son assumes in the economy has always already been given a space in the life of God. The Son's assumption of humanity, with both the joys and the suffering, the life and the death, the sin and its overcoming, is incorporated in a real way into God's life, but without fundamentally changing God in God's self. Balthasar does walk a dangerous edge here, and he may even take a step off with one foot, but within the whole corpus of his work, he does retain the vital distinction between the immanent and the economic Trinity—yet that distinction is more permeable that some would want to allow.

However, Balthasar would argue that the traditional conceptions of God's immutability and impassibility are not big enough. If we take seriously the one person, then all predicates—including suffering and death—can properly be said of Christ. However, the concern is to what extent and to what effect Balthasar posits this suffering. Does he cross the classical and crucial distinction between the divine Son in the economy and the divine Son in his immanent Trinitarian life? In the end, Balthasar's position simply refuses the polarity between

---

25. Weinandy, *Does God Suffer?* 200–201.

absolute immutability and absolute mutability. On the one hand, he adamantly insists that God experiences no creaturely suffering and that creation is not necessary for God. He lifts up Christ's redeeming power with a full accounting both of Christ's divinity and humanity. But Balthasar does this by arguing that creaturely suffering and violence are not a threat to God, but rather that these creaturely consequences of the sinful refusal of love have already been overcome and reconciled by the ever-greater, super-event of God's love. Balthasar's insistence on reading the incarnation as a pattern of the Trinitarian life moves him to allow for a carefully qualified and non-necessary mutability within the life of God itself. While Balthasar roundly criticizes and nicely deconstructs any notion of process theology's positing of creaturely suffering in God, he also wants to take seriously the suffering and alienation on the cross—this too must be assumed if it is to be redeemed. He insists that the cross is a Trinitarian event that can accommodate and overcome the utmost in alienation without in any way succumbing to it. He does so not because he has assented to the modern notion of suffering, but because he wants to show that God, in God's self, has space even for the most extreme forms of refusal and alienation, and that these refusals are already always reconciled without violating the freedom of loving response and obedience. Further, because he pushes the wondrous exchange to include the uttermost depths of human experience and the heights of God's self-giving love, for Balthasar, Christ assumes the absolute furthest reaches of human alienation from God so that he can *overcome* them in his one person and open the way to life with God.

Balthasar is following through on what he sees as the logic of the incarnation. In this event, God has truly entered human history, has become a full human being, has lived, suffered, assumed the full depths of human sin and alienation from God through his death, and has been resurrected. In his ascension back to the Father, he does not leave that event or his incarnation behind. So while God has not changed in God's essence or being, nonetheless this event has "affected" God in the sense that it is the Incarnate Son who ascends to heaven. So God, in his Trinitarian life, mysteriously and freely draws what is other into God's life—not out of any lack, but precisely because God is always already so complete and full that this in no way threatens God but is rather welcomed by God. Balthasar has moved in the direction of a conception that allows for this movement, without, in his view, positing a change in God. This willingness to receive what is "other" is who God is as the being of love, and therefore God does not have to change in order to draw humanity—Jesus' humanity and by participatory extension ours—into the divine life.

Nature and Grace:
Analogical Participation

Having plumbed and assumed the depths of all that alienates humanity from God, Balthasar then scales the heights and tells us that, because every last bit of sin and suffering and even death itself have been assumed and redeemed in this one person, now a way has been opened into the very life of God through Christ's resurrection and ascension. Humans have been transformed both ontologically and morally through their participation in him. Humanity in Christ is now given a place in the Trinitarian life of God, which has eternally created space for what is other. In addition, Balthasar's conception of this human participation in God's life is enriched by his stress on reciprocity as a vital feature of analogy, combined with his distinctive view of receptivity as an active perfection of love rather than a merely passive lack. God's very being can be redefined to include receptivity, without endangering God's distinctiveness from creation or threatening God's wholly-otherness. In Balthasar's hands, receptivity becomes a divine perfection, an openness to the love and self-giving between the Trinitarian persons and, through the incarnation, is extended to include creation. Redeemed humanity now becomes properly repositioned in this space that God intends for it. But Balthasar does not stop there. He also assures us that creation becomes a non-necessary enrichment in the life of God.

But does such a conception blur the distinction between divine and human, and between grace and created nature in ways that are detrimental to both? We have already visited the issue of Balthasar's conception of divine impassibility and immutability in God. While Balthasar walks the edges of a daring line between divine and human, he would argue that God has already walked precisely that line in Jesus Christ, without blurring the distinction between divine and human and without evacuating either. We turn now to the effect of these affirmations on Balthasar's treatment of the relationship between grace and created nature and the way in which his conception of analogy flows from his understanding of the incarnation.

Balthasar reminds us that humans are created to receive God's grace, and creation is intended to be in a continual participatory relationship with its creator. There is no creaturely reality outside this relationship. It does not exist. Affirming that reality does not evacuate created nature of its content, rob it of its integrity, or make grace less gratuitous. Rather, creaturely reality—in its full creatureliness—is, moment-by-moment, first the recipient of and then the mediator of divine grace in the world. It's what human nature, at its deepest, most creaturely level, is designed to be. We know this and participate in it because of Jesus, who as the divine Son enters into union with the fullness of humanity, irradiates that humanity with power and grace, and enacts what it means to be fully and completely human in the world as God intends. The incarnation is the redemption, perfection, and fulfillment of creaturely reality in the one person of Jesus Christ, who draws all of humanity into that redemption, perfection, and fulfillment, and allows each person to truly inhabit his or her own humanity, to become a true person, and to enact that personhood in the world.

Balthasar's treatment of Jesus' humanity argues that the fullness of his humanity is not evacuated by union with the divine, nor are divine and human in an antithetical or competitive relationship. Rather, in a manner reminiscent of Cyril, Balthasar argues that the humanity comes to its true fullness and perfection *in* this harmonious union of divine and human. Grace perfects and elevates nature. Because Balthasar does not have a competitive conception of the relationship between God and creation, he has no difficulty with a concept in which the divine enters a union with humanity without becoming less divine and without threatening the integrity of created nature. Jesus' human nature perfectly is and does what created nature is designed to be and to do—actively receive and respond to God's grace. In fact, Balthasar's theology revolves around this conception of the incarnation, which orders the way in which divine goodness, truth, and beauty truly do show forth and irradiate the world—through the real creaturely realities of the world—without erasing those realities or evacuating them of their own content. This is what Steven A. Long misses in his analysis of Balthasar's treatment of created nature.

While Balthasar does consistently give priority to the supernatural, because this supernatural grace is precisely what creates, sustains, and redeems the created order, he draws definite distinctions between divinity and humanity. But these distinctions are drawn within an analogically participatory framework that does not place them in a competitive relationship with one another. Balthasar can make the argument that creation enriches the divine life because the conception of God's very being as love can be redefined to include receptivity, *without* endangering God's distinctiveness from creation or threatening God's wholly-otherness, and also *without* endangering the integrity of created nature. Creatures retain the freedom of their acting space and must say "yes" or "no" to God's love in Christ and freely live out their authentic roles. Yet this created freedom and acting space are always already embraced by the love of God. Even in the midst of humanity's rebellion, suffering, and violence, humans are already redeemed if they choose to accept God's gift. The dramatic tension between God and creatures remains and human response to God is open to the future, but Balthasar reminds us that there is indeed nothing outside God. There is nothing in our experience Jesus has not experienced. There is no place we can go that God in Christ has not already been and has not lovingly redeemed. This confidence in God's redemptive love and power secures Christ's ability to descend even to the depths of hell and alienation. There is space and love enough in God even—perhaps especially—for this. God in God's self is immense, loving, and lively enough to make genuine room for all that is not God without in any way being threatened by this otherness or overpowering it.

Further, given his conviction that love by its nature includes reciprocity, Balthasar is being consistent in applying this analogical framework to his conception of participation. His primary accent is always on God's descent to humankind in the incarnation. God participates in and takes on what is utterly dissimilar—humanity—in order to open a way for humans to participate in God's life. But this gracious gift of God also requires an active receptivity from humanity, and this activity of obedient participation in Christ's mission becomes a non-necessary enrichment in God's life. Love always makes room for response and a mutual reciprocity.

Because Balthasar's analogical understanding can hold grace and nature in a harmonious distinction and tension without dissolving the differences, he also does not see the concept of infused grace as one that creates the problems envisioned by Barth. Human nature can be infused with grace, which is always a gift and never owed to or possessed by the creature. This infusion does transform humanity. This transformation is not the evacuation of its authentic creatureliness, but rather the perfection and elevation of its true, intended nature. Because Balthasar believes that sin seriously damages and perverts, but does not completely destroy, any human capacity to receive grace or to respond to it, he can view the perfection of that nature in and through the humanity of Christ as one that redeems, frees, heals, and perfects created nature into what God truly intends. While salvation and atonement are an objective event for Balthasar, they also have subjective aspects that can begin to be realized here and now.

While Balthasar is often criticized for failing to develop extended treatments of moral or ethical topics, he consistently points to the lives of the saints as ample evidence that ontological and moral transformation of life is made possible by the event of Jesus Christ. Redemption, while it certainly has an eschatological telos, nonetheless is present and walking around in the world in the lives of those who, like Mary, say "yes" and open their lives to the reception of God and the discovery of their mission in Christ.[26] Further, because Balthasar envisions human moral life as one in which each

---

26. Contrast this to Barth's treatment of Mary, in which she is really simply a vessel used by the Spirit to bring about the incarnation in ways that assure the full humanity and full divinity of Jesus. Mary has no truly active role. See Karl Barth, *Church Dogmatics, Vol. 1.2, The Doctrine of the Word of God*, ed. G. W. Bromiley and T. F. Torrance, trans. G. T. Thomson and Harold Knight (London: T&T Clark, 1956), 136–146.

person becomes a true theological actor in Christ, people discover who they truly are and receive the ability to take the world stage to enact the unique part God has given them to play. Balthasar trusts that those roles will be enacted through the Spirit, within the supportive structures of the church, and with the continual empowerment of the sacraments. While there is an overall script, there is also a dynamic openness as the play unfolds. What each person's role will look like and the way in which his or her role will interact with the others on the stage is open to the ever-greater surprise of God's love and the movement of the Spirit among them. Given that perspective, Balthasar does not offer extensive prescribed developments of ethical issues, although that may have been helpful in developing a better and fuller understanding of the ways in which human response interacts with God in the mutual reciprocity that Balthasar envisions.

As we have seen, Balthasar is quite at home affirming the similarity within an always-greater dissimilarity between God and creatures. This conviction gives him a boldness and assurance in speaking of human participation in God's life. Like Cyril, he is drawn to the biblical image of vine and branches. There is a clear priority for the vine, but there is also a rich appreciation for the significant fruit that branches bear when attached to that vine. This is no merely eschatological vineyard either. While the final harvest awaits the future coming of the Lamb, there is real fruit to be grown and shared in the present as well. Human lives participate in Christ's mission within the divine life, both now and eternally.

Despite an underdevelopment of specific issues, one catches in Balthasar's work a confidence about the role and work of human beings in the world in the present age, as well as in the age to come. Redeemed and freed from sin and death, humans can now act as real human persons, empowered by the Spirit, and sustained by the practices of the church and the sacraments to cooperate with Christ's ongoing work in the world in an ongoing and ever greater participation in Christ.

While there may be differences between Cyril and Balthasar in the area of how human participation is received, if at all, in the inner life of God, Balthasar's approach does carry forward many of Cyril's key insights: the two-fold, ontological and spiritual or moral aspects of deification; the transformation of humanity into something more fully human; a dynamic conception of participation in which humans constantly grow into greater participation in Christ's mission now, while awaiting the future fullness of life with God; and a harmoniously conceived relationship between nature and grace. Cyril may provide a helpful check against some of Balthasar's more speculative tendencies that, if read without care, can be conceived as transgressing the boundaries between human and divine. Cyril provides a reminder that such conversations rightly belong within the boundaries of the incarnation in the economy of salvation, and that this is a Christic space large enough for every kind of vital human participation in God's life.

However, read carefully with an eye to the intricate nuances of his thought, Balthasar's ideas can be seen as an extension of Cyril's understanding of single-subject Christology, the wondrous exchange, and the transformation of human life through participation in God's life. Additionally, Balthasar may be seen as extending Cyril's conception of the receptivity of humanity to God's divine grace. While both stress this receptivity of humanity, Balthasar also works with an analogical pattern of reciprocity to argue that human receptivity is a reflection of receptivity in the divine inner life of God—not as a lack but as a perfection, as simply a quality of the way self-giving love is given and received. Working from that premise, Balthasar has no difficulty with seeing creation as an enrichment in

God's life, not in the sense of adding something that God needs or is lacking, but as the fullness of love and grace received and offered back in thanksgiving.

Conclusion

We live in an era in which people search for meaning and a secure anchor in a world that is buffeted by the currents of the false hope of an Enlightenment-bequeathed humanism and the cynical nihilism that deconstructs hope but offers nothing in its place. In such a world, Christianity is faced with the urgent need to recover its story of human life secured and made whole by the gracious love of God. The theologies of Barth and Balthasar seek to recover the ancient and more radical notion that creation is a gift from God that is not inherently violent or meaningless or closed in on itself, but rather created for a relationship with God, which is secured by the gracious self-giving of the Trinity. Cyril, Barth, and Balthasar all remind us of the ancient Christian story that is rooted in God's profound love for what God has graciously created, a story that takes seriously the consequences of human sin and rebellion and celebrates the sheer magnitude of God's action in Jesus Christ to save creation and restore humanity to the end God intends—life with God.

The questions and concerns raised in this chapter do not undermine the great power of Barth and Balthasar's theological conceptions, but are rather offered in the hope that they provide a way forward in extending their thought through the insights of Cyril. These theologians continually remind us that God moves into the world as self-giving love and grace in Jesus Christ so that through the ongoing power of the Holy Spirit, humans may truly participate in God's life.

5

Reclaiming God's Vision for Human Life

"Robert, the Scriptures are well aware of the power latent within us, and they are urging us to harness that power . . . urging us to build the temples of our minds." . . . "The Second Coming is the coming of man—the moment when mankind finally builds the temple of his mind."[1]

"We are creators, and yet we naively play the role of 'the created.' We see ourselves as helpless sheep buffeted around by the God who made us. We kneel like frightened children, begging for help, for forgiveness, for good luck. But once we realize that we are truly created in the Creator's image, we will start to understand that we, too, must be Creators. When we understand this fact, the doors will burst wide open for human potential." . . . "The most amazing part," Katherine said, "is that as soon as we humans begin to harness our true power, we will have enormous control over our world. We will be able to design reality rather than merely react to it."[2]

—Dan Brown, *The Lost Symbol*

1. Dan Brown, *The Lost Symbol* (New York: Doubleday, 2009), 499.
2. Brown, *The Lost Symbol*, 501.

In short, he took what was ours to be his very own so that we might have all that was his.[3]

Indeed, the mystery of Christ runs the risk of being disbelieved precisely because it is so incredibly wonderful.[4]

—Cyril of Alexandria, *On the Unity of Christ*

In many ways, we would do well to remember Barth's cautions about the whole notion of deification as a concept that can lead to an array of atrocities undertaken in the name of human advancement and the resulting deep disillusionment and hopelessness in the wreckage left behind. These *are* the dangers of a conception of deification stripped of its explicitly Christian parameters and applied through a humanistic confidence in the inherent capacities of humans to develop and to transcend the currently perceived boundaries of human existence. From the horrors of genocide and the drive toward technological developments that outpace ethical considerations in fields like bioengineering, to the devastation wrought by irresponsible mortgage lending and an emphasis on short-term financial gain—all promulgated in the name of humanistic, religious, or political causes, or simply in the name of capitalistic opportunity—humans remain capable of exactly what Barth feared. When humans become ensnared in a world closed in on itself, anchored by and accountable to nothing larger than itself—a world that sees its own desires and strivings as its only true end—false hope and the resulting failures and disillusionment are what remain.

3. Cyril of Alexandria, *On the Unity of Christ* trans. John McGuckin (Crestwood, N.Y.: St. Vladimir's Seminary Press, 1995), 59.
4. Cyril, *On the Unity of Christ*, 61.

Unmoored from a properly Christian framework, improperly conceived understandings of the deification of humankind under the guise of many other names brings with them deleterious consequences. In a western world that becomes increasingly secular and privatized, the pendulum swings in one of two directions. On the one hand, we cling to a positive vestige of Enlightenment humanism that asserts human beings can evolve and ascend by developing their inherent human capacities with no real need of God as anything other than a placeholder for things that currently cannot be explained. In an increasingly individualized society, concepts of deification as the right, even duty, of self-actualization are undertaken in ways that "work for me" and that involve truncated conceptions of participation in or responsibility to anything larger than self, with detrimental consequences for our economic, political, and social life together. In addition, the growing undercurrent of Gnosticism and the return of a Platonically-conceived ascension through increasing knowledge can be seen in purveyors of every kind of self-improvement program imaginable. We are surrounded by the culturally approved message that with enough of the right kind of knowledge—which really already lies deep within us—and enough discipline, we can transcend the difficulties of the world, which itself is viewed as an increasingly hostile and even inherently evil place. Of course, the catch is that humans cannot and do not transcend themselves by their own efforts or by their own inherent capacities—and so we live through repeated failures and deep disappointments when this idol of our own making continually exhibits its feet of clay.

In response, we swing to a negative rejection of Enlightenment humanism and its idea of universal truths that could be learned and embraced by all humankind. Instead we engage in an endless series of postmodern deconstructions designed to expose the ugliness of the human condition and our self-deception, an ugliness and horror from which there's no real way out beyond self-deception. There are no shortages of philosophers telling us that there is no truth, goodness, or beauty in which we might participate in the first place. There is nothing but our longing for an Absolute that leaves only a trace of the human longing for it on the nothingness of an empty space that was never really occupied in the first place.[5] We must live to and for ourselves and there's nothing beyond the assertion of individual will and power.

A proper Christian understanding of participation in the life of God has a crucial vision to offer to a western world that has lost its moorings in such disturbing ways. Cyril of Alexandria, Karl Barth, and Hans Urs von Balthasar point us toward this vision, though in different ways, and remind us that what Christianity has to offer to such a world is a vision for a radically different form of human life—a Christic form that secures human life, draws humanity into God's life, and enables a participation in God's truth, beauty, and goodness. The only anchor that is secure must continually be received as a gift from outside ourselves. And it can be continually received because it is continually given from the inexhaustible self-giving of God's own self.

As we have seen, Barth's conceptions beautifully convey that God establishes a covenant relationship with humanity, which God keeps even in the face of human rebellion and disobedience, through the offering of God's very self in Jesus Christ. Barth beautifully affirms the single subject of the incarnation as the divine Son who comes among us to live a fully human life and to offer love, gratitude,

---

5. See the work of Slavoj Zizek, *The Fragile Absolute: or Why is the Christian legacy worth fighting for?* (London: Verso, 2000). See also the work of Jacques Derrida, "Faith and Knowledge: the Two Sources of 'Religion' at the Limits of Reason Alone" in *Religion: Cultural Memory in the Present*, ed. Jacques Derrida and Gianni Vattimo (Stanford: Stanford University Press, 1998) and Gianni Vattimo, *The End of Modernity* (Baltimore: John Hopkins University Press, 1988).

and obedience in the place of our sinful rebellion and to restore us to a proper relationship with God in which we can live out our calling as covenant partners. Barth also offers a helpful caution about the collapsing of the distinction between divine and human, seen in the falsely grounded Enlightenment humanism that promises humanity can ascend to divine knowledge and status through the development of its own inherent capacities. Barth lived with the disastrous consequences of the human ability to twist and promote selfish ambition, prejudice, and even hatred as a participation in God's intent. Thus, despite his strong affirmation of the covenant of election in which God accepts humiliation so that humanity might be exalted, throughout Barth's theology runs a deep reserve about bringing divine and human into participatory relationship in which humanity is truly transformed.

Cyril has something to offer to Barth—the confidence that, as a result of the union of divine and human in Christ, humanity can now truly transcend its original condition and become a new creation solely and only through the gracious act of God. Grace can perfect and elevate nature and allow for a genuine participation by humanity in the divine life without blurring the distinction between divine and human. Cyril offers a vision of participation that is both a dynamic process of obedience and growth toward God's purposes, and a transformation of humanity itself into something fuller and truer through Christ, both empowered by the Spirit. Cyril acts as a corrective to what Balthasar calls Barth's radical eschatological tendencies—a delay of the transformation and participation of humanity into a future *eschaton*—by emphasizing the here and now possibilities of participation. In addition, Cyril balances Barth's tendencies toward a forensic view of justification that often fails to see the current, dynamic relationship between justification and sanctification, and the ways in which the restored relationship between God and creatures is more than simply a change in status that removes barriers to obedience.

Cyril also assumes that transformed life will be lived out in the community of the church and in the reception of the sacraments, which continually both nurture and call to account Christians' participation in the gracious new life they have received. This move is made possible by Cyril's strong pneumatology and his view of sacraments as an effective means of grace and participation. Cyril thus offers robust concepts of church and sacraments that can augment Barth's cautious reserve about the ability of both to mediate grace and form Christian patterns of life.

We have also seen that Balthasar builds on much of Barth's conceptual framework. But Balthasar augments Barth with a fuller analogical understanding that allows him to develop a larger framework for human participation in the life of God. Balthasar's work is strong in some of the areas in which Barth has trouble. His trinitarian inversion gives a full-bodied exposition to his pneumatology and recognizes the fullness of the Holy Spirit, both in the immanent Trinity and in the economy of salvation. In addition, Balthasar's ability to draw on Mary, as a concrete and particular person who says "yes" and, in her obedience, gives birth to Christ in the world through the church, gives Balthasar's work an ecclesial and sacramental strength that Barth lacks. Further, Balthasar captures Cyril's insight that, within the hypostatic union, divinity and humanity are seen in their perfection, and humanity is indeed made perfect. While the distinction between divinity and humanity is maintained, there is harmonious participation rather than the antithesis and confrontation one finds so strongly in Barth.

Balthasar reminds us that there is indeed nothing outside God—nothing that God in Christ has not already fully and lovingly redeemed. God in God's self is immense, loving, and lively enough to make space for all that is not God without in any way being threatened by this otherness. This conception creates a large space for human activity and participation in Christ's mission in the world, and in the trinitarian life of God. Balthasar seeks to open the drama of self-giving trinitarian love enacted in human history though Christ to our view, enabling us to see ourselves as caught up in the divine drama of full healing and redemption. He places before us the dramatic event of God's love, beckoning us to see the role we are invited to play and to actively take our place in the world as we are directed and empowered by the Spirit. To a postmodern world whose gaze is too often captured and held by the horrific and hopeless, Balthasar reminds us that Christ's salvific work is truly effective. A new way of living anchored in something beyond ourselves in the life of God has truly changed all of life. The possibility of a new life is opened for us. There is room in God's embrace for humanity, and humans have the gift of new life and of cooperating in God's vision for creation. They can participate in Christ's mission, a mission that is truly transforming for themselves and others.

However, if Barth is in places too hesitant about the participation of human life in God, Balthasar can be accused of being too daring. Cyril provides a helpful lens through which to examine the more daring edges of Balthasar's conceptions. While Cyril consistently argued that Nestorius and the Antiochenes were so worried about protecting God's impassibility that they could not grasp the true union of humanity and divinity in the incarnation, his argument should not be taken to mean that he would wholeheartedly approve Balthasar's approach either. Cyril consistently argued that in the incarnation the impassible suffers, but he was careful to note that this was solely within the economy of God's salvation—not a feature of God's immanent life. Cyril provides a reminder that if the one subject of Christ in the incarnation is properly understood, there is simply no need even to flirt with an internal passibility or mutability in the life of God. Within Cyril's Christology, it is still possible to see the incarnation as an event that changes humanity without changing God. This in no way makes God a static, unmovable, or removed being, but precisely preserves God's ability to participate in and redeem humanity for the participation Balthasar envisions. Cyril provides a necessary check to the more radical edges of Balthasar's notions of participation that push against boundaries of analogical participation and the real distinction between human and divine. Second, Cyril's conception of the ways in which participation in Christ results in an ontological change that then empowers or requires a response of continual progress in holy living could lend a fuller account of the moral life to Balthasar's thought, particularly through further development of the notion of active receptivity.

Throughout our discussion, we have also seen the ways in which the Protestant and Roman Catholic divide over imputed righteousness and infused grace have come into play in the differences between Barth and Balthasar—differences that would have been foreign to Cyril's conceptual framework. Cyril's approach envisions both an ontological and moral transformation through participating in the life of God. Both of these transformations can occur in, and only in, the grace and person of Jesus Christ. Are, then, the concepts of imputed righteousness and infused grace as diametrically opposed and incompatible as so many Protestants and Catholics seem to believe? Is it either/or? Or is there a possibility of both/and? Is it possible that on the basis of Christ's righteousness and saving activity on our behalf, we receive an infusion of grace that makes this action transformative in us as a result of the Holy Spirit's work within us? Can we not be at once *accounted* righteous as a result of Christ's alien righteousness, but also—as a pure gift of God relying solely on the power of the Holy Spirit—be *made* righteous as we are infused by grace and transformed into the people God intends us to be as a result of the life, death and resurrection of Jesus Christ?

To affirm only one side or the other leads to the very difficulties we have seen arise between Barth and Balthasar, and points to the ways in which we need both aspects to achieve the fullness of the vision one sees in Cyril. The benefits of an emphasis on imputed righteousness are that one is constantly reminded that no inherent capacity or work on the part of humans can remove our sin or restore us to right relationship with God. God's salvific activity in Jesus Christ is solely God's action on our behalf and requires nothing inherent in us to be efficacious—salvation is an objective fact. We are freed from endless internal self-gazing, worrying about whether our works are sufficient to merit salvation and reward. However, while imputed righteousness assures us of our changed status before God—and asserts that this change in relationship is an ontological change—a sole emphasis on imputation and a rejection of infused grace does not sufficiently attend to the ways in which that change of imputed status results in a change of life here and now. If human nature has not really been changed—but instead is merely viewed differently by God in the sense that our sin is "overlooked" and Christ's righteousness alone is what is seen—then how are humans really freed to be and live differently in light of the miracle of the resurrection? We can affirm that we are freed to follow Christ in lives of gratitude and obedience, as Barth so eloquently does, but the fact is that most adherents of imputed righteousness are always quick to remind us that we still remain sinners, caught up in the power of sin—even though sin has ultimately been defeated—and that we live in a constant seesawing between sin and righteousness. We have not fundamentally transformed and therefore any change in our lives here and now is provisional at best. We can never surely put both feet down on the journey toward living differently.

On the other hand, the concept of infused grace has no difficulty in dealing with the inward and outward transformation of humanity. God's word and action are always effective and this truly changes who we intrinsically *are,* as well as changing our status before God. If God pronounces us saved and righteous in Christ, then we really become righteous. Human nature has actually been freed from the power of sin and death and given a new birth, solely as an unmerited gift of grace from God. That transformation can and should result in a new way of being and acting in the world—in progress toward holy living. One is encouraged, indeed commanded, to put both feet down on the path toward continual growth in good works as a fruit of salvation. Proponents of imputed righteousness will here remind us that this concept or emphasis on bearing fruit often leads to the idea that our works somehow contribute to our salvation and merit reward, and that it also leads to unnecessary doubt and confusion about the state of one's inward being and rightness with God. It is a necessary caution. But just because it *can* lead in that direction does not mean that it *must.*

Anthony Lane has argued that just such a response to the Reformers concerns was originally offered at the meeting of Catholic theologians at Regensburg in 1541.[6] Moving through the articles drafted at Regensburg, Lane notes that these theologians insisted that we receive justification by being accepted as righteous on the basis of Christ's merit—imputed righteousness—and that simultaneously, through the Holy Spirit, we receive inherent righteousness, which through an infusion of grace allows us to receive participation in the divine life and begin to live in accordance with God's intentions. Justification and sanctification are "parallel and inseparable" gifts that

---

6. See Anthony N. S. Lane, "A Tale of Two Imperial Cities: Justification at Regensburg (1541) and Trent (1546–1547)" in *Justification in Perspective: Historical Developments and Contemporary Challenges,* ed. Bruce L. McCormack (Grand Rapids: Baker Academic, 2006), 119–145.

are given by grace and received by faith.[7] Lane argues the insight here is that imputed righteousness is necessary because "our inherent righteousness and the righteousness of our works remain imperfect and it is not on that basis that we stand before God," but only through Christ's righteousness.[8] However, trusting in God's grace and righteousness means that we also trust God to make effective *in* us what God pronounces *of* us. In addition, Lane argues that Regensburg reminds us that there is "the good news of free grace but there is also the call to discipleship."[9] "While good works do not cause our justification . . . they are necessary as consequences," Lane notes.

In combining the objectively focused concept of imputed righteousness and the subjectively focused concept of infused grace, do we not have a more comprehensive account of the fullness of God's gracious activity on our behalf in Jesus Christ? Do we not see more clearly Cyril's vision of an ontological transformation of humanity that is intimately tied to a new ability to take real and sure steps to living as God's people in the world, freed *from* the power of sin and death and freed *for* newness of life?

While we are surely right and wise to heed Barth's cautions about our ability to be self-deceptive and to characterize even the most heinous of acts as God's intent, must we then move to another extreme where we can have no confidence in our ability to live as God intends? Surely, in the light of Christ, we can have a humble confidence in God's grace at work, changing us and empowering our lives through the Spirit. Such a transformation is never a result of our own inherent capacities that are developed through the humanly achieved enlightenment of our minds, nor is it a result of our good

---

7. Lane, "A Tale of Two Imperial Cities," 126, with reference to the Articles of Regensburg.
8. Lane, "A Tale of Two Imperial Cities," 130.
9. Anthony N. S. Lane, "Two-Fold Righteousness: A Key to the Doctrine of Justification?: Reflections on Article 5 of the Regensburg Colloquy (1541)," in *Justification: What's At Stake in the Current Debates* (Downer's Grove, Ill.: Intervarsity, 2004) 219.

works and moral striving. But such newness of being and life are simply and solely the gift of a God who, in nearly unimaginable power and grace, has united himself with our humanity in order to save us from our own rebelliousness and disobedience, to redeem us from sin and death, and to restore us to fullness of life as God's beloved people. If we mean what we say—that through Jesus Christ, who is fully human and fully divine in one person, God has acted to defeat sin and death and to restore us to life and fellowship with God and one another—then how is living with a diffidence about the new reality that Christ has ushered in a faithful act? Certainly we live in a world that provides more than ample evidence of the destructive consequences of human arrogance and self-deceit, of what happens when humanity becomes encapsulated in itself, convinced that its own enlightened inherent capacities will provide all the necessary resources for abundant life. And we've certainly seen the continual ways in which that belief so often is exhibited as a self-driven quest for power and advantage. On the other hand, we've also seen the reactions to the failure of that enlightenment worldview in a host of philosophical deconstructions that merely expose the failures of humanity in their rawest and ugliest forms and then leave us staring at the ruins with the cynical admonishment that nothing will ever change and there is no escape. We live in a world that oscillates between false hope and false cynicism, between falsely grounded confidence in human abilities and falsely grounded disparagement and despair. What resources in the Christian tradition offer an alternative vision, one that is grounded in the reality of God's gracious love and action on our behalf? I would argue that such an alternative requires the fullness of Cyril's vision of human life participating in God's life—a life received as gift and secured by the love and power of God.

Cyril's understandings provide ongoing resources for assessing and augmenting the theology of Karl Barth and Hans Urs von Balthasar, addressing the redemption and the restoration of creation brought about by Jesus Christ. Cyril's vision of human life as a participation in the life of God made possible by Jesus Christ through the power of the Holy Spirit offers the world an alternative to its false narrative of a self-made world locked in a continuous loop of pseudo-improvements that ultimately only disillusion. It offers the vision of transformed humanity made possible and secured by the sheer gift of God's grace, a grace that empowers and urges us to purposeful and holy living as God's people.

This gift of ontological and moral transformation is to be lived out in the community of the church, in which Christians are continually formed through the practices of worship, confession, reconciliation, and the sacraments. Living in humble confidence as God's people in the world requires sustained practices that remind us we are constant recipients of God's grace and initiative. These practices help us listen for the voice and work of the Spirit, subject such guidance to communal accountability and discernment, and encourage us with the fellowship of others who journey with us. Our participation in God's life is always lived in community with God and one another through the church that Jesus established and the Spirit sustains and empowers. We need never be stranded and alone on the shoals of the world's oscillations between false hope and false despair.

Instead, we can reaffirm with Cyril that, in the life, death, and resurrection of Jesus Christ, all evil and suffering are finally redeemed and creation is made a truly new reality, transformed by the life-giving love of Christ. A new reality has begun in the incarnation. All of creation is transformed. This unique union of God and humanity has changed the cosmos, and reality is seen really and truly only in the light of Christ. Human life—both now and eternally—has changed.

We have been given a share in the divine life that empowers our present with hope and moves us toward the future through graced participation in the very life of God. Cyril, Barth, and Balthasar each proclaim that the truth, goodness, and beauty of that vision shine on us, lighting our path, and they invite and empower us to take our places in the great drama of God's ongoing redemptive work in the world.

Bibliography

Anatolios, Khaled. *Athanasius: The Coherence of His Thought*. London: Routledge, 1998.

Athanasius. *Orations Against the Arians*. In *The Trinitarian Controversy*. Translated and edited by William G. Rusch. Philadelphia: Fortress Press, 1980.

Balthasar, Hans Urs von. *A Theology of History*. New York: Sheed and Ward, 1963.

———. *Cosmic Liturgy: The Universe According to Maximus the Confessor*. Translated by Brian E. Daley. San Francisco: Ignatius, 2003.

———. *Explorations in Theology*, Vol. IV: *Spirit and Institution*. Translated by Edward T. Oakes, S. J. San Francisco: Ignatius, 1995.

———. *Mysterium Paschale*. With introduction by Aidan Nichols. San Francisco: Ignatius, 1990.

———. *The Glory of the Lord*, Vol. I: *Seeing the Form*. Translated by Erasmo Leiva-Merikakis. San Francisco: Ignatius, 1982.

———. *The Glory of the Lord*, Vol. VII: *The New Covenant*. Translated by Brian McNeil. T&T Clark, 1990.

———. *The Theology of Karl Barth: Exposition and Interpretation*. Translated by Edward T. Oakes. San Francisco: Ignatius, 1992.

———. *Theo-Drama: Theological Dramatic Theory* Vol. II: *Dramatis Personae: Man in God.* Translated by Graham Harrison. San Francisco: Ignatius,1990.

———. *Theo-Drama: Theological Dramatic Theory* Vol. III: *Dramatis Personae: Persons in Christ.* Translated by Graham Harrison. San Francisco: Ignatius, 1992.

———. *Theo-Drama: Theological Dramatic Theory,* Vol. IV: *The Action.* Translated by Graham Harrison. San Francisco: Ignatius, 1994.

———. *Theo-Drama: Theological Dramatic Theory,* Vol. V: *The Last Act.* Translated by Graham Harrison. San Francisco: Ignatius, 1998.

———. *Theo-Logic:* Vol. II: *The Truth of God.* Translated by Adrian J. Walker. San Francisco: Ignatius, 2004.

———. *Church Dogmatics,* Vol. 1.1, *The Doctrine of the Word of God.* Edited by G. W. Bromiley and T. F. Torrance. Translated by G. W. Bromiley. London: T&T Clark, 1936.

———. *Church Dogmatics,* Vol. 1.2, *The Doctrine of the Word of God.* Edited by G. W. Bromiley and T. F. Torrance. Translated by G. T. Thomson and Harold Knight. London: T&T Clark, 1956.

———. *Church Dogmatics,* Vol. 2.1, *The Doctrine of God.* Edited by G. W. Bromiley and T. F. Torrance. Translated by T. H. L. Parker, W. B. Johnston, Harold Knight, and J. L. M. Haire. London: T&T Clark, 1957.

———. *Church Dogmatics,* Vol. 2.2, *The Doctrine of God.* Edited by G. W. Bromiley and T. F. Torrance. Translated by G. W. Bromiley, J. C. Campbell, Iain Wilson, J. Strathearn McNab, Harold Knight, and R. A. Stewart. Edinburgh: T&T Clark, 1957.

———. *Church Dogmatics,* Vol. 3.1, *The Doctrine of Creation.* Edited by G. W. Bromiley and T. F. Torrance. Translated by J. W. Edwards, O. Bussey, and Harold Knight. Edinburgh: T&T Clark, 1958.

———. *Church Dogmatics,* Vol. 3.2, *The Doctrine of Creation.* Edited by G. W. Bromiley and T. F. Torrance. Translated by Harold Knight, G. W. Bromiley, J. K. S. Reid, and R. H. Fuller. Edinburgh: T&T Clark, 1960.

———. *Church Dogmatics*, Vol. 3.4, *The Doctrine of Creation*. Edited by G. W. Bromiley and T. F. Torrance. Translated by A. T. MacKay, T. H. L. Parker, Harold Knight, Henry A. Kennedy, and John Marks. Edinburgh: T&T Clark, 1961.

———. *Church Dogmatics*, Vol. 4.1, *The Doctrine of Reconciliation*. Edited by G. W. Bromiley and T. F. Torrance. Translated by G. W. Bromiley. Edinburgh: T&T Clark, 1956.

———. *Church Dogmatics*, Vol. 4.2, *The Doctrine of Reconciliation*. Edited by G. W. Bromiley and T. F. Torrance. Translated by G. W. Bromiley. Edinburgh: T&T Clark, 1958.

———. *Church Dogmatics*, Vol. 4.3.1, *The Doctrine of Reconciliation*. Edited by G. W. Bromiley and T. F. Torrance. Translated by G. W. Bromiley. Edinburgh: T&T Clark, 1961.

———. *Church Dogmatics*, Vol. 4.3.2, *The Doctrine of Reconciliation*. Edited by G. W. Bromiley and T. F. Torrance. Translated by G. W. Bromiley. Edinburgh: T&T Clark, 1962.

———. *Community, State, and Church*. Translated and with an introduction by David Haddorff. Eugene, Ore.: Wipf & Stock, 1960.

———. *Ethics*. Translated by G. W. Bromiley. New York: Seabury, 1981.

Bauerschmidt, Frederick. "Aesthetics: The theological sublime." In *Radical Orthodoxy*. Edited by John Milbank, Catherine Pickstock, and Graham Ward. London: Routledge, 1999.

Betz, John, R. "Beyond the Sublime: The Aesthetics of the Analogy of Being." *Modern Theology* 21, no. 3 (July 2005): 367–411 and 22, no. 1 (January2006): 1–50.

Boulnois, Marie-Odile. "The Mystery of the Trinity according to Cyril of Alexandria: The Deployment of the Triad and Its Recapitulation into the Unity of Divinity." In *The Theology of St. Cyril of Alexandria: A Critical Appreciation*. Edited by Thomas G. Weinandy and Daniel A. Keating. London: T&T Clark, 2003.

Brown, Dan. *The Lost Symbol*. New York: Doubleday, 2009.

Clayton, Paul B. *The Christology of Theodoret of Cyrus: Antiochene Christology from the Council of Ephesus (431) to the Council of Chalcedon (451).* New York: Oxford University Press, 2007.

Coakley, Sarah. "What Does Chalcedon Solve and What Does it Not? Some Reflections on the Status and Meaning of the Chalcedonian 'Definition.'" In *The Incarnation.* Edited by Stephen T. Davis, Daniel Kendall, and Gerald O'Collins. Oxford: Oxford University Press, 2004.

Cyril. *Against Nestorius.* Translated by Norman Russell. In Norman Russell, *Cyril of Alexandria.* New York: Routledge, 2000.

———. *Commentary on Isaiah.* Translated by Norman Russell. In Norman Russell, *Cyril of Alexandria.* New York: Routledge, 2000.

———. *Commentary on John.* Translated by Norman Russell. In Norman Russell, *Cyril of Alexandria.* New York: Routledge, 2000.

———. *Commentary on John.* Translated by Daniel A. Keating. In Daniel A. Keating, *The Appropriation of Divine Life in Cyril of Alexandria.* Oxford: Oxford University Press, 2004.

———. *Commentary on the Gospel of John.* In Library of the Fathers, Two Volumes. Translated by P. E. Pusey and T. Randall. London: W. Smith, 1885. Also available at archive.org.

———. *Explanations of the Twelve Chapters.* Translated by John McGuckin. In John McGuckin, *Saint Cyril and the Christological Controversy: Its History, Theology, and Texts.* Crestwood, N.Y.: St. Vladimir's Seminary Press, 2004.

———. *First Letter to Succensus.* Translated by John McGuckin. In John McGuckin, *Saint Cyril and the Christological Controversy: Its History, Theology, and Texts.* Crestwood N.Y.: St. Vladimir's Seminary Press, 2004.

———. *Homilies on Luke.* Translated by R. Payne Smith from *A Commentary upon the Gospel according to S. Luke by S. Cyril, Patriarch of Alexandria.* New York: Studion, 1984. In Daniel A. Keating, *The Appropriation of Divine Life, in Cyril of Alexandria.* Oxford: Oxford University Press, 2004.

———. *Homily Given at Ephesus on St. Stephen's Day in the Church of St. John.* Translated by John McGuckin. In John McGuckin, *Saint Cyril and the Christological Controversy: Its History, Theology, and Texts.* Crestwood, N.Y.: St. Vladimir's Seminary Press, 2004.

———. *Letter to Eulogius.* Translated by John McGuckin. In John McGuckin, *Saint Cyril and the Christological Controversy: Its History, Theology, and Texts.* Crestwood, N.Y.: St. Vladimir's Seminary Press, 2004.

———. *Letter to the Monks.* Translated by John McGuckin. In John McGuckin, *Saint Cyril and the Christological Controversy: Its History, Theology, and Texts.* Crestwood, N.Y.: St. Vladimir's Seminary Press, 2004.

———. *On the Unity of Christ.* Translated by John McGuckin. Crestwood, N.Y.: St. Vladimir's Seminary Press, 1995.

———. *Scholia on the Incarnation.* Translated by John McGuckin. In *Saint Cyril and the Christological Controversy: Its History, Theology, and Texts.* Crestwood, N.Y.: St. Vladimir's Seminary Press, 2004.

———. *Second Letter to Nestorius.* Translated by Lionel Wickham. In *Cyril of Alexandria, Select Letters.* Oxford Early Christian Studies. Oxford: Oxford University Press, 1983.

———. *Second Letter to Succensus.* Translated by John McGuckin. In John McGuckin, *Saint Cyril and the Christological Controversy: Its History, Theology and Texts.* Crestwood, NY: St. Vladimir's Seminary Press, 2004.

———. *Third Letter to Nestorius.* Translated by Lionel Wickham. In *Cyril of Alexandria, Select Letters.* Oxford Early Christian Studies. Oxford: Oxford University Press, 1983.

Daley, Brian. "Nature and the 'Mode of Union': Late Patristic Models for the Personal Unity of Christ." In *The Incarnation.* Edited by Stephen T. Davis, Daniel Kendall, and Gerald O'Collins. Oxford: Oxford University Press, 2004.

————. "The Fullness of the Saving God: Cyril of Alexandria on the Holy Spirit." In *The Theology of St. Cyril of Alexandria: A Critical Appreciation.* Edited by Thomas G. Weinandy and Daniel A. Keating. London: T&T Clark, 2003.

De Lubac, Henri. *The Mystery of the Supernatural.* Translated by Rosemary Sheed. New York: Herder & Herder, 1998.

Derrida, Jacque, "Faith and Knowledge: the Two Sources of 'Religion' at the Limits of Reason Alone" in *Religion: Cultural Memory in the Present.* Edited by Jacques Derrida and Gianni Vattimo. Stanford: Stanford University Press, 1998.

Fairbairn, Donald. *Grace and Christology in the Early Church.* Oxford: Oxford University Press, 2003.

————. "The One Person Who Is Jesus Christ: A Patristic Perspective." In *Jesus in Trinitarian Perspective.* Edited by Fred Sanders and Klaus Issler. Nashville: B&H, 2007.

Farag, Lois M. *St. Cyril of Alexandria, A New Testament Exegete: His Commentary on the Gospel of John.* Piscataway, N.J.: Gorgias, 2007.

Farrow, Douglas. *Ascension and Ecclesia: On the Significance of the Doctrine of the Ascension for Ecclesiology and Christian Cosmology.* Grand Rapids: Eerdmans, 1999.

Gavrilyuk, Paul. "Theopatheia: Nestorius's main charge against Cyril of Alexandria." *Scottish Journal of Theology* 56, no. 2 (2003): 190–207.

Gilson, Etienne. *Being and Some Philosophers.* Toronto: Mediaeval Studies of Toronto for The Pontifical Institute of Mediaeval Studies, 1949.

Griffiths, Paul. "Is There a Doctrine of the Descent into Hell?" *ProEcclesia,* Vol. 17, no. 3. (Summer 2008): 257–268.

Grillmeier, Aloys. *Christ in Christian Tradition,* Vol. I: *From the Apostolic age to Chalcedon (451).* Translated by John Bowden. Atlanta: John Knox, 1975.

Gunton, Colin. "Salvation." In *The Cambridge Companion to Karl Barth.* Edited by John Webster. Cambridge: Cambridge University Press, 2000.

Harnack, Adolph von. *History of Dogma*, Volume 1. Translated by Neil Buchanan from Third German Edition. Boston: Little, Brown, and Company, 1902.

Hart, David Bentley. *The Beauty of the Infinite: The Aesthetics of Christian Truth.* Grand Rapids: Eerdmans, 2003.

Hart, Trevor. "Revelation." In *The Cambridge Companion to Karl Barth.* Edited by John Webster. Cambridge: Cambridge University Press, 2000.

Hauerwas, Stanley. *With the Grain of the Universe: The Church's Witness and Natural Theology.* Grand Rapids: Brazos, 2001.

Healy, Nicholas, and David Schindler. "For the life of the world: Hans Urs von Balthasar on the Church as Eucharist." In *The Cambridge Companion to Hans Urs von Balthasar.* Edited by Edward T. Oakes and David Moss. Cambridge: Cambridge University Press, 2004.

Hunsinger, George. *Disruptive Grace: Studies in the Theology of Karl Barth.* Grand Rapids: Eerdmans, 2000.

———. "Election and the Trinity: Twenty-five Theses on the Theology of Karl Barth." *Modern Theology* 24, no. 2 (April 2008): pg. 179–198.

———. "Karl Barth's Christology." In *The Cambridge Companion to Karl Barth.* Edited by John Webster. Cambridge: Cambridge University Press, 2000.

———. "Karl Barth's doctrine of the Holy Spirit." In *The Cambridge Companion to Karl Barth.* Edited by John Webster. Cambridge: Cambridge University Press, 2000.

———, ed. *For the Sake of the World: Karl Barth and the Future of Ecclesial Theology.* Grand Rapids: Eerdmans, 2004

Husbands, Mark and Daniel J. Treier, eds., *Justification: What's at Stake in the Current Debates.* Downer's Grove, Ill.: InterVarsity, 2004.

Johnson, Keith L. *Karl Barth and the Analogia Entis.* London: T&T Clark, 2010.

Jones, Paul Dafydd. *The Humanity of Christ: Christology in Karl Barth's Church Dogmatics.* London: T&T Clark, 2008.

Kalantzis, George. "Is there Room for Two?: Cyril's Single Subjectivity and the Prosopic Union," St. Vladimir's Theological Quarterly, 52, no.1 (2008): 95–110.

Karkkainen, Veli-Matti. *One with God: Salvation as Deification and Justification.* Collegeville, Minn.: Liturgical, 2004.

Keating, Daniel A. *The Appropriation of Divine Life in Cyril of Alexandria.* Oxford: Oxford University Press, 2004.

———. "Divinization in Cyril: The Appropriation of Divine Life." In *The Theology of St. Cyril of Alexandria: A Critical Appreciation.* Edited by Thomas G. Weinandy and Daniel A. Keating. London: T&T Clark, 2003.

Lamont, John. "The Nature of the Hypostatic Union," Heythrop Journal 47, no. 1 (2006): 16–25.

Lane, Anthony N. S. "A Tale of Two Imperial Cities: Justification at Regensburg (1541) and Trent (1546–1547)." In *Justification in Perspective: Historical Developments and Contemporary Challenges.* Edited by Bruce L. McCormack. Grand Rapids: Baker Academic, 2006.

———. "Two-Fold Righteousness: A Key to the Doctrine of Justification? Reflections on Article 5 of the Regensburg Colloquy (1541)." In *Justification: What's at Stake in the Current Debates.* Downer's Grove. Ill.: Intervarsity, 2004.

Long, Stephen A. "Divine and Creaturely 'Receptivity': The Search for a Middle Term." *Communio* 21 (Spring, 1994): 151–161.

———. *Natura Pura: On the Recovery of Nature in the Doctrine of Grace.* New York: Fordham University Press, 2010.

MacIntyre, Alasdair. *Three Rival Versions of Moral Enquiry: Encyclopaedia, Genealogy, and Tradition.* Notre Dame, Ind.: University of Notre Dame Press, 1990.

McCabe, Herbert. *God Matters.* London: Geoffrey Chapman. 1987.

McCormack, Bruce L. "Grace and being: the role of God's gracious election in Karl Barth's theological ontology." In *The Cambridge Companion to Karl*

Barth Edited by John Webster. Cambridge: Cambridge University Press, 2000.

———, "Justitia aliena: Karl Barth in Conversation with the Evangelical Doctrine of Imputed Righteousness." In *Justification in Perspective: Historical Developments and Contemporary Challenges.* Edited by Bruce L. McCormack Grand Rapids: Baker Academic, 2006.

———. *Karl Barth's Critically Realistic Dialectical Theology: Its Genesis and Development 1909-1936.* Oxford: Oxford University Press, 1995.

———. *Orthodox and Modern: Studies in the Theology of Karl Barth.* Grand Rapids: Baker Academic, 2008.

———. "What's at Stake in Current Debates over Justification?" The Crisis of Protestantism in the West." In *Justification: What's at Stake in the Current Debates.* Edited by Mark Husbands and Daniel J. Treier. Downer's Grove, Ill.: InterVarsity, 2004.

———, ed. *Justification in Perspective: Historical Developments and Contemporary Challenges.* Grand Rapids: Baker Academic, 2006.

McGuckin. John. *Saint Cyril and the Christological Controversy: Its History, Theology, and Texts.* Crestwood, N.Y.: St. Vladimir's Seminary Press, 2004.

McIntosh, Mark A. *Christology from Within: Spirituality and the Incarnation in Hans Urs von Balthasar.* Notre Dame: Notre Dame Press, 1996.

———. "Christology." In *The Cambridge Companion to Hans Urs Balthasar.* Edited by Edward T. Oakes and David Moss. Cambridge: Cambridge University Press, 2004.

———. "Review of Pitstick, Alyssa, *Light in Darkness: Hans Urs von Balthasar and the Catholic Doctrine of Christ's Descent into Hell.*" In *Modern Theology* 24, no. 1 (January 2008): 137–139.

McLeod, Frederick. *The Image of God in the Antiochene Tradition.* Washington, D.C.: The Catholic University of America Press, 1999.

————. *The Roles of Christ's Humanity in Salvation: Insights from Theodore of Mopsuestia*. Washington, D.C.: Catholic University of America Press, 2005.

McKinion, Steven, A. *Words, Imagery & The Mystery of Christ: A Reconstruction of Cyril of Alexandria's Christology*. Leiden: Brill, 2000.

Meyendorff, John. *Byzantine Theology: Historical Trends and Doctrinal Themes*. New York: Fordham University Press, 1974.

Milbank, John. *Theology and Social Theory: Moving Beyond Secular Reason*. Oxford: Blackwell, 1990.

Mosser, Carl. "The Earliest Patristic Interpretations of Psalm 82, Jewish Antecedents, and the Origin of Christian Deification." *Journal of Theological Studies*, NS, 56, Pt. 1 (April 2005): 30–74.

Neder, Adam. *Participation in Christ: An Entry into Karl Barth's Church Dogmatics*. Louisville: Westminster John Knox, 2009.

Norris, Richard, A. "Christological Models in Cyril of Alexandria." *Studia Patristica*, 13, pt. 2 (1975): 255–268.

————. *Manhood in Christ: A Study in the Christology of Theodore of Mopsuestia*. Oxford: Clarendon, 1963.

O'Hanlon, Gerard. *The Immutability of God in the Theology of Hans Urs von Balthasar*. Cambridge: Cambridge University Press, 1990.

O'Keefe, John, J. "Impassible Suffering? Divine Passion and Fifth-Century Christology." *Journal of Theological Studies* 58, no. 1 (March 1997): 39–60.

Oakes, Edward T. *Pattern of Redemption: The Theology of Hans Urs von Balthasar*. New York: Continuum, 1994.

————. "Hans Urs von Balthasar: The Wave and the Sea," *Theology Today* 62, no. 3 (October 2005): 364–374.

————. "The Internal Logic of Holy Saturday in the Theology of Hans Urs von Balthasar." *International Journal of Systematic Theology*, 9, no 2 (April 2007): 184–199.

Oakes, Kenneth. "The Question of Nature and Grace in Karl Barth: Humanity as Creature and as Covenant-Partner." *Modern Theology*, 24, no. 4 (October 2007): 595–616.

Pitstick, Alyssa Lyra. *Light in Darkness: Hans Urs von Balthasar and the Catholic Doctrine of Christ's Descent into Hell*. Grand Rapids: Eerdmans, 2007.

Przywara, P. Erich. *Polarity: A German Catholic's Interpretation of Religion*. Translated by A. C. Bouquet. London: Oxford University Press, 1935.

Quash, Ben. "The theo-drama," in *The Cambridge Companion to Hans Ur von Balthasar*. Edited by Edward T. Oakes and David Moss. Cambridge: Cambridge University Press, 2004.

———. *Theology and the Drama of History*. Cambridge: Cambridge University Press, 2005.

Rowland, Tracy. "Review of Alyssa Pitstick, *Light in Darkness: Hans Urs von Balthasar and the Catholic Doctrine of Christ's Descent into Hell*." In *International Journal of Systematic Theology*, 10, no. 4, (October 2008): 479–482.

Russell, Norman. *Cyril of Alexandria*. New York: Routledge, 2000.

———. *The Doctrine of Deification in the Greek Patristic Tradition*. Oxford: Oxford University Press, 2004.

Schindler, David C. "Towards a Non-Possessive Concept of Knowledge: On the Relation between Reason and Love in Aquinas and Balthasar." *Modern Theology* 22, no. 4 (October 2006): 577–607.

Sonderegger, Katherine. "Barth and feminism." In *The Cambridge Companion to Karl Barth*. Edited by John Webster. Cambridge: Cambridge University Press, 2000.

Sullivan, Francis A. *The Christology of Theodore of Mopsuestia*. Rome: Analectia Gregoriana, 1956.

Torrance, Alan. "The Trinity." In *The Cambridge Companion to Karl Barth*. Edited by John Webster. Cambridge: Cambridge University Press, 2000.

Vattimo, Gianni. *The End of Modernity*. Baltimore: John Hopkins Press, 1988.

Ward, Graham. "Introduction, or, A Guide to Theological Thinking in Cyberspace." In *The Postmodern God: A Theological Reader*. Edited by Graham Ward. Oxford: Blackwell, 1997.

Webster, John. *Barth*, second edition. New York: Continuum, 2004.

———. *Barth's Earlier Theology: Four Studies*. London: T&T Clark, 2005.

———. *Barth's Ethics of Reconciliation*. Cambridge: Cambridge University Press, 1995.

———. *Barth's Moral Theology: Human Action in Barth's Thought*. London: T&T Clark, 1998.

———. "Webster's Response to Alyssa Lyra Pitstick, *Light in Darkness*." In *Scottish Journal of Theology*, 62, no. 2 (2009): 202–210.

———., ed. *The Cambridge Companion to Karl Barth*. Cambridge: Cambridge University Press, 2000.

Weinandy, Thomas. *Athanasius: A Theological Introduction*. Farnham, U.K.: Ashgate, 2007.

———. "Cyril and the Mystery of the Incarnation." In *The Theology of St. Cyril of Alexandria: A Critical Appreciation*. Edited by Thomas G. Weinandy and Daniel A. Keating. London: T&T Clark, 2003.

———. *Does God Suffer?* Notre Dame: University of Notre Dame Press,2000.

Wesche, Kenneth Paul. "Eastern Orthodox Spirituality: Union with God in Theosis." In *Theology Today*, 56, no. 1, 1999, 31.

White, Thomas Joseph. "On the Possibility of Universal Salvation." *Pro Ecclesia* Vol. 17, no. 3 (Summer 2008): 269–280.

Wigley, Stephen D. *Karl Barth and Hans Urs von Balthasar: A Critical Engagement*. London and New York: T&T Clark, 2007.

Williams, A. N. *The Ground of Union: Deification in Aquinas and Palamas*. Oxford: Oxford University Press, 1999.

Wilkin, Robert L. *Judaism and the Early Christian Mind: A Study of Cyril of Alexandria's Exegesis and Theology*. New Haven: Yale University Press, 1971.

———. *The Spirit of Early Christian Thought: Seeking the Face of God.* New Haven: Yale University Press, 2003.

Young, Frances. "A Reconsideration of Alexandrian Christology." *Journal of Ecclesiastical History*, 22 (1971).

———. "Theotokos: Mary and the Pattern of Fall and Redemption In the Theology of Cyril of Alexandria." In *The Theology of St. Cyril of Alexandria: A Critical Appreciation.* Edited by Thomas G. Weinandy and Daniel A. Keating. London: T&T Clark, 2003.

Zizek, Slavoj. *The Fragile Absolute: or Why is the Christian legacy worth fighting for?* London: Verso, 2000.

Index of Authors

Anatolios, Khaled, 21, 24, 25, 26, 27, 42, 43, 44, 50, 55, 56, 57, 58, 59, 61, 65, 66, 68, 71

Athanasius, 21, 22, 23, 24, 25, 26, 27, 28, 42, 43, 44, 50, 56, 57, 60, 68, 71, 168, 170

Balthasar, Hans Urs von, 9, 10, 11, 12, 13, 17, 70 78, 79, 80, 84, 85, 86, 87, 88, 89, 90, 104, 114, 125, 145, 147, 148, 149, 150, 151, 152, 153, 154, 155, 156, 157, 158, 159, 160, 161, 162, 163, 164, 165, 166, 167, 168, 169, 170, 171, 172, 173, 174, 175, 176, 177, 178, 179, 180, 181, 182, 183, 184, 185, 186, 187, 188, 189, 190, 191, 192, 193, 194, 195, 196, 197, 198, 199, 200, 201, 202, 203, 204, 205, 206, 207, 208, 209, 210, 211, 212, 215, 238, 239, 240, 241, 242, 243, 244, 245, 246, 247, 248, 249, 250, 251, 252, 256, ac257, 258, 259, 260, 262, 265, 266

Barth, Karl, 9, 10, 11, 12, 13, 17, 19, 70, 75, 76, 77, 78, 79, 80, 81, 82, 83, 84, 85, 86, 87, 88, 89, 90, 91, 92, 93, 94, 95, 96, 97, 98, 99, 100, 101, 102, 103, 104, 105, 106, 107, 108, 109, 110, 111, 112, 113, 114, 115, 116, 117, 118, 119, 120, 121, 122, 123, 124, 125, 126, 127, 128, 129, 130, 131, 132, 133, 134, 135, 136, 137, 138, 139, 140, 141, 142, 143, 144, 145, 146, 147, 148, 149, 150, 151, 152, 153, 167, 184, 190, 191, 192, 194, 200, 201, 202, 203, 304, 208 209 211, 212, 215,

216, 217, 218, 219, 220, 221,
222, 223, 224, 225, 226, 227,
228, 229, 230, 231, 232, 233,
234, 235, 236, 237, 238, 239
242, 249 252, 254, 256, 257,
258, 259, 260, 261, 263, 265,
266

Bauerschmidt, Frederick, 3, 6, 165

Betz, John, R., 79

Boulnois, Marie-Odile, 65, 67, 71

Brown, Dan, 1, 6, 253

Clayton, Paul B., 32, 33, 34, 35,
36, 37, 40, 49, 56

Coakley, Sarah, 47

Cyril, 1, 7, 8, 9, 10, 11, 12, 13, 15,
16, 17, 18, 19, 21, 22, 23, 24,
25, 26, 27, 28, 29, 30, 31, 33,
34, 37, 38, 39, 40, 41, 42, 43,
44, 45, 46, 47, 48, 49, 50, 51,
52, 53, 54, 55, 56, 57, 58, 59,
60, 61, 62, 63, 64, 65, 66, 67,
68, 69, 70, 71, 72, 73, 76, 77,
78, 92, 93, 95, 101, 102, 111,
112, 114, 117, 121, 133, 143,
144, 145, 146, 148, 149, 150,
158, 161, 167, 168, 169, 170,
172 180, 191, 192, 193, 196,
198, 207, 208 209 211, 212,
213, 214, 215, 216, 217, 218,
220, 222, 223, 224, 227, 228,

229, 234, 235, 236, 237, 238,
239, 241, 242, 247, 250, 251,
252, 254, 256, 257, 258, 259,
260, 261, 263, 264, 265

Daley, Brian, 41, 72

DeLubac, Henri, 79, 160, 163, 197

Derrida, Jacque, 256

Fairbairn, Donald, 21, 22, 24, 32,
38, 43, 48, 213

Farag, Lois M., 43, 45, 50 51, 53,
64

Farrow, Douglas, 136, 137

Gavrilyuk, Paul, 8, 57

Griffiths, Paul, 188

Grillmeier, Aloys, 39, 49

Gunton, Colin, 128, 135, 136, 142

Harnack, Adolph von, 17, 19, 20,
21, 77, 102

Hart, David Bentley, 22

Hart, Trevor, 109, 110, 127

Hauerwas, Stanley, 90, 129, 130,
135, 230

Healy, Nicholas, 240

Hunsinger, George, 96, 99, 106,
107, 131, 132, 134, 135

Husbands, Mark, 21, 89, 200, 201

Johnson, Keith L, 85, 86, 88, 89, 110, 126, 133, 135, 164, 220, 231, 232, 233

Jones, Paul Dafydd, 82, 85, 98, 100, 101, 103, 104, 110, 111, 113, 119, 127, 217, 223, 224

Kalantzis, George, 36, 57

Karkkainen, Veli-Matti, 22, 23, 24

Keating, Daniel A., 1, 18, 22, 25, 26, 28, 42, 43, 44, 52, 53, 55, 59, 60, 61, 62, 63, 64, 65, 66, 67, 68, 69, 70, 71, 72, 214

Lane, Anthony N. S., 89, 200, 262, 263

Long, Stephen A., 158, 159, 163, 164, 165, 204, 247

MacIntyre, Alasdair, 4

McCabe, Herbert, 8

McCormack, Bruce L., 21, 78, 79, 80, 82, 84, 89, 90, 93, 98, 99, 100, 101, 108, 109, 118, 120, 127, 131, 190, 201, 202, 262

McGuckin. John, 16, 28, 29, 30, 37, 38, 39, 40, 41, 44, 45, 46, 47, 49, 50, 51, 54, 55, 56, 58, 60, 93, 113, 180, 237, 254

McIntosh, Mark A., 12, 153, 157, 167, 168, 171, 172, 173, 174, 175, 176, 177, 178, 183, 184, 186, 187, 189, 197, 205

McLeod, Frederick, 31, 32, 33, 34, 35, 36, 37, 41, 56, 57, 113

McKinion, Steven, A., 44, 45, 49, 50, 51

Meyendorff, John, 20, 23, 24, 28, 42, 44, 45, 46, 47, 50, 51, 52, 55, 67, 68

Milbank, John, 3, 5, 79, 165

Mosser, Carl: 20

Neder, Adam, 82, 85, 87, 90, 96, 98, 100, 107, 108, 112, 113, 118, 121, 122, 125, 126, 127, 128, 129, 133, 134, 139, 141, 143, 216, 217, 218, 219, 220, 224, 232, 235

Norris, Richard, A.:31, 32, 33, 35, 36, 47, 49

O'Hanlon, Gerard, 153, 154, 155, 156, 157, 158, 160, 183, 192, 196, 198

O'Keefe, John, J., 8, 52

Oakes, Edward T., 12, 80, 147, 152, 157, 168, 173, 178, 185, 186, 204, 205, 240

Oakes, Kenneth, 79, 80, 81, 88, 90, 222

Pitstick, Alyssa Lyra, 152, 187, 188, 189, 190, 191, 192, 193, 194, 241

Przywara, P. Erich, 150, 151, 152, 205

Quash, Ben, 173, 178, 184, 205, 206

Rowland, Tracy, 187, 189, 190

Russell, Norman, 15, 19, 20, 21, 22, 24, 25, 26, 27, 42, 44, 45, 47, 50, 51, 53, 59, 60, 61, 62, 64, 65, 66, 68, 69, 71, 76, 211, 213, 214

Schindler, David C., 153, 154, 240

Sonderegger, Katherine, 125

Sullivan, Francis A., 33, 34, 35, 36, 38, 40, 49, 57

Treier, Daniel J., 21, 89, 200, 201

Vattimo, Gianni, 3, 4, 5, 6, 256

Ward, Graham, 3, 5, 165

Webster, John, 80, 81, 82, 89, 96, 129, 133, 137, 138, 139, 152, 188, 189

Weinandy, Thomas, 8, 26, 39, 44, 45, 56, 57, 58, 67, 72, 191, 192, 242, 243

Wesche, Kenneth Paul, 24

White, Thomas Joseph, 194

Wigley, Stephen D., 12, 152, 173, 186, 195, 197, 198, 200, 203, 206, 207

Williams, A. N., 17, 24, 25, 60, 71, 72, 213, 214

Wilkin, Robert L., 20, 58, 68

Young, Frances, 44, 55, 63, 68

Zizek, Slavoj, 256

Index of Subjects

abyss, 175, 177, 185, 241

acting space, 12, 146, 187, 197, 205, 213, 248

active subject, 30, 46, 105 226

Adam: First Adam: 23, 31, 32, 42, 63, 68, 73, 237; Second Adam: 44, 52, 56

agent, 33,55, 138, 215, 217

agential, 100, 110, 111, 217, 223

Alexandrian, 19, 24, 27, 34, 38, 43, 48, 57, 59, 60, 61, 65, 67, 73, 111, 118, 168, 237

alien, 79, 84, 86, 89, 102, 106, 120, 125, 201, 220, 260

alienation, 11, 148, 177, 182, 183, 184, 185, 195, 196, 207, 208, 210, 241, 244, 248

Antiochene, 24, 32, 33, 34, 35, 36, 37, 40, 48, 49, 50, 60, 111, 168, 193, 237, 259

analogia entis, 79, 80, 85, 129, 149, 150, 242

analogia fidei, 79, 80, 90, 229

analogy, 11, 78, 80, 94, 110, 149, 158, 159, 204, 208, 216, 225, 231, 233, 245, 246

analogy of being, 79, 80, 126, 147, 149, 150, 151, 152, 164, 199, 203, 204, 205, 216, 221, 233, 242; Christological: 147, 152, 154, 166, 167, 196, 197, 204, 238, 239

analogical pattern, 79, 80, 95, 150, 158, 160, 161, 167, 206, 225, 251

analogy of faith, 11, 151, 152

anhypostasis, 93

antithesis, 78, 79, 81, 87, 107, 108, 113, 114, 145, 209, 219, 225, 226, 227, 236, 258 ascension, 16, 44, 122, 136, 137, 185, 238, 245, 255

ascent, 137, 199, 207

assumed, 33, 43, 45, 50, 52, 75, 91, 97, 106, 111, 120, 122, 126, 164, 165, 180, 191, 193, 194, 196, 215, 240, 243, 244, 245

assumes, 11, 12, 26, 92, 145, 163, 164, 165, 182, 189, 195, 196, 197, 208, 241, 243, 244, 258

assumption, 3, 44, 53, 184, 221, 243

atonement, 75, 82, 97, 116, 121, 126, 181, 184, 188, 193, 194, 215, 232, 249; forensic: 89, 147, 199, 200, 201, 202, 203, 204, 257; penal: 181, 183, 194; substitutionary: 188, 193, 194

attributes, 26, 33, 57, 59, 108, 118, 119, 121, 168, 169, 189, 193

Baptism, 21, 44, 65, 66, 89, 107, 200, 201, 202, 216

beatific vision, 89, 161, 189

beauty, 2, 6, 22, 61, 65, 69, 70, 144, 159, 165, 205, 210, 230, 247, 256, 266

being as action, 112

capacity: inherent, 6, 7, 73, 79, 86, 88, 89, 90, 118, 133, 201, 203,
212, 217, 227, 229, 234, 236, 261; natural, 79

Chalcedon, 47, 49, 84, 98, 109, 137, 148, 157, 166, 167, 168, 169, 170, 176

Chalcedonian, 9, 91, 96, 106, 108, 111, 134, 183, 209, 212

Christ: abandonment of, 173, 183, 186; as agent, 55, 215, 217; consciousness of, 3, 46, 169, 173, 174, 175, 177, 190; crucifixion of, 83, 115; descent into hell of, 150, 184, 185, 187, 208; as divine Word, 34, 52, 53, 167; as forsaken, 186; as Logos, 24, 25, 38, 40, 44, 45, 46, 47, 49, 50, 51, 54, 55, 59, 92, 93, 97, 99, 101, 108, 109, 113, 169, 172, 183, 185, 237; mission of, 149, 153, 167, 171, 173, 174, 175, 176, 177, 178, 179, 181, 186, 189, 194, 197, 198, 205, 206, 238, 250, 251, 259; passivity of, 178, 184, 185 191; as recipient: 55, 56, 215, 217, 223, 233; self-understanding of, 170, 173, 174

Christology: Logos asarkos, 99, 101, 190; Logos sarx, 168, 170

Christological: analogy of being, 11, 147, 166, 167, 196, 197, 204, 238

communication: gratiae, 103; idiomatum, 36, 40, 46, 101, 103, 118, 171; operationum, 101, 105

communication of idioms, 36, 101, 112

competitive relationship, 70, 165, 205, 218, 226, 235, 240, 247, 248

confrontation, 11, 16, 84, 91, 106, 108, 112, 114, 124, 125, 133, 143, 145, 216, 218, 219, 220, 225, 235, 236, 258

conjunction, 40, 113

conversion, 130, 134, 232

cooperate with divine, 65, 69, 78, 134, 135, 139, 215, 218, 224, 251

cooperation with divine, 23, 106, 118, 134, 168, 218, 226, 238

correspond, 110, 127, 143, 219, 232

correspondence between human and divine, 107, 110, 118, 122, 142, 218, 232

corresponding to divine, 81, 103, 108, 133

corruption of sin and death, 23, 44, 60, 88, 97, 219, 237

covenant, 76, 80, 82, 84, 85,86, 87, 89,91, 94, 96, 108, 117, 127, 129, 144, 145, 216, 221, 235, 257; fellowship: 76, 81, 114; partnership: 10, 12, 75, 76, 80, 81, 88, 114, 117, 144, 146, 215, 216, 217, 218, 234, 257

created nature, 84, 163, 165, 166, 212, 216, 219, 229, 234, 240, 246, 247, 248, 249

creation: as covenant, 80, 82, 83, 84, 85; as enrichment, 12, 157, 158, 198, 242, 246, 248, 251; as gift, 13, 158, 252; dependent upon God, 78; distinction between God and, 27, 151, 183, 196, 246, 248; God's intent for, 259; new creation, 21, 213, 238, 257, 265; non-necessary, 11, 99, 155, 156, 157, 198, 244, 246; otherness, 157, 207; relationship between God and, 32, 109, 157, 160, 161, 164, 167, 209, 226, 240, 247; resituation of, 205; repositioning of, 187, 196; restoration of, 265; space for, 148, 152, 204, 205

creatureliness, 61, 81, 89, 97, 151,
    165, 246, 249
cross, 34, 40, 68, 130, 137, 148,
    152, 154, 156, 165, 181, 182,
    183, 184, 186, 188, 195, 208,
    210, 229, 233, 241, 244

death: and corruption, 23, 44, 60,
    98, 237; as enemy, 23; fall and,
    22, 32, 72, 74; freedom from,
    45, 53, 55, 91, 148, 213, 215,
    229, 237, 250, 262, 263; Jesus'
    experience of, 180, 183, 184,
    185, 186, 188, 191, 194, 196,
    208; overcoming/defeating, 8,
    12, 13, 15, 16, 22, 23, 32, 44,
    53, 55, 63, 67, 68, 71, 98, 142,
    152, 197, 215, 231, 233, 235,
    243, 245, 263, 264
deification, 2, 7, 9, 10, 11, 12, 16,
    17, 18, 19, 20, 21, 22, 24, 26,
    27, 28, 29, 48, 54, 58, 60, 63,
    65, 72, 73, 77, 102, 113, 118,
    119, 120, 121, 141, 144, 145,
    146, 149, 199, 209, 212, 213,
    214, 215, 216, 222, 233, 251,
    254, 255
deified, 26, 55, 59, 118, 120, 121,
    122
descent to hell, 182, 184

dialectic(s), 11, 77, 78, 79, 80, 81,
    84, 90, 93, 107, 108, 109, 163,
    164, 218, 225, 226, 227, 228
disobedience, 22, 23, 32, 53, 76,
    86, 87, 144, 177, 196, 208, 256,
    264
distortion of sin, 20, 23, 164
divine: drama, 259; nature, 26, 33,
    34, 44, 45, 53, 57, 59, 61, 69,
    71, 75, 92, 103, 119, 121, 127,
    159, 161, 170, 171, 183, 193;
    perfection, 150, 153, 158, 167,
    246
divinization, 55, 108, 117, 119,
    120
divinizing, 119
dynamic growth, 8, 218

early church, 10, 18, 20, 21, 22,
    23, 25, 42, 76, 126, 160
economy of salvation, 15, 16, 28,
    30, 42, 54, 55, 67, 99, 148, 191,
    251, 258
election, 10, 76, 77, 80, 84, 85, 86,
    91, 96, 97, 99, 100, 114, 127,
    131, 135, 144, 145, 194, 216,
    218, 222, 224, 229, 232, 235,
    257; subject of, 76, 82, 91, 94,
    98, 100, 117, 202, 216, 223,
    224, 233; object of, 76, 81, 85,

91, 94, 98, 100, 117, 202, 216, 223, 224

enhanced humanity, 58, 113, 121, 124, 145, 224, 233

enhancement, 123, 124, 126 145, 226, 227, 228

enhypostasis, 93, 110 129

Enlightenment, 2, 3, 6, 7, 9, 163, 252, 255, 257, 264

enrichment, 11, 12, 157, 158, 198 209, 239, 246, 249, 251

epistemological, 3, 221

eschatological, 67, 140, 141, 147, 198, 203, 204, 215, 232, 249, 250, 257

eternal life, 21, 24, 60, 73, 135,156, 158, 179

eternity, 82, 99, 103, 105, 137, 149, 150, 155, 156, 157, 167

event of Incarnation, 11, 55, 83, 94, 97, 99, 100, 101, 103, 106, 108 119, 122, 123, 137, 138, 139, 147, 148, 152, 153, 156, 168, 172, 206, 213, 217, 220, 226, 232, 243, 245

evil, 25, 86, 87, 88, 185, 229, 255, 265

exaltation, 11, 26, 27, 75, 96, 100, 113, 115, 117, 118, 121 122, 123, 124, 125, 126, 127, 130, 132, 136, 137, 140, 141, 142, 144, 145, 146, 199, 202, 215, 217 218, 222

exalted, 26, 75, 114, 115, 117, 119, 122, 124, 126, 127, 136, 137, 141, 178, 199 218, 237, 257

exchange formula, 10, 19, 21, 24, 61, 73, 126, 193, 212, 214

extrinsic change, 126, 220, 223, 236

extrinsic union, 60, 113, 185, 223, 224, 226, 233

faith, 2, 14, 65, 66, 69, 80, 126, 130, 131, 134, 139, 143, 180, 220, 230, 232, 263

Fall, 11, 22, 25, 28 42, 43, 63, 65, 71, 72, 77, 86, 87, 89, 149,160, 161, 162, 193, 213,

fellowship, 22, 76, 81, 82, 97, 100, 114 117, 122, 126, 127, 128 131, 144, 146, 216, 232, 234, 235, 264, 265

forgiven, 132

forgiveness, 71, 253

formed reference, 142

freedom: finite, 150, 197, 205, 206; infinite, 205, 206

free will, 23, 31, 32, 42, 65, 113, 169

God's divine: freedom, 76, 81, 192; purpose, 41, 166; purposes, 83, 257; self-disclosure, 166; self-giving, 158, 207, 244; self-determination, 103; self-disclosure, 166; sovereignty, 78, 152, 164, 233; transcendence, 17, 27, 41, 56, 150, 151, 155; will, 23, 31, 32, 52, 89, 227

goodness, 2, 73, 144, 159, 165, 210, 224, 230, 247, 256, 266

grace: analogical, 1, 2, 23, 25, 70; cooperation with, 65; gift, 13, 23, 28, 62, 63, 69, 72; hypostatic union and, 36, 40, 41; infused: 60, 89, 124, 133, 143, 200, 201, 202, 220, 236, 237, 249, 260, 261, 262, 263; indwelling of Spirit, 70, 71; irradiates, 166, 240, 246; participation through, 26, 42, 61, 63, 65, 66, 67; perfecting nature, 11, 70; prevenient, 72; possession of, 62; recovering grace, 53; receptive to, 68, 71; recipients of, 22, 26, 27, 62, 65; supernatural, 72, 78

harmony of divine and human in Incarnation, 36, 118, 217, 226, 235

harmonious relationship, 13, 168, 218, 220, 222, 233, 240, 247, 249, 251 258

hell, 11, 150, 182, 185 186, 187, 188, 191, 194, 196, 208, 209, 241, 248

holiness, 142, 235

Holy Spirit: empowerment of, 236; gift of, 22, 28, 42, 43, 64, 69, 72, 142, 202, 260, 265; indwelling, 69, 72; proceeds, 153, 178; stable base for, 43, 66

human acting space, 12, 146, 187, 197, 205, 213, 248

human being: God's intent for, 23, 32, 60, 63, 117, 144, 160, 161, 177, 195, 215, 229, 257, 262, 263

human nature, 9, 18, 19, 24, 25, 26, 33, 34, 40, 42, 44, 45, 47, 48, 51, 52, 58, 61, 62, 63, 64, 65, 68, 71, 72, 77, 79, 85, 86, 89, 92, 96, 98, 105, 110, 118, 119, 121, 122, 124, 133, 134, 142, 161, 163, 164, 165, 170, 177, 180, 181, 183, 190, 193, 199, 205, 211, 219, 220, 227,

228, 230, 232, 233, 234, 239, 241, 242, 246, 247, 249, 261, 262

humanism, 2, 117, 162, 163, 252, 255, 257

humanity: Christ's, 8, 9, 33, 44, 45, 48, 49, 50, 51, 54, 55, 56, 57,63, 68, 73, 98, 113, 117, 121, 136, 144, 145, 148, 167, 169, 172, 173, 178, 179, 182, 189, 191, 193, 194, 195, 196, 207, 208, 212, 215, 217, 218, 223, 227, 228, 251, 256, 264; enhanced, 58, 113, 121, 124, 145, 224, 233

humility, 83, 115, 234

humiliation, 96, 98, 103, 113, 115,117, 118, 124, 127, 136, 218, 257

hypostasis, 33, 34, 35, 37, 38, 39,40, 45, 46, 59, 101, 169, 189, 240

hypostatic union, 9, 10, 30, 34, 39, 42,45, 54, 55, 64, 76, 77, 91, 92, 94, 95, 97, 100, 101, 11, 112, 149, 170, 175, 178, 186, 187, 192, 205, 215, 217, 225, 240, 258

identity: of action, 100, 105, 106, 110, 115, 122, 123, 167; of

mission, 172, 173, 174, 176, 190, 198, 205, 206, 209, 238

image, 21, 22, 25, 27, 31, 42, 43, 62, 65, 68, 70, 71, 72, 73, 158, 162, 213, 237

immanence, 5, 27, 150, 151, 155

immanent, 84, 99, 101, 106, 142, 149, 154, 155, 159, 178, 183, 188, 189, 190, 192, 194, 208, 239, 241, 242, 243, 258, 259

immutability, 41, 102, 113, 149, 157, 158, 183, 188, 193, 208, 209, 242, 243, 244, 246

impassible, 47, 183, 192, 241, 259

impassibility, 30, 40, 41, 55, 58, 102, 149, 183, 188, 208, 209, 241,242, 243, 246, 259

imputation, 89, 201, 220, 261

imputed righteousness, 125, 131, 201, 202, 203, 220, 260, 261, 262, 263,

incarnate, 25, 26, 30, 34, 38, 42, 43, 46, 47, 48, 51,52, 55, 57, 63, 68, 71, 73, 92, 93, 169, 170, 172, 177, 181, 184, 190, 191, 196, 208, 243, 245

Incarnation as pattern of Trinitarian activity, 172

incorruption, 53, 60, 64

indwelling of Spirit, 22, 27, 32, 42, 43, 56, 66, 69, 70, 71, 72, 107, 133, 179, 236, 237

infused grace, 89, 124, 133, 143, 200, 201, 202, 220, 236, 237, 249, 260, 261, 262, 263

infused habitus, 120, 126

infusion, 66, 89, 112, 119,121, 125, 139, 143, 146, 201, 202, 204, 218, 235, 236, 249, 260, 262

inherent capacity, 6, 7, 73, 79, 88, 89, 90, 118, 133, 201, 203, 212, 217, 227, 229, 234, 261

initiative, God's, 23, 67, 69,78, 81, 83, 110, 144, 152, 181, 215, 216, 217, 218, 238, 265

intrinsic, 17, 61, 161, 164, 214, 221, 223, 233, 240, 262

Jesus: abandonment of, 173, 183, 186; as agent/agential, 33, 55, 100, 110, 111, 215, 217, 223; ascension of, 16, 44, 122, 136, 137, 185, 238, 245, 255; assumption/taking on of sin, 193; crucifixion of, 83, 115; death, experience of, 180, 183, 184, 185, 186, 188,191, 194, 196, 208; divine mission of, 173, 174; as elect one, 81, 82, 85, 99; as fully divine, 33, 48, 50, 53, 55, 57, 98, 113, 117, 136, 148, 167, 173, 179, 189, 191, 196; as fully human, 8, 9, 33, 44, 45, 48, 49, 50, 51, 54, 55, 56, 57,63, 68, 73, 98, 113, 117, 121, 136, 144, 145, 148, 167, 169, 172, 173, 178, 179, 182, 189, 191, 193, 194, 195, 196, 207, 208, 212, 215, 217, 218, 223, 227, 228, 251, 256, 264; hour of, 175, 178; historical existence of, 172, 175; human consciousness of, 46, 169, 174, 175, 190; human knowledge of, 88, 162, 189; identity of, 30, 100, 103, 110, 122, 167, 173, 174, 176, 189, 238; incarnate, 25, 26, 30, 34, 38, 42, 43, 46, 47, 48, 51,52, 55, 57, 63,68, 71, 73, 92, 93, 169, 170, 172, 177, 181, 184, 190, 191, 196, 208, 243, 245; as judge, 76, 91, 94, 115, 116, 184, 216; as judged, 76, 91, 94, 115, 116, 184, 216; as object of election, 76, 91, 94, 98, 99, 202, 216, 223, 224; mission of, 149, 153, 156, 171, 172, 173, 174, 175, 176, 177, 178, 179, 181, 182, 186, 189, 194, 197,

198, 205, 206, 238, 249, 250, 251, 259; one subject, 16, 45, 46, 49, 63, 76, 94, 105, 106, 259; as savior, 120, 185; as second person of the Trinity, 16, 39, 52, 92, 99, 106, 144, 194, 196, 207, 237; as single subject/subjectivity, 8, 9, 10, 16, 18, 27, 28, 29, 36, 38, 42, 45, 47, 49, 50, 52, 54, 58, 59, 63, 76, 77, 91, 92, 93, 95, 101, 106, 110, 111, 113, 114, 117, 121, 144, 145, 148, 164, 169, 179, 182, 183, 189, 196, 207, 212, 214, 215, 216, 217, 219, 222, 223, 224, 225, 226, 237, 238, 239, 240, 241, 242, 243, 245, 251, 256; as subject of election, 76, 91, 94, 98, 99, 202, 216, 223, 224; suffering of, 11, 40, 44, 46, 51, 52, 59, 105, 115, 116, 121, 142, 168, 169, 180, 181, 183, 187, 188, 191, 192, 193, 194, 195, 205, 208, 209, 231, 237; as recipient, 55, 56, 215, 217, 223, 233, 246; two states of, 96, 145; redemption of, 13, 18, 22, 29, 42, 43, 54, 55, 68, 72, 85, 88, 140, 141, 147, 162, 183, 186, 188, 190, 196, 198, 232, 241, 247, 249, 259, 265; resurrection of, 8, 10, 11, 12, 16, 22, 23, 23, 44, 55, 61, 66, 71, 72, 83, 90, 109, 110, 115, 122, 132, 134, 135, 137, 139, 142, 143, 165, 171, 180, 185, 186, 201 206 208 209 212, 213, 214, 215, 216, 219, 228, 229, 230, 231, 232, 233, 234, 238, 239, 245, 261, 265; self-surrender of, 174, 178, 182, 189

judgment, humanity's, 98, 115, 184

judgment, God's, 87, 115, 125, 127, 184

justice, 104, 123, 171, 172, 183

justification, 89, 135, 141, 184, 201, 202, 203, 220, 235, 262, 263; relationship to sanctification, 72, 89, 200, 201, 257, 262

kenosis: Trinitarian, 150, 152, 153, 157, 167, 178, 189

kenotic, 83, 84, 149, 152, 153, 182

knowing, 5, 79, 162, 174, 221, 223, 231, 232

knowledge, human: 3, 7, 11, 60, 71, 85, 88, 90, 129, 142, 151, 162, 202, 203, 221, 223, 230, 233, 235, 255, 257

knowledge of God, 46, 104, 173
knowledge of Jesus, 136, 175, 188, 189

life of God, 2, 7, 8, 9, 10, 11, 12, 13, 22, 23, 42, 45, 55, 72, 73, 83, 92, 133, 147, 148, 150, 152, 155, 156, 158, 159, 161, 165, 195, 196, 198, 207, 208, 212, 213, 214, 215, 238, 242, 243, 244, 245, 246, 251, 256, 258, 259, 260, 265, 266
life with God, 7, 8, 11, 16, 44, 76, 89, 117, 121, 196, 210, 214, 244, 251, 252
likeness, 1, 21, 22, 23, 26, 27, 42, 61, 62, 70, 72, 71, 73, 198, 237
Logos, 9, 24, 25, 38, 40, 44, 45, 46, 47, 49, 50, 51, 54, 55, 59, 92, 93, 97, 108, 109, 113, 169, 172, 183, 185, 237
love of God, 7, 13, 40, 62, 73, 76, 79, 91, 92, 104, 115, 123, 140, 142, 147, 148, 155, 157, 158, 161, 165, 174, 178, 181, 194, 195, 198, 207, 210, 216, 217, 241, 243, 244, 245, 248, 250, 252, 264, 265; reciprocal, 154, 158, 159, 160, 175, 178, 245, 249, 252; self-giving, 69, 153, 158, 159, 160, 175, 177, 182, 185, 186, 196, 208, 244, 246, 248, 251, 252, 259

Mary, 29, 30, 33, 44, 55, 249, 258
mediation, 99, 136, 137, 138
mediating, 31, 135, 138
metaphysical, 3, 4, 5, 22, 28, 35, 37, 41, 164, 172, 220, 230
mia physis, 38
miracle(s), 46, 54, 88, 90, 129, 134, 229, 230, 231, 233, 261
miraculous, 19, 25, 134, 231, 232, 233
mission, 3, 12, 149, 153, 156, 171, 173, 174, 175, 176, 177, 178, 179, 181, 182, 186, 189, 194, 197, 198, 205, 206, 209, 238, 249, 250, 251, 259
modalities, 155, 156, 196, 198
mode of being, 91, 97
mode of existence, 8, 41, 64, 93, 101, 104, 167, 169, 171, 172, 176, 178, 191, 192, 193, 194, 196, 207, 208, 228, 239
moral life, 23, 27, 67, 205, 237, 249, 260; as performance, 205

narrative, 3, 4, 5, 6, 7, 19, 67, 265
nature: created, 84, 163, 165, 166, 212, 216, 219, 229, 234, 240, 246, 247, 248, 249; divine, 26,

33, 34, 44, 45, 53, 57, 59, 61, 69, 71, 75, 92, 103, 119, 121, 127, 159, 161, 170, 171, 183, 193; human, 9, 18, 19, 24, 25, 26, 33, 34, 40, 42, 44, 45, 47, 48, 51, 52, 58, 61, 62, 63, 64, 65, 68, 71, 72, 77, 79, 85, 86, 89, 92, 96, 98, 105, 110, 118, 119, 121, 122, 124, 133, 134, 142, 161, 163, 164, 165, 170, 177, 180, 181, 183, 190, 193, 199, 205, 211, 219, 220, 227, 228, 230, 232, 233, 234, 239, 241, 242, 246, 247, 249, 261, 262; pure nature, 90, 160, 162, 163, 165, 166, 236; renewed/ renewal of, 43, 65, 68, 147, 201; transformed nature, 51, 52, 58, 64, 199; two natures, 9, 18, 26, 29, 33, 34, 35, 36, 37, 38, 40, 44, 45, 46, 47, 48, 49, 51, 52, 56, 57, 58, 59, 64, 77, 92, 95, 96, 97, 101, 103, 106, 107, 108, 109, 111, 113, 114, 117, 125, 149, 157, 167, 170, 177, 193, 219, 222, 240, 241

new birth, 28, 66, 262

new life, 14, 47, 62, 66, 69, 71, 130, 131, 132, 143, 234, 258, 259

nihilism, 2, 3, 252

non-competitive, 220, 240

obedience: 22, 31, 32, 48, 56, 65, 68, 69, 76, 86, 87, 88, 96, 100, 104, 105, 108, 110, 112, 113, 115, 116, 117, 121, 122, 123, 124, 125, 131, 132, 134, 140, 141, 142, 146, 171, 173, 175, 176, 177, 178, 182, 183, 202, 208, 214, 217, 220, 227, 232, 235, 239, 244, 257, 258, 261

objective, 116, 128, 129, 133, 134, 138, 139, 140, 141, 142, 146, 179, 200, 231, 249, 261, 263

one person: Christ as, 8, 9, 11, 16, 27, 29, 42, 46, 50, 55, 57, 59, 70, 77, 93, 94, 95, 98, 101, 106, 107, 108, 109, 110, 111, 112, 113, 117, 118, 119, 144, 145, 154, 165, 167, 169, 171, 172, 175, 179, 182, 184, 185, 191, 192, 193, 104, 195, 197, 207, 212, 214, 215, 217, 218, 220, 222, 224, 226, 227, 228, 229, 233, 237, 238, 239, 241, 243, 244, 245, 247, 264

ontology, 13, 21, 112, 118, 127, 137, 177, 197, 220, 221, 223

ontological(ly), 1, 5, 6, 8, 9, 16, 22, 25, 27, 28, 36, 40, 41, 42, 45, 47, 51, 54, 55, 56, 57, 63, 65,

66, 67, 70, 73, 81, 87, 89, 112, 126, 127, 128, 133, 142, 146, 148, 163, 177, 183, 198, 199, 200, 202, 203, 207, 215, 218, 231, 235, 236, 238, 245, 249, 251, 260, 261, 263, 265

otherness, 6, 157, 204, 207, 209, 246, 248, 259

overcome, 13, 53, 98, 231

paradox, 55, 173, 232

partners/partnership, 10, 12, 76, 80, 81, 86, 87, 88, 114, 117, 130, 131, 142, 144, 146, 215, 216, 217, 234, 257

partake(s), 43

partakers, 1, 53, 61, 62, 66, 69

participation: analogical, 2, 12, 21, 22, 26, 27, 60, 61, 73, 120, 151, 199, 204, 221, 231, 238, 248, 258, 260; and Holy Spirit, 19, 22, 25, 28, 32, 43, 53, 61, 63, 65, 66, 68, 71, 121, 135, 206; and human response, 69, 89, 143, 200, 202, 205, 206, 219, 248, 256, 258; and salvation, 16, 23, 25, 28, 45, 60, 63, 64, 67, 74, 150, 213, 238, 251, 260; as gift, 28, 42, 62, 63, 64, 65, 66, 73, 129, 133, 149, 166, 209, 210, 214, 219, 238, 263; as

event, 89, 96, 103, 107, 108, 122, 128, 218; as intent for human life, 23, 24, 78, 128, 161, 166, 198, 257; effects of, 13, 19, 147, 213, 251, 256, 259, 265; in/through Christ, 21, 24, 25, 26, 27, 53, 61, 63, 64, 66, 71, 82, 89, 96, 103, 107, 131, 137, 142, 187, 251, 265; in life of God, 2, 7, 8, 9, 11, 12, 13, 22, 23, 27, 28, 42, 45, 59, 60, 63, 66, 72, 95, 100, 121, 147, 148, 150, 212, 250, 251, 256, 257, 262, 265; moral, 28, 60, 67, 69, 73, 128, 129, 143, 148, 187, 198, 200, 202, 203, 206, 214, 215, 236, 238, 245, 251, 257, 262; ontological, 8, 28, 59, 60, 63, 64, 65, 66, 71, 73,128, 133,142, 148, 200, 203, 204, 213, 214, 215, 216, 217, 220, 232, 235, 236, 238, 245, 259, 262; pattern of, 205, 206; proper understanding of, 20, 25, 26, 27, 28, 59, 60, 61, 73, 214

passible, 7, 47, 242

possibility, 192, 193, 242, 260

passive, 26, 68, 79, 204, 208, 245

patristic, 20, 23, 24, 42, 183

pattern: of life, 63, 67, 70, 172, 215; of redemption, 18, 22, 42, 55, 196

perfection: divine, 150, 153, 158, 167, 246

physis, 37, 38, 40, 169

post-modern, 2

post-modern philosophy, 2

pneumatology, 258

pneumatological, 28, 66, 71, 73

predicate(s), 36, 46, 105, 164, 191, 193, 239, 241, 243

predicated, 33, 46, 48, 118, 159, 191, 192, 194, 195, 214, 222

predication, 25, 26, 46, 57, 108, 191, 239

presupposition, 59, 84, 85, 156, 179

properties, 25, 37, 110, 191, 192, 214

prosopa, 33, 35, 40, 41

prosopic union, 30, 32, 35, 36, 41

prosopon, 33, 34, 35, 36, 37, 38, 40, 46

provisional, 140, 141, 142, 143, 230, 232, 234, 261

pure nature, 90, 160, 162, 163, 165, 166, 236

purpose, God's, 4, 83, 166, 257

purposes, 83, 257

ransom, 181, 188

real distinction, 2, 17, 19, 129, 151, 183, 196, 217, 228, 260

reappropriate, 7, 8, 43

reappropriation, 7, 43

recapitulate, 53, 60

receptivity, 26, 27, 55, 65, 68, 149, 150, 157, 158, 159, 160, 164, 167, 208, 239,

recipient(s), 22, 55, 56, 62, 79,132, 215, 217, 223, 233, 246, 265

reconciliation, 82, 83, 87, 111, 114, 115, 116, 117, 121, 124, 129, 132, 135, 139, 140, 141, 144, 146, 218, 227, 228, 231, 235, 265

reconstruct, 9

recovering, 7, 53, 76, 137

redeemed, 3, 7, 10, 45, 50, 55, 109, 114, 120, 141, 148, 157, 164, 165, 180, 181, 187,193, 195, 205, 215, 239, 240, 244, 245, 246, 248, 250, 258, 265

redemption, 13, 18, 22, 29, 42, 43, 54, 55, 68, 72, 85, 88, 140,141, 147, 162, 183, 186, 188, 190, 196, 198, 232, 241, 247, 249, 259, 265

refusal, 87, 88, 144, 162, 194, 207, 244

regenerate, 25, 130, 134, 236

regeneration, 53, 54, 58, 128, 134, 135, 216

relational, 99, 131

relationship: between nature and grace, 10, 11, 70, 72, 89, 90, 134, 160, 162, 229, 239, 251

reposition(ed), 187, 197, 208, 246

repositioning, 198

resituate, 197

respond, 23, 65, 70, 80, 81, 89, 90, 122, 127, 128, 131, 146, 151, 152, 191, 194, 213, 219, 231, 234, 238, 247, 249

restore(d), 7, 8, 13, 22, 24, 44, 54, 60, 71, 76, 117, 144, 165, 214, 234, 237, 252, 257, 261, 264

restoration, 21, 22, 42, 134, 265

resurrection, 8, 10, 11, 12, 16, 22, 23, 23, 44, 55, 61, 66, 71, 72, 83, 90, 109, 110, 115,122, 132, 134, 135, 137, 139, 142, 143, 165, 171, 180, 185, 186, 201, 206, 208, 209, 212, 213, 214, 215, 216, 219, 228, 229, 230, 231, 232, 233, 234, 238, 239, 245, 261, 265

revelation, 7, 11, 79, 80, 81, 83, 88, 90, 99, 110, 132, 136, 137, 138, 151, 159, 164, 165, 166, 190, 200, 203, 204, 226

salvation:15, 16, 22, 24, 28, 29, 30, 32, 42, 47, 54, 55, 57, 60, 65, 67, 78, 95, 97, 99, 113, 128, 134, 138, 141, 148, 149, 155, 175, 179, 181, 182, 186, 188, 191, 194, 200, 213, 217, 218, 223, 224, 228, 233, 238, 241, 249, 251, 258, 259, 261, 262

sanctifying, 43, 53

sanctification, 43, 44, 65, 72, 89, 130, 142, 200, 201, 204, 257, 262

save(d), 51, 53, 73, 76, 89, 144, 146, 179, 184, 186, 201, 207, 216, 234, 252, 262, 264

scripture, 1, 14, 21, 62, 168, 188, 253

scriptural, 21, 24, 33, 84, 152

self-giving, God's, 158, 207, 244

simul justus et peccator, 125

simultaneously sinners and justified, 143, 231, 234

sin, overcoming of death and, 8, 12, 13, 15, 16, 22, 23, 32, 44, 53, 55, 63, 67, 68, 71, 98, 142, 152, 197, 215, 231, 233, 235, 243, 245, 263, 264

sin, power of, 67, 215, 232, 233, 234, 261, 262, 263

single subject/subjectivity, 8, 9, 10, 16, 18, 27, 28, 29, 36, 38, 42,

45, 47, 49, 50, 52, 54, 58, 59, 63, 76, 77, 91, 92, 93, 95, 101, 106, 110, 111, 113, 114, 117, 121, 144, 145, 148, 164, 169, 179, 182, 183, 189, 196, 207, 212, 214, 215, 216, 217, 219, 222, 223, 224, 225, 226, 237, 238, 239, 240, 241, 242, 243, 245, 251, 256

Son of God, 47, 48, 57, 93, 96, 97, 98, 100, 101, 102, 106, 108, 115, 117, 119, 122, 123, 127, 133, 145, 167, 175, 183, 224, 242

Son's mission, 153, 178

soteriology: 9, 10, 16, 18, 21, 25, 28, 29, 30, 32, 43, 54, 63, 100, 117, 137, 148, 150, 152, 164, 169, 177, 179, 181, 183, 191, 194, 196, 207, 212, 215, 233, 236

space, 12, 90, 94, 140, 146, 148, 151, 152, 154, 155, 156, 157, 162, 167, 187, 192, 194, 196, 197, 198, 204, 205, 206, 207, 208, 213, 238, 240, 243, 244, 245, 246, 248, 251, 256, 259

stable base, 43, 66

subjective, 46, 128, 132, 133, 139, 146, 179, 232, 235, 249

subjectively, 134, 138, 139, 141, 263

substance, 36, 37

substantial, 36, 41, 45, 56, 227

suffering, 11, 13, 40, 44, 46, 51, 52, 59, 105, 115, 116, 120, 121, 142, 154, 168, 169, 180, 181, 182, 183, 187, 188, 191, 192, 193, 194, 195, 205, 208, 209, 231, 237, 239, 241, 242, 243, 244, 245, 248, 265

supernatural, 21, 72, 78, 89, 133, 160, 162, 163, 164, 166, 196, 197, 198, 199, 202, 208, 214, 236, 240, 247

supernaturally, 71

synergism, 134, 227

synergistic, 78, 226

telos, 3, 7, 15, 16, 89, 146, 208, 216, 249

teleological, 7, 8, 13, 14, 77, 209

temporal, 67, 154, 155, 156, 158

transcendence, 17, 27, 41, 56, 150, 151, 155

transcendentals, 153, 158, 159, 164

transform, 47, 52, 53, 60, 68, 73, 101, 126, 144, 167, 181, 212, 218, 220, 236, 237, 240, 249

transformed, 8, 13, 19, 20, 24, 26, 44, 51, 52, 54, 55, 58, 59, 62,

64, 71, 74, 128, 143, 170, 199, 206, 214, 215, 245, 257, 258, 261, 265

transformation, 2, 8, 10, 17, 19, 21, 27, 44, 45, 55, 56, 59, 60, 64, 67, 68, 128, 130, 146, 199, 203, 211, 216, 231 237, 249, 257; cognitive, 202, 203, 221, 232; moral, 60, 66, 67, 73, 143, 148, 198, 199, 202, 203, 208, 214, 215, 218, 221, 235, 238, 245, 249, 260, 262, 263, 265; ontological, 60, 63, 66, 67, 73, 118, 121, 128, 143, 147, 148, 198, 199, 200, 202, 204, 208, 215, 218, 219, 232, 233, 235, 236, 238, 245, 249, 251, 257, 260, 262, 263, 265

Trinity, 13, 21, 82, 99, 153, 156, 157; economic, 153, 154, 155, 178, 183, 188, 192, 258; immanent, 99, 153, 154, 155, 156, 159, 178, 183, 188, 189, 193, 194, 208, 258; immutability, 188, 191, 192, 239, 241, 244; impassibility, 188, 191, 192, 239, 241; inner-relationship, 110, 122, 123, 131, 148, 150, 152, 153, 155, 156, 157, 158, 159, 160, 172, 176, 178, 183, 189, 192, 194,

196, 198, 240, 243, 244; inversion, 178, 258; kenosis, self-giving, 7, 68, 150, 152, 153, 157, 158, 159, 160, 167, 173, 174, 175, 176, 177, 178, 183, 185, 186, 187, 189, 196, 198, 206, 207, 208, 244, 246, 251, 252, 256, 259, second person of: 16, 39, 52, 92, 99, 106, 123, 144, 159, 172, 177, 181, 186, 194, 196, 207, 237; relationship between immanent and economic, 99, 149, 154, 155, 178, 188, 190, 192, 243; receptivity, 150, 157, 158, 159, 160, 164, 167, 208, 239, 242, 245, 246, 248, 251, 260

Trinitarian: salvation as, 28, 42, 64, 70, 71, 73, 83, 144, 148, 152, 153, 154, 155, 172, 178, 181, 182, 183, 184, 185, 186, 191, 206, 207, 209, 213, 244; immutability, 101; immanent, 106; perichoresis, 175

Truth, 2, 3, 4, 88, 93, 97, 104, 127, 129, 131, 132, 133, 142, 144, 146, 159, 165, 186, 210, 247, 255, 256, 266

two-fold, 28, 52, 73, 115, 236, 251

two natures, 9, 18, 26, 29, 33, 34, 35, 36, 37, 38, 40, 44, 45, 46, 47, 48, 49, 51, 52, 56, 57, 58, 59, 64, 77, 92, 95, 96, 97, 101, 103, 106, 107, 108, 109, 111, 113, 114, 117, 125, 149, 157, 167, 170, 177, 193, 219, 222, 240, 241

unity, 8, 16, 32, 35, 36, 37, 40, 41, 46, 48, 49, 67, 91,92, 96, 97, 104, 106, 107, 108, 127, 130, 132, 133, 150, 151, 153, 155, 160, 161, 166, 169, 171, 173, 184, 189, 197, 210, 215

unveiling, 4, 81

violence, 5, 6, 8, 13, 116, 142, 193, 230, 244, 248

vision: Christian vision, 7, 9, 10, 13, 18, 58, 77, 78, 114, 143, 146, 149, 256, 264, 265; God's vision, 8, 9, 13, 70, 146, 160, 210, 256, 259, 265; of human life, 7, 8, 9, 10, 12, 13, 18, 58, 77, 78, 89, 114, 121, 141, 143, 146, 149, 150, 151, 161, 209, 210, 212, 232, 256, 257, 264, 265

vocation: human, 198, Christian, 132, supernatural, 162

will: God's, 23, 31, 32, 52, 89, 227; human, 32, 33, 65, 107, 142, 177, 194, 202, 217

will-to-power, 3, 6

witness, 100, 129, 130, 131, 134, 146, 203, 217, 230, 233

wondrous exchange, 9, 10, 11, 74, 148, 149, 150, 179, 180, 181, 182, 187, 191, 193, 194, 195, 196, 202, 207, 208, 209, 217, 218, 238, 239, 240, 244, 251

Word: incarnate, 16, 26, 38, 43, 44, 45, 46, 50, 51, 54, 63, 66, 67, 93, 104, 106, 167, 175, 184, 189, 193; single subject, 16, 27, 32, 37, 39, 50, 57, 63, 93, 167, 215, 237

world: 2, 3, 4, 6, 7, 12, 13, 20, 31, 48, 51, 65, 76, 82, 86, 88, 90, 99, 100, 109, 115, 116, 123, 132, 138, 139, 151, 153, 154, 155, 157, 160, 161, 173, 174, 175, 178, 181, 182, 184, 185, 186, 187, 188, 189, 198, 200, 203, 204, 207, 209, 211, 217, 220, 230, 232, 239, 246, 247, 249, 250, 251, 252, 253, 254, 255, 256, 258, 259, 262, 263, 264, 265, 266